I0704381

2020
TRUMP
EXISTENTIAL

- A WARNING to EVANGELICALS -
- A GIFT to PROGRESSIVES -
- A PERIOD of CHANGE -
- It's ORWELLIAN -

In 2015, Microsoft's Bill Gates detailed a warning of the next big threat to the world – something that kills over ten million or more people – likely caused by an infectious virus not a nuclear war.

He detailed what would be needed to prepare for that pandemic "war". Military expenditure that politicians bragging about was not the answer.

Coronavirus provided that answer: M4A & UBI.

~~~~~~

They're idiots, losers, they're scum
Taking advantage of everyone
You're a dog, they're your fleas
Doing everything they can to spread disease
They'll whine, they'll bitch,
they'll fuck you if you're rich
They'll leach, they'll latch,
they are the itch you can't scratch
...
~ "The Moron Brothers"
by Mike Burkett

~~~~~~

My time is finally near
And I can feel the change in the wind right now
Nothing's in my way
And they're not gonna hold me down no more
No, they're not gonna hold me down
...
~ "Where My Heart Will Take Me"
by Diane Warren

~~~~~~
~~~~~~

CHAPTERS

CHAPTER ONE – Existential Virus

**"If our conversation led to no practical outcome,
it was merely 'excessive talk." ~ Rabbinical Saying**

Throughout 2019 and into 2020, the word *"Existential"* had perforated through everyday language as a *"threat"* or *"crisis"* that must be deemed important. But, looking back through the media approach to issues, we discover this newly popularized term had its origins in a speech, delivered in Florida, by candidate Donald John Trump.

"For those who control the levers of power in Washington, and for the global special interests, they partner with these people that don't have your good in mind. Our campaign represents a true existential threat like they haven't seen before.

"Our movement is about replacing a failed and corrupt— now, when I say "corrupt," I'm talking about totally corrupt — political establishment, with a new government controlled by you, the American people..

"This election will determine whether we are a free nation or whether we have only the illusion of democracy, but are in fact controlled by a small handful of global special interests rigging the system, and our system is rigged. This is reality, you know it, they know it, I know it, and pretty much the whole world knows it. The establishment and their media enablers will control over this nation through means that are very well known. Anyone who challenges their control is deemed a sexist, a racist, a xenophobe, and morally deformed.

"They will attack you, they will slander you, they will seek to destroy your career and your family, they will seek to destroy everything about you, including your reputation. They will lie, lie, lie, and then again they will do worse than that, they will do whatever is necessary." – 13 October 2016 - 5:49 PM ET.

In a race-free society, any society where people to not invoke race and are not inherently racist, there can be no such thing as the xenophobic – there is an exhibition of dislike or prejudice against those of other countries. Xenophobia is either racist or culturalist – it does not matter which spin you place on, even if it is the same spin I place on cultural heritage in my books.

When speaking of a virus or disease of any sought, we must accept that there is a place of origin and it is quite proper to identify the variation on the disease by the origin location. Wuhan Flu is a Coronavirus (a crown virus) that originated in Wuhan China – or it was first recognized there.

When we look back on the disease we are going to recognize – or we should recognize – that it is a *culling* disease. It is not like smallpox or bubonic plague. It does not kill for the sake of killing.

A culling disease is one that would not harm the host unless that host already suffers from a life-threatening condition or some physical problem that restricts the body's natural ability to combat biological, chemical, or viral attacks.

Culling diseases are related to biological life forms who live off their host – they are parasitic in a way that requires a healthy host in their initial stage of establishing residence within their host. They are the tenant who moves in, hangs a picture on the wall, and then discovers the rotted stud that, when shaken by the hammer driving the nail breaks and causes the wall to crack or crumble.

I love to invoke evangelicals – because they often get words they quote so horribly wrong. In Revelation we are told that – in a period that, most likely, falls in the decade from 2030 to 2040 – a third of life shall die. We know that Climate Change will cause the extinction of many species. For those whose translations focus on humanity, we know the Baby-Boom will be the bulk of the third that is to die in that period. That can be a natural death, or it can be a death accelerated by a culling virus.

For the event to have meaning, first the population must cease to expand and, in the United States, the Census Bureau has said 2019 was the first year when the population did not grow, but might have shrunk relative to 2018. When that can be said for the global population, we are at the point where the population could easily drop by a third within a year to ten-years.

If we consider food shortages or general instances of physical stress of the type that once had the average global life expectancy at 35, a culling virus could easily damage those nations where Climate Change is creating average temperatures exceeding human tolerance levels. As a result, those in equatorial regions would be culled from the human herd as rapidly as those with defined medical conditions.

As we look at the Wuhan coronavirus, we can see a life form that jumps between people. There may be intermediary animals – nothing that eats a cadaver or simply bites an infected person and becomes a carrier. This is not the era of the ancient plagues where humans were dealing with mosquitoes, flea-infested rats, mice or a contaminated surface. Then there is a human-to-human pandemic involving a disease that does not want to kill its host and therefore does not contaminate the bloodstream.

The Wuhan virus is transmitted by respiratory system vapors, droplets, or small particles. This requires either close interpersonal contact or nearly immediate contact with a contaminated surface.

Knowing that it becomes obvious that any heavily populated area would be a natural habitat for the virus. Given the population of China and population density of the Wuhan region, it makes sense that any virus created in pigs and ducks – mainstays of the Chinese diet – would emerge there.

When we deal with the spread to other countries, population density is also associated with international airports – hubs of both commercial and tourist travel. Once we accept population density as a pandemic threat, we can look at why certain cities see spreading of the disease to a larger degree than others of similar importance – cities that are economic hubs, like New York City and Los Angeles, or Educational hubs like Boston, New York, and New Haven.

Both cities are commercial hubs. NYC, with a population of about 8.7 million, have finance in the form of Wall Street, along with several major Universities. Los Angeles has a population of about 4 million and, because of Hollywood, is an entertainment capital. If go north, there is San Francisco, with 885 thousand residents who serve to fill Northern California's cultural, commercial, and financial needs.

We can look at the "college town" environment in a city like Boston, where Universities – Harvard, MIT, BU, and Northeastern – contribute to the population of 4.9 million that links the city with 'hometown' cities and towns across the nation. This is a contrast to Yale University, in New Haven, Connecticut – where the population is 862 thousand and there is no international airport, but students can, if exposed, still introduce the virus.

There are party towns: Las Vegas, Nevada, with 650 thousand residents and countless tourists; then there is the smaller tourist destination, of New Orleans, Louisiana with 390 thousand residents and noted for crowds drawn to Creole restaurants augmented by the annual Mardi Gras which packs people together in celebrations seen as costumed parades and masquerade balls.

In 2020, festivities began Saturday, 1 February and extended through 25 February – nobody in government told them to cancel their month-long party. But then, the first United States death was reported in Washington State on Saturday, 29 February. Therefore, the timeline does not infer fault or error.

If we recognize and accept the realities of socialization within the context of both commerce and recreation, the contamination pattern of any virus can be computer modeled and the spread of any future pandemic or epidemic can be anticipated.

There are inherent differences between communities which have a direct effect on commutative patient totals.

Consider that New York City emerged to become an epicenter of the Wuhan virus – it's a rather large population within a relatively small area, with considerable interpersonal contact without social contact. You can stand in Times Square on New Year's Eve, be part of the celebration and yet be totally alone.

When I was in High School, I lived in the Flatbush section of Brooklyn – a county and borough whose population of 2.5 million people is five times the population of the State of Wyoming, roughly four times the population of Alaska (the biggest state in the union and twice the size of the second-biggest state, Texas) – when I had a book to read and wanted the true privacy necessary to ensure you could concentrate, I would go to the corner of Flatbush Avenue and Church Street.

That's arguable the busiest corner in Brooklyn; it is a few hundred feet from Erasmus Hall High School which, at the time had about 7,000 students attending in three shifts. I would sit on the steps of the Flatbush Reform Church and, though there was a steady flow of pedestrian traffic, it was the only neighborhood location that nobody would bother or even pass within twenty feet of you.

On the opposite extreme, if you wanted a can of sardines to be an example of "social distancing," all you need to do was go on the subway or bus during the morning or evening rush hour. New York City is a place where people are packed together throughout the day.

New York is the city that never sleeps.

Because it never sleeps, and because it has multiple airports, highways, trains, and buses that are busy at all hours, contamination and the spreading of disease is rather easy.

In contrast, Los Angeles is car-centered – everyone drives and are therefore "self-isolated" during the period when New Yorkers are being the most exposed – during commuting time, pushed together standing on crowded subways grasping the same hand-poles while the car sways, bumping people against each other in an era of social distancing. NYC is a natural hotbed of contamination, where any virus easily transmitted by breath or touch finds a natural accelerant for their spread.

From the City, white-collar commuters carry the virus to New Jersey and Connecticut, or Westchester County and Long Island. It is a base reality that resulted in Gov. Andrew M. Cuomo disclosing that, as of Sunday, 22 March, New York State had roughly 5 percent of global coronavirus cases – with about half of them in the City.

Thank's to New York and the surrounding areas, 3 days after publication of book 8 in this series – on 30 March, American virus cases surpassed 104,500 with 1,702 deaths – the mortality rate was in 1.63% range; two days later, there were 137,000 cases, with 2,400 deaths, for a rate of 1.75%. In New York State, the death rate was one every 6 minutes. The previous decade, saw influenza kill between 12,000 and 61,000 Americans a year or an average of 1-5 thousand a month.

On 30 March, Germany showed a record number of cases in the context of a record low death rate; besides, there were more vacant beds than the total hospital capacity in Italy or several other nations. As a result, Germany was bringing patients in from those other countries.

With that in mind, on 30 March Dr. Anthony Fauci said the U.S. could have over 100,000 coronavirus deaths. In keeping with caution, he went pessimistic and said:

"We're going to have millions of cases. ... As I have said before, it's true the virus itself determines that timetable. You can try and influence that timetable by mitigating against the virus, but, ultimately, it's what the virus does."

At a White House press briefing, the media wanted to talk per capita testing, while making it a point to ignore the demographic and geographic realities of where and why testing is done. President

Trump quickly shut them down for their snide slant to what should be serious journalism.

Using their example of South Korea, with its total population of 51,471,614 in a 38,691 square mile area (1,302 people per square mile), with the United States population of 330 million (90 people per square mile) it's a bit harder to test people. But the MSM will lie, distort, and misrepresent – they practice Lawyer's Lies by stating a fact without the appropriate context. Trump has called them on this repeatedly, and those who follow coverage of the Democratic candidate see them using the same technique to defend Joe Biden and attack his political opponents.

In that context, the 9.86 million population of Seoul South Korea is roughly equal to that of the New York City metropolitan or commuter area, and for Korea represents a quarter of the nation. It is natural for them to have a higher per capita testing ability – which is why the media liars select that criteria for their attacks on Trump, but refrain from any mention of it in terms of infections or deaths.

This can be seen in a sample of numbers at 5:00 PM EST, on 1 April 2020, with the Global percent as the baseline a nation would want to be below:

        11.90% - 13,155 / 110,574 cases Italy

        08.94% - 9,131 / 102,179 cases Spain

        07.89% - 2,357 / 29,857 cases United Kingdom

        07.00% - 4,043 / 57,749 cases France

        06.37% - 3036 / 47,593 cases Iran

        Global Baseline 05.02% - 46,252 / 921,924 cases

        04.03% - 3,316 / 82,361 cases China

        02.20% - 4,542 / 206,207 cases United States

        01.15% - 891 / 77,558 cases Germany

        01.13% - 108 / 9,539 cases Canada

As seen, global mortality rates were 5.02% of identified cases; when dealing with a culling virus, high exposure and a low mortality rate combine as evidence that the health care system or policies of a nation are succeeding or failing. In terms of identified cases, the United States exceeds those of many other industrial nations, but in terms of mortality, except for Germany, it was doing far better than the European Union. How it is doing when this volume is ready to be published, we will see at the end of the final chapter.

But why, when the EU nations have some form of Universal Health coverage, is the U.S. mortality rate lower than theirs? Does Trump deserve any part of the credit?

It seems, while they had the same information Trump did, EU governments worsened their predicament by overestimating their response capacity, while Trump publically voiced optimism, while engaging in actions driven by pessimism. He practiced the old saw about *"Hoping for the best and preparing for the worst."*

On 5 February, one day after the State of the Union address, and about two weeks after China instituted a locked-down of nearly 60 million people in Hubei province, EU state representatives were informed by a European Commission official that they had *"things under control"* and that *"There is strong level of preparedness in member states, most have measures in place."*

Two weeks later, Italy had its first coronavirus death, and six weeks later, the Italian death toll was four times that of China.

During that period, as the lack of preparation and seriousness of the problem became self-evident, rather than focusing on joint action many of the member States encased themselves in defensive cocoons defined by trade barriers which, if Trump were instituting them would have been termed xenophobic by his detractors. There intended effect was to hamper the export of medical equipment and enhance the protectionist measures against fellow EU members. It might be seen as a BREXIT type default self-preservation position.

Think about the very real, life-threatening, xenophobic acts of some EU members; compare them to Nancy Pelosi's 15 July 2019 "Dear Colleague" letter to House Democrats about Trump's policies in opposition to illegal immigration – a letter in which she showed she was, in truth, a Reagan Democrat: *"The House cannot allow the President's characterization of immigrants to our country to stand. Our Republican colleagues must join us in condemning the President's xenophobic tweets."* She went on to invoke references made by other House members who had quoted *"President Ronald Reagan's last speech as President in which he said, 'Thanks to each wave of new arrivals to this land of opportunity, we're a nation forever young, forever bursting with energy and new ideas, and always on the cutting edge, always leading the world to the next frontier... If we ever closed the door to new Americans, our leadership in the world would soon be lost.'"*

Keep in mind that Reagan is the one who created the policy of runaway National Debt based on the idea that runaway inflation would monetize it and thereby negate it; he was also the one who was for open borders, opposed a Democratic-sponsored fence along the Southern Border and declared unrestricted amnesty for many of those who violated American immigration laws. The record shows Pelosi supported Reagan's unrestricted immigration approach and voted <u>against</u> the 2006 Secure Fence Act, which funded the segment of "wall" built by Obama and she now opposes completion of that work by Trump.

In response to her letter, Trump tweeted, "*So interesting to see 'Progressive' Democrat Congresswomen, who originally came from countries whose governments are a complete and total catastrophe, the worst, most corrupt and inept anywhere in the world (if they even have a functioning government at all), now loudly ... and viciously telling the people of the United States, the greatest and most powerful Nation on earth, how our government is to be run. Why don't they go back and help fix the totally broken and crime-infested places from which they came.*"

As we move forward in the decade, we will see the number of *"totally broken and crime-infested places"* increase. The European Union and its response to the current virus provide an example of its fractured nature which was initially exposed by the 2016 BREXIT vote.

As it stands, as of this writing, Americans need to focus on a comparison with other nations of similar international importance, geographical structure, or population density. It is only then that we can evaluate the final data by comparing American mortality and exposure rates with those nations.

America is a very open and mobile nation; it follows that an easily communicated virus would spread quickly. The degree of that spread is exposed by testing, and positive result exposes the travel pattern of commerce or individuals. The spread pattern has military applications for any who might want to engage in biological warfare attacks in the future.

The Chinese response to Wuhan flu was interesting. Not only did they closed the region, engage in a lock-down that would stop the spread, they artificially inflated their mortality rate by under-reporting exposures – they did not count or report as exposed those people who were asymptomatic. Unless there were clear symptoms, China did not consider the person exposed.

While having a high mortality rate is a negative, media focus has been on exposure and testing. From a propaganda standpoint, it is beneficial to have a high-mortality-low-exposure rate. It makes the disease seem more deadly and more frightening, thus it is more disnerving and disruptive to the next nation in which it appears.

Trump has stated confronting the coronavirus was a state of war and conceptually, if it were a war, it might fall into the definition set forth by political science Wolf Graf von Baudissin. By its nature, war is a spiritual endeavor, the underlying reasons are derived from a viewpoint conflict. Those with a more sustainable viewpoint must ultimately emerge victorious. When viewed in terms of disease and pandemic, the conflict is between biological species.

With disease, as with war, there are two forces – the resident population and the invader. As I've cited in previous books, there is a Greek Oracle about two opposing armies separated by a river: *"The first one in the water will lose."*

As we have seen in the attack tactics taken against Trump, it was assumed that the *"in the water"* was the literal meaning and so, when one army was seen splashing around in the river, it was taken to mean they were destined to lose, so the other army attacked and thus disclosed the true meaning. Since the attacker had to go into the water to attack, it was those who attacked across the water who lost both the battle and the war.

"The first one [TO ATTACK] will lose."

Trump understands this and is therefore positive and friendly until the opponent attacks. On 8 November 2016, Swamp Denizens began their attack – yielding the title of book 3, *"The Swamp Fights Back."* As the MSM and denizens showed, they only know attacks; it was the same mistake the Tea Party denizens made with Obama.

To illustrate the Oracle, I utilize both Napoleonic France and Germany attacking Russia, Russia invading Afghanistan, The United States-Vietnam War, and how they tie back to Scythian tactics which allowed the Colonial forces to win against Britain and the Resistance to defeat Germany in the Second World war.

How does this relate to Wuhan Flu and differentiate it from a Bubonic plague? The answer is the objective.

Bubonic plague kills its host, it spreads via blood. This means the creation of a cadaver that is consumed by predators, or as "road-kill" – hence the Biblical prohibition against eating an animal whose cause of death is unknown. But, as mentioned, Wuhan coronavirus conforms to a respiratory flu category consistent with culling disease characteristics – it only kills the weak or those with an underlying condition that has already extensive stress on the immune system.

Accordingly, this is not a war – there is no aggressive invader in the sense of a military context – coronavirus is more like what we experience with uncontrolled immigration. When we vaccinate, we are placing restrictions on that immigration through the controlled introduction of a disease in a form the immune system can identify and adjust for.

The war analogy is interesting, especially in a conceptualist like Trump who is attacked when speaking of his *"gut feeling"* or instinctive sense something is the correct answer.

A conceptualist understands the commonality between things in a way that allows the general application of any given pattern that is known to work in a related context. As such, when told of a medication that successfully treats malaria and that coronavirus has characteristics that mimic those of malaria, it is easy to accept any medical speculation that the medication might also address those characteristics of Wuhan flu.

Trump was attacked for suggesting, as his medical people did, that chloroquine and hydroxychloroquine could prove valuable in the treatment of Wuhan Flu. His statement, like many others he has made, was distorted by the MSM, who cited the head of the Food and Drug Administration's statement that the drug needed testing before its potential benefits in containing the virus were certified.

Of course, it didn't take long for Trump's FDA sources to see the wisdom of using the approved medications on virus patients – in a context for which approval had yet to be granted.

At the end of March, an FDA decision affirmed Trump's *"gut feeling"* about the applicability of malaria within the context of a medically sound decision – *"Based on the totality of scientific evidence available to FDA, it is reasonable to believe that chloroquine phosphate and hydroxychloroquine sulfate may be effective in treating COVID-19."*

Consistent with the pattern of attacks on Trump's decisions, the FDA refuted those who attacked Trump's reliance on his form of *"instinct and gut feeling."*

Trump was functioning from reports that Clinicians in China, Italy, and France had been testing existing pharmaceuticals into the fight, and had observed anti-malaria drugs – and an unlicensed antiviral remdesivir (RDV) which *"has demonstrated in vitro and in vivo activity in animal models against the viral pathogens that cause MERS and SARS, which are coronaviruses structurally similar to SARS-CoV-2 (Wuhan Flu)"* – were all proving effective. Therefore, he could assert, with reasonable certainty, there would be something available soon.

True to form, rather than doing their due diligence research, the anti-Trump pundits and elements of the MSM immediately went on the attack. These attacks ignored the fact that more than 1,000 patients in New York were being successfully treated with the drugs and chose to focus on the cautious statements made by Dr. Anthony Fauci, who emphasized the treatments have not yet been proven to be safe and effective – a process that could take a year or more.

Even so, at his dying patient's request, an infectious disease doctor in Florida administered the medications. But not until after he explained all the ramifications and that there were *"no trials, there's no testing, it was not something that was approved,"* for the treatment of Wuhan flu. Within an hour of taking the medication, there was a sign of improvement accompanied by minor discomfort as his body fought off the disease – five days later he was discharged from the hospital.

Allowing that the success rate was still antidotal, on 24 March Health and Human Services (HHS) Secretary Alex Azar, labeled Trump the *"Right to Try president"*, as befits one who supports the right of patients in immediate need to use exploratory treatments.

Six days later, reports from New York spoke of Dr. Vladimir Zelenko having treated 699 coronavirus patients with 100% success using Hydroxychloroquine Sulfate, Zinc, and Z-Pak. One common response reported by Dr. Zelenko was that the shortness of breath symptom was resolved within four to six hours of treatment.

The media was reporting on a shortage of ventilators, though, if only the alleviation of the breathing difficulty were achieved, that need for additional ventilators would be eliminated based on the reported results of zero patients died, zero patients incubated, and four hospitalizations among the 699 treated.

Subsequent to Trump's mention of the treatment and vicious media attacks the idea that Trump could make a medical suggestion, Secretary Azar had tweeted: "*Scientists in America and around the world have identified multiple potential therapeutics for COVID19, including chloroquine and hydroxychloroquine.*"

As seen with the FDA approval, Trump refers to "*instincts*" when he is really expressing facts predicated on expert knowledge from those not yet ready to formally commit to an "on the record" statement or commitment. Trump's detractors make it a point to jump on and exploit boilerplate modifiers about "trials" and lengthy ethically sound procedures usually conducted over extended periods in a controlled environment.

We can even think in terms of the "Wall" that those who were opposed to Trump's anti-coronavirus positions or attacked as racist and xenophobic should now see as an appropriate response to the defense of the National Health and Welfare.

Michigan Governor Gretchen Whitmer apparently authorized threatening "administrative action" against doctors who prescribed the *chloroquine phosphate and hydroxychloroquine sulfate* which Trump had suggested could potentially help coronavirus patients. But, not long after, when FDA Chief Scientist Denise M. Hinton had formally stated the benefits outweigh the risks, and after numerous attacks her threatening of healthcare workers within her state, she relented.

When we look to the Southern Border – by 1 April it had been closed by Mexico. Obama's "Fence" or Trump's "Wall" was proving to be the proper response to what is known to be a threat created by Climate Change, the warning being the coronavirus in Mexico and the unsanitary conditions which, on 16 March, were cited as a basis for El Salvador to blocking flights from Mexico City. As of 1 April, there were 1215 cases and 29 deaths in Mexico (mortality: 2.38%).

CHAPTER TWO - Existential Angst

"A good name is more desirable than great riches;
to be esteemed is better than silver or gold."
~ Proverbs (22:1)

Existential, such a popular word in the age of Impeachment and COVID-19. And with it, the nation gained angst – anxiety, dread, or anguish – which is manipulated by those who profit by keeping the masses in an unfocused state by tricking them into focusing on the trivial and all that, in the long-term, is meaningless in terms of their survival.

The nation should be concerned with existence, but it chose to focus on finding excuses to impeach Trump. Granted, a second impeachment attempt is temporarily off the table – at least it should be until after the November 2020 election affirms Trump retains his role as the occupant of the Oval Office.

In an existential context, if the nation rids itself of Trump, it likely gets Biden – dispelling any consideration of America's concern for its continued existence. Depending on who the Vice President is, may well have decided to end its historical meaningful existence. It will be reduced to a nation ruled by meaningless rhetoric.

On Wednesday, 22 January, Representative Adam Schiff said that *"The president has shown that he believes that he's above the law and scornful of constraint."*

This is the same Adam Schiff that accepted Administration Policy negated the law against extortion and blackmailing of foreign officials. He can excuse negating laws, he can lie, he can tarnish the name of a political opponent and when called upon to prove his claims, he declares existence of what he asserts to be "overwhelming evidence", but when called upon to produce it, he produces nothing; then says the judge and jury must investigate and find the evidence.

If you do not understand the lie, answer a simple question: What law or statute code did Trump violate when, functioning *sub rosa* so as not to embarrass or accuse without evidence, he acted in accordance with a Clinton era treaty covering shared investigation evidence, and sought any data Ukraine officials might uncover as they delved into their investigations into domestic corruption?

When mention of any data related to Burisma, Hunter Biden or Joe Biden in relationship to boast of violating Federal Law came up, Schiff was quick to accept that blackmail and extortion were the acceptable "Government Policy" of the Obama-era; the world even watched as MSM defended Biden by saying *"there was no evidence of any wrongdoing"* and so used the lack of evidence from ongoing Ukraine investigations to be evidence that none would emerge in the future.

Think about the Clinton "Oral in the Oval' impeachment that was conducted by guys who would leave the hearings to visit their mistresses before heading home to their wives. As hypocritical as they were, even they knew there needed to be a legal violation before there could be an impeachment, so they manipulated things to elicit a deviation in definition that they could brand a lie – the meaning of *"Sexual Relations"*, a term normally used to describe intercourse, but which normally excludes kissing, hugging and forms of oral sex or mutual masturbation.

Perjury is a crime, even when it is simply to keep one's private life private. So there was a basis to impeach Clinton. But where was the basis to impeach Trump? They had been seeking on since the election results were announced on 8 November 2016.

Even as the pandemic was spreading, the anti-Trump forces could not refrain from denouncing Trump for asserting others did not prepare for the pandemic. We know that Obama experienced the problem with H1N1 and know the depleted resources were not replenished.

Who was responsible? Obama, Biden, Congress?

If it was Congress, we need to remember many of them are there now and are botching things again. Adam Schiff is diverting Congressional resources into an "investigation' he hopes will provide and new basis to attack Trump.

On CNN, commentators were asserting, *"he's been in office three years"* and claimed nobody saw this coming. For them, Trump is a liar. But what about Italy, Spain, France, Iran, and the point of origin for Wuhan virus, China? Why weren't they prepared and why are their spread or mortality rates so much worse than America – surely, for Trump not to have prepared, they would have had to have known and prepared.

More important, since the 2016 election, various elements of Congress and MSM had worked diligently to distract Trump from the duties they were now claiming he failed to perform. As we saw in Book-8 of this series, Nancy Pelosi engaged in activities to delay the transfer of the Impeachment Articles that were synchronized to the emergence and spread of Wuhan virus. A week after release the of the book on *Amazon Barron's* published an article saying Pelosi's husband had done exactly what was posited on page 40 of the book – *Did her family do any buying in late March?*": "*Nancy Pelosi's Husband Bought Up Slack, Microsoft, and Alphabet Securities*"

The article informed readers: "*From Feb. 21-28, Paul Pelosi paid between $850,003 and $1.75 million for Microsoft stock options. He acquired a total of 150 call-option contracts to buy Microsoft stock at $130 each, and 100 call-option contracts to buy the stock at $140 each. The options expire March 31, 2021. ... Microsoft shares, which traded in March for as little as $135.00—within the range of the purchase price of his options—were trading Thursday for $153.63 for a loss of 2.6% year to date.*"

That means, the answer to the question posed in Book-8 was a resounding YES. When I mentioned this on QUORA's discussion board, someone thought I was mistaken and said I meant California Senator Dianne Feinstein.

I googled it and discovered she and three colleagues had sold "*off stocks worth millions of dollars in the days before the coronavirus outbreak crashed the market.*"

Senator Feinstein was a ranking Senate Judiciary Committee member and therefore was in a position to know the game Pelosi was playing during the impeachment who shook things up by saying she was somewhat biased "toward acquitting Trump" because, with "*nine months left to go, the people should judge. We are a republic, we are based on the will of the people – the people should judge.*"

Obviously, with the votes to acquit, there was no reason for Feinstein to break with the Democrats. The coronavirus was still on the way to crashing the markets, so it was doing what impeachment would have done if the Nixon-Clinton pattern had held – as it would have if there had been an actual crime cited in the Articles.

Naturally, Feinstein denied any insider trading: "*During my Senate career I've held all assets in a blind trust of which I have no control.*" But it conformed to a standard lawyer's lie scenario where there was no "pillow talk", and her spokesman, Tom Mentzer, would say, *"All of Senator Feinstein's assets are in a blind trust. She has no involvement in her husband's financial decisions."*

According to the news report, Republicans Richard Burr of North Carolina, James Inhofe of Oklahoma, and Kelly Loeffler of Georgia were the other three Senators.

On 13 February, Richard Burr, the chairman of the Senate Intelligence Committee, apparently used 30 transactions to unload $628,000 to $1.72 million in holdings roughly a week before the markets fell. Burr's spokesperson placed this obfuscation spin on the trades: *"Senator Burr filed a financial disclosure form for personal transactions made several weeks before the U.S. and financial markets showed signs of volatility due to the growing coronavirus outbreak. As the situation continues to evolve daily, he has been deeply concerned by the steep and sudden toll this pandemic is taking on our economy."*

As author of the Pandemic and All-Hazards Preparedness Act of 2019, Burr was well versed in potential dangers of the pandemic which would emerge five months after it was signed into law. Five months is hardly sufficient time for preparation, but it is sufficient to set the process in motion to ensure a quick response that would allow for the recovery that Trump viewed so optimistically.

As for the other Senators – Loeffler and Inhofe.

Loeffler's husband is Jeffrey Sprecher, chairman of the New York Stock Exchange, and they began to sell stock on 24 January, the same day Loeffler was privy to a briefing from two members of Trump's Coronavirus Task Force. The couple continued to sell until 14 February – the sales are estimated to have totaled between $1.2 million and $3.1 million, with the proceeds used to purchase stock in a software company that facilitates working at home. Loeffler later claimed – and the Senate Ethics committee later agreed – these miraculously coincidental trades happened without the knowledge of either herself of her husband:

"This is a ridiculous and baseless attack. I do not make investment decisions for my portfolio. Investment decisions are made by multiple third-party advisors without my or my husband's knowledge or involvement. As confirmed in the periodic transaction report to Senate Ethics, I was informed of

these purchases and sales on February 16, 2020 — three weeks after they were made."

As for Inhofe, it was reported he *"sold as much as $400,000 in stock all on Jan. 27, in companies such as PayPal, Apple, and real estate company Brookfield Asset Management."*

The timing of the Pelosi purchase options was the same 24 February period when Nancy Pelosi lead the media on a tour of San Francisco's Chinatown encouraging people visit the restaurants and shops – to do exactly the opposite of sheltering in place or social distancing. According to Pelosi, *"That's what we're trying to do today is to say everything is fine here. Come because precautions have been taken. The city is on top of the situation."*

So there we have it, Nancy Pelosi clearly declaring its safe in San Francisco *"because precautions have been taken. The city is on top of the situation."*

In another statement, she underscored what was known to be a virus spreading fantasy: *"Come to Chinatown. Precautions have been taken by our city, we know that there's concern about tourism, traveling all throughout the world, but we think it's very safe to be in Chinatown and hope that others will come."*

But, for her husband to make money on the pandemic, to be able to exercise his options, the virus needed to panic the markets. The only way for that to happen was for the virus to spread. Had the impeachment followed the path seen with Clinton and Nixon, then the stocks would have lost between 22% and 49%. Instead, because there was no cited crime, the markets blew it off and continued to rise. Then, current with the impeachment vote, intelligence officials were telling the Congressional Intelligence Committee that there was an emerging pandemic – and Pelosi sat on the Articles until the emerging news started to affirm the intelligence reports.

That's when the House Intelligence Committee played games.

They started yelling the Senate needed more or new witnesses to prove what House Managers had asserted was a case based on *"overwhelming evidence"* – even though it was a case without a crime, without any clearly delineated or defined definition of wrong-doing. It distracted the media from the pandemic and allowed the delayed response to happen. The Swamp Denizens were busy with The Most Harm to the Most People policies we saw described in my 2013 & 2014 political books.

Of course, on 29 March, Pelosi was on CNN deflecting from the actions she leads by accusing Trump of not acting while she was distracting attention from the emerging problem: *"The president, his denial at the beginning, was deadly. His delaying of getting equipment to where it — his continued delay in getting equipment to where it's needed is deadly ... as the president fiddles, people are dying."*

But when it came to fiddling while Rome burnt, Pelosi was in charge of both the music and setting the fires.

Yelling *"Abuse of Power"* and *"Obstruction of Congress"* are what she was doing while the pandemic was growing. It was what she was dedicated to when, in January, the famed Doomsday Clock was set at two minutes to midnight this year, the metaphorical point of the Earth's destruction.

Where Trump is attacked for saying that *"in theory"* America could be back in business by Easter. Though many Swamp Denizens have presented it as a firm commitment, what Trump really said on 24 March was *"I'd love to have it open by Easter. I would love to have that. It's such an important day for other reasons, but I'll make it an important day for this too. I would love to have the country opened up and just raring to go by Easter."* So, we see the president presenting it as a symbolic goal; not something intended to be based on medical or scientific evidence.

A year earlier, on 11 March 2019, Pelosi told the media, *"I've been thinking about this: Impeachment is so divisive to the country that unless there's something so compelling and overwhelming and bipartisan, I don't think we should go down that path, because it divides the country."* She then added, *"And he's just not worth it."*

Pushed to elaborate, she failed to mention any valid reason for impeachment, instead, she asserted, *"Are we talking ethically? Intellectually? Politically?"*

Then answered her own question: *"All — All of the above. No. No. I don't think he is. I mean, ethically unfit. Intellectually unfit. Curiosity-wise unfit. No, I don't think he's fit to be president of the United States."*

But as has been reported, her position changed as soon as there was a way for her family to have a financial gain as the Wuhan pandemic coincided with the transfer of the Impeachment Articles to the Senate. In holding the articles, Pelosi rebuffed calls from top

Democrats to submit them; during a 9 January press conference she said: "*I will turn them over when I'm ready, and that will probably be soon.*"

In terms of timing, the WHO "Rolling updates on coronavirus disease (COVID-19)" web page informs us that, on 5 January, "*WHO published its risk assessment and advice and reported on the status of patients and the public health response by national authorities to the cluster of pneumonia cases in Wuhan.*"

Then it tells us, the day after her statement, on 10 January, "*WHO issues its first guidance on the novel coronavirus*" stating:

"*Developed with reference to other coronaviruses, such as SARS and MERS, WHO issued a tool for countries to check their ability to detect and respond to a novel coronavirus.*

"*This information is to help with identifying main gaps, assessing risks and planning for additional investigations, response and control actions.*"

Five days later, after the House vote to approve the managers, Pelosi formally presented two articles of impeachment to the Senate.

The timeline seems perfectly synchronized to an adjustment of the impeachment process to the emergence of the Wuhan virus.

The world watched Pelosi's attempts to dictate Senate rules and procedural actions. And, when that delaying tactic failed, House Managers rebuffed their own "*overwhelming evidence*" assertions and called for new witnesses – if they had been allowed, they would have stretched the process out over for at least an additional eight weeks or easily into the end of March when the pandemic forced the creation of stimulus legislation that could not have passed during an impeachment.

The timeline and sequence of known events and informed projections all came together to infer Pelosi manipulated things and held her no impeachment that position until her family saw a way of profiting from it; then attempted to manipulate things to maximize the detrimental effect on both national health and the economy. Of course, it depends on whether we wish to grant Pelosi the intellect or guile to engage in such deceitful conduct.

On 26 January, House Manager and Florida Representative Val Demings appeared on ABC's "This Week" spouting the bogus talking point, "*Regardless of what you say, the truth still matters and the evidence against the president is overwhelming. ... I do believe the testimony when you put it all together is as clear as two plus two equals four.*" Still, a week later the President was acquitted and to this day nobody can enumerate the overwhelming evidentiary points – without asserting hearsay that also includes the extortion Biden boasted of, and Trump had declared "horrible", was Obama Administration policy.

With no clearly definable evidence, other than hearsay, there was no case – but, clearly, a number of Congressional Managers had no difficulty lying about the existence of nonexisting evidence. That works – when the real intention is to crash the financial markets.

Distraction becomes easy when there is a president whose key point of focuses is on the positive and beneficial human outcomes that will yield a legacy which will place him in high historic regard. All that is needed, during a medical "emergency" is to get the masses to think in terms of the traditional point of focus for doctors – those things that constitute the technical and biomedical aspects of a case. The medical focus downplays the patients' values and feelings.

The words of Dr. Fauci betray that technocratic focus.

During the final stages of an impeachment, Swamp Denizens had been striving to find a justification for over the four-years since the 8 November 2016 announcement of Trump's victory – that the national "*basket of deplorables*" had rejected the New York City and Southern California champion of corruption – they were gifted with the Wuhan virus.

On 19 March 2020, Trump set aside reality to say: "*Nobody knew there'd be a pandemic or an epidemic of this proportion.*" It was a message of humanity, one that deflected responsibility or the media practice of making shotgun blast assertions of blame aimed to incite their audiences, which Trump was seeking to use to force the public to focus on the current issue – and not get distracted by a blame game which deflects from reality and positive actions.

On 26 March, Trump said, "*nobody would have ever thought a thing like this could have happened.*" As those stock trades made – either directly or via third parties – by Burr, Feinstein, Loeffler, Inhofe, and Pelosi show, the statement was an obvious lie.

Those who chose to ignore the known timeline tend to focus on a 29 January 2020 Peter Navarro memo, to the National Security Council, which said, "*risk of a worst-case pandemic scenario should not be overlooked.*" The memo included a clear warning: "*The lack of immune protection or an existing cure or vaccine would leave Americans defenseless in the case of a full-blown coronavirus outbreak on U.S. soil."*

But, we know the CDC was already screening Wuhan arrivals, and that Trump had already warned the airlines of the travel ban he would initiate on 31 January – 2-days after Navarro's memo. And Navarro had issued a second warning in February when Pelosi was encouraging people to engage in close personal consumerism in San Francisco's Chinatown. If people had followed her advice, resulting in a widespread outbreak that would have been blamed on Chinese Americans – so was a means of inciting racism that would then be deflected to become Trump's fault.

The second Navarro warning, on 23 February, informed the president of an *"increasing probability of a full-blown COVID-19 pandemic that could infect as many as 100 million Americans, with a loss of life of as many as 1-2 million souls. The lack of immune protection or an existing cure or vaccine would leave Americans defenseless in the case of a full-blown coronavirus outbreak on U.S. soil."*

Think about what he said, and consider a media environment that was devoutly anti-Trump, so anti-American and pro-harm.

Anti-Trump media persisted in asserting Trump should listen to the medical experts – whose bias, based on a 24 May 2011 Journal of Medicine article, which asserted doctors *"directed the focus away from personal meanings onto medical facts,"* – touted the warnings of medical projections made by an economist.

Based on the study reported in the Journal article, *"the doctors showed little curiosity about the individual and neglected more personal aspects of the patients' conditions, showing little or no existential care."* In the pandemic context, existential care is the concern for the stresses imposed by social isolation, the economic impacts which are the concerns of those speaking of Universal Basic Incomes and income replacements or augmentation in the stimulus packages.

On 31 March, Dr. Anthony Fauci stated that between 100,000 and 240,000 deaths were *"a number that we need to anticipate, but we don't necessarily have to accept it as being inevitable."*

Dr. Deborah Birx offset the negative by invoking the positive, *"We really believe we can do a lot better than that."* And she did so with the knowledge that the numbers represented four or five times as many cases being identified before the pandemic ended. It also meant they were projecting the possibility of as many American deaths as occurred in World War Two, but only a fraction of the initial projections which allowed a possibility the death toll might approach two million.

With that level of death supposedly looming on the horizon, on 2 April, Adam Schiff and Nancy Pelosi announced the creation of the House Select Committee on the Coronavirus Crisis which was to investigate the Trump administration's handling of the pandemic emergency. Their goal was to find "mistakes" and deflect attention from solving current problems by focusing attention away from any lack of preparation connected with Obama-Biden or state failure to prepare for the level of pandemic, epidemic or plague which Climate scientists had, for decades, warned could emerge by the third decade of the 21st century.

There is a WHO problem with – as President Trump tweeted on 7 April:

"The W.H.O. really blew it. For some reason, funded largely by the United States, yet very China-centric. We will be giving that a good look. Fortunately I rejected their advice on keeping our borders open to China early on. Why did they give us such a faulty recommendation?"

That recommendation was given on 3 February and stated that none of the widespread travel restrictions were necessary to stop the spread of the Wuhan coronavirus – that name referring to its place of origin in Wuhan, the capital of China's Hubei province. As we know, Trump went against the "*expert advice*" presented by WHO and, on 31 January, formally introduced the travel restrictions that have since been duplicated wherever the virus has appeared.

Had Trump done as his impeachment promoting adversaries have said he should, the travel ban would not exist and Pelosi's State would probably exceed New York City in both infections and deaths? But, as she demonstrated in Chinatown, that would doubtless have pleased the House Speaker and facilitated more stock trades by her husband.

As is, Adam Schiff has suggested various lines of inquiry that, as chairman of the Intelligence Committee, he has already begun to pursue under the heading of "fact-finding" in preparation for the next nonsense impeachment – based on the idea Schiff described or justified with the idea: "*There needs to be oversight to make sure the representations we're hearing about the availability of testing are true — or if they're not true, then the administration needs to be held accountable.*" And that accountability is predicated on two election – both Trump and Schiff would need to be re-elected.

It can be anticipated Adam Schiff – a 59-year-old, 10-term, congressman – has a lock on re-election. Therefore, his preparation anticipates a less than decisive Trump victory which will then turn into a 2nd impeachment and disrupt the government in a way the first one failed to do. Schiff seems to thrive on imposing angst.

The Bolton book, which was supposedly such a case making revelation has vanished. And, months later, there was the comical reality – wherever we find a vocal figure for impeachment we find the pandemic working overtime. This presents an existential crisis for those who either support or deny prophecy. Swamp Denizens fought back, lost, and those who voted them into power are being punished with the threat of death. In 2014, it was "*Death Over Life: Secret of Revelation: A Prophecy of America's Destruction*", along with "*Biblical Prophecy: Are we in the Revelation Era*" – things that an Evangelical Republican might consider, but are outside the mental bias of secular whatever types.

Still, attempting to fulfill the ancient prophecies is something that gives life to many – Schiff has begun to make a career of it, Nancy Pelosi is a daughter of Thomas D'Alesandro Jr, who entered Congress when he was 36, and then became Mayor of Baltimore at 44 and held the office for 12-years. In 1958, after a professional life as a politician, D'Alesandro lost his bid for the Senate and at the age of 55, apparently was out of elective politics. He died August 1987, the same year Nancy was elected to the House of Representatives. It is a family that makes its living off the public dime and, from Nancy's actions toward Trump, hates those who are productive members of the national economy.

By holding the Article of Impeachment and trying to force the Senate to obey her rules rather than follow the Constitution, Pelosi engaged in the obstruction of Constitutional due process and rights to a speedy trial. She also obstructed the working of the Senate and ability of Senate Presidential candidates to conduct their campaigns in an orderly and productive manner – she was actively engaged in rigging the nomination for Joe Biden.

As we know from the transcript, Biden bragged of engaging in an act of extortion against Ukraine for the express purpose of having their Prosecutor General fired. How would America feel if Saudi Arabia and Russia withheld oil until such time as all members of Congress were removed from office? Or maybe just sought the removal of the Attorney General, Speaker of the House, or Minority Leader of the Senate?

If declared their *"Government Policy"*, under house legal in standards, an Oil nation's actions would be quiet legal and proper in the same way Biden's actions were. Biden claimed to have imposed a six-hour clock on what appears to have been a six-month process. As the official record shows, Congressman Jerry Nadler told the Senate, as *"Administration Policy"* such extortion is quite legal.

Thus, based on the "established legal standard" argued to protect Biden – and, by extension, Obama – the U.S. would quietly comply with oil-based extortion by the top five nations with proven reserves: Venezuela; Saudi Arabia; Canada; Iran; Iraq. Russia is eighth in the world, the United States is tenth and has half the oil of Russia, meaning America will, at some point, be dependent on the Russians – unless it goes Green and shifts all normal daily energy needs to electric in the same way China is.

There are multiple levels of existential angst derived from the conflagration of impeachment, coronavirus, and a 59th quadrennial presidential election.

Climate Change has placed both the planet and America into a Zeitgeist-era – one where the defining spirit or mood of one period of history came into direct conflict with the one that was to replace it. The ideas, beliefs, and social mores which defined the twentieth century can no longer be justified in the twenty-first or the centuries to follow.

Where America will fit – or if it will continue as a meaningful representation of anything – is being decided. Americans seem to be arguing they want someone who openly brags about the extortion of foreign officials. It does NOT matter if Hunter Biden profited, or if the idea was to shield the own of Burisma from investigation and prosecution. The fact is the extortion occurred and was declared American National Policy.

The alternative is four more years of Donald John Trump.

CHAPTER THREE – Existential Change

"It's a Barnum and Bailey world
Just as phony as it can be
But it wouldn't be make-believe
If you believed in me"
~ Billy Rose, 'It's Only a Paper Moon'

So many in America have failed to comprehend they elected PT Barnum to be President through the 58th and 59th quadrennial period. At the same time, they can only see the negative in phrases like *"you reap what you sow."* They infer a hindsight condemnation for what, at the time, was an intentional act diligently carried out.

True, we sometimes do things which seem correct at the time, we have a reason – however much it proves, in the context of future events, to have been wrong, it should have been right at the time.

But there are times when people and things are simply stupid to begin with. We saw this repeatedly with Chuck Schumer, who, when the Articles of Impeachment reached the Senate, asserted his version of the Californian House mismanagement claim that their perfect case had *"No witnesses; no documents,"* for the trial.

Schumer even tweeted that, *"America will remember this day. Senate Republicans turned away from truth and went along with a sham trial. If President Trump is acquitted with no witnesses, no documents, the acquittal will have no value because Americans will know this wasn't a real trial."*

Clearly, he had totally dismissed reality, and knew he could because he knew the base demographic wasn't too bright; he could do it with a straight face after the House Democrats had deposed 18 witnesses, 17 witnesses in public; the Senate had heard 192 clips of testimony from 13 witnesses during trial and received 28,578 pages of "overwhelming evidence".

Of course, when the pandemic reached America, Schumer and the rest were happy to yell that Trump denies evidence and the expert facts. And, as Good Friday approached and there was talk of rebooting the economy, the Republican *Lincoln Project* decided to attack its own and launched an ad campaign saying, *"Coronavirus has now killed three times more Americans than 9/11. So what's Donald Trump been up to? Blaming the impeachment hearings for distracting him from preparing for the pandemic."*

Attacking your own is an interesting gambit, one that can be taken to deflect any opposition attacks or be a meaningful rebellion by the "troops" that reflects an existential change in perception. It may well be that the Republican Swamp denizens believe they profit more from a President Biden than they could from keeping Trump in power for another four years.

The ad, entitled *"Distracted,"* claims Trump was very busy in January – not with impeachment related matters, but rather that he *"had plenty to do, like campaign rallies and golfing."*

The narration even posits the question, on the *"day before the first American died, where was Trump? Where do you think he was?"* And then, answers its own question: *"At another rally. By March, the world was calling coronavirus a pandemic. Where was Trump? On Twitter, as usual, blaming everyone else."*

As we know from the timeline, the first death was in January and at the time WHO was downplaying the emerging pandemic. So it would seem the *Lincoln Project* was playing at being Democratic and holding Trump accountable for not being smarter than "The Medical Experts" who saw no reason to close borders, ban travel, or take any extraordinary action of the type which became universal in March. Moreover, the juxtaposition of recognizing a pandemic in March with events prior to 21 January shows a level of cognitive dissonance or blatant dishonesty we have come to associate with the Swamp Denizens in both the Republican and Democratic Party.

The Republican perspective asserts Trump *"just didn't care. He still doesn't. He was never distracted. And Americans have been paying attention."* And if they can sell that point to voters in all fifty states, Biden should be able to garner the 270-plus Electoral College votes needed to grant him the Oval Office in January 2021.

On 9 April, political strategist and co-founder of *The Lincoln* Project, Reed Galen stated: *"The President's dishonest, incompetent, and delusional press conferences have veered into disturbing territory. The President is aware he lacks the competency to deal with this crisis, though he refuses to hold himself accountable. Instead, he'd rather place blame for his ineptitude on an irrelevant issue."*

Thus we see how *"The Swamp Fights Back."* (6 July 2017)

In the case of *The Lincoln Project*, which was founded in 2019 for the express purpose of removing Trump from office, we have a web page (lincolnproject.us) that describes their swamp denizen objective: *"We understand that action must be taken, now, to protect the institutions that have made the United States the greatest nation the world has ever known."*

They then say:

"Our Mission

"Defeat President Trump and Trumpism at the ballot box.

> *"We do not undertake this task lightly nor from ideological preference. Our many policy differences with national Democrats remain. However, the priority for all patriotic Americans must be a shared fidelity to the Constitution and a commitment to defeat those candidates who have abandoned their constitutional oaths, regardless of party. Electing Democrats who support the Constitution over Republicans who do not is a worthy effort."*

Consistent with the joint New York City and California based actors in the impeachment, the principle 'advisor' for *The Lincoln Project* is a New York attorney, George Conway, who is identified as *"a founding member of Checks & Balances, a group of conservative and libertarian lawyers organized to defend the rule of law."*

For those who have gleefully supported Biden over Sanders, they should derive great solace from the certain knowledge that the Pelosi/Schiff/Nadler talking points are derived directly from the standard Conservative Republican playbook. It is no surprise that Biden could boast of committing extortion against a foreign nation – with no observable benefit for the nation, but an implicit benefit for his son and a corrupt Ukraine oligarch – and earn support and endorsement from Conservative and Libertarian Republicans.

As with everything else in this crazy time of change, White House counselor Kellyanne Conway is the wife of the anti-Trump leader – in February she was on Fox News' "America's Newsroom" and said of those whose talking points her husband emulates:

> *"I think it shows you how petty and peevish and partisan the Democratic Party has come. And for all the people out there who fancy themselves the armchair psychiatrist trying to analyze certain people, they ought to shift their craft over to Nancy Pelosi."*

Pelosi is symbolic of the age of cynicism in which we now live and which is the antithesis of the profitable real estate culture that defines New York City-based firms. However, it defines the political culture which prospers through attack without specifics or providing any solution.

Those who have not been fully taken in by the con will be able to look and listen – then they will ask, "*What's the answer?*" They will want to know "the bottom line" solution.

Whenever you hear an attack, whenever someone gives you a statement like that provided by Bernie Sanders, and subsequently by Joe Biden – on 12 March, Sanders said, "*Unfortunately, in this time of international crisis, it is clear to me at least that we have an administration that is largely incompetent.*" But, what, specifically, is the incompetence of which he speaks?

We need to demand that such statements be accompanied by specifics. If necessary, the speaker should have a list prepared that enumerates BOTH the incompetence and the proper or appropriate response to each and every example.

It's easy to be a cynic. Especially when nobody demands you provide "the answer" or "bottom line" solution.

If we look at the COVID-19 situation, we see that there is a need for universal testing and treatment at government expense – Medicare for All (M4A), as advocated by Bernie Sanders – which would not be needed if the United States had not followed a pattern of gross incompetence for 108 years... the period since 1912 when the former President Theodore Roosevelt ran as a Progressive Party candidate.

Curiously, their platform, "*A Contract with the People*", had stated as its goal "*To destroy this invisible Government, to dissolve the unholy alliance between corrupt business and corrupt politics is the first task of the statesmanship of the day.*"

Today we might see that "*invisible Government*" as the "*Deep State*" and realize that nothing has changed. Instead, those who come to power and are showing they can impose change are called "disastrous", "horrible", the "worst in history", or "incompetent", when it is over a century of incompetence that they are trying to undo.

What is interesting is the degree to which those who profess change work so hard to ensure things remain the same. We see this in the presumptive nomination of Joe Biden which was presented by Adam Schiff as the presumptive basis for a "quid pro quo" against a political opponent who, at the time, was a private citizen – and even during the impeachment itself was little more than a candidate who met stiff opposition from Bernie Sanders and his supporters.

If we look at Biden and the extortion Trump – in the phone call – termed "horrible", we see the existence of an *"unholy alliance"* of corruption that continues and is supported by all those who we saw actively promote the impeachment since the 2016 election.

The House Managers knew Biden was the presumptive 2020 presidential candidate – even when he had 24-opponents for that nominatio63n. Then attacked Trump for "quid pro quo extortion" that never exceeded asking a favor in accordance with a 1998/9 treaty between the United States and Ukraine, but dismissed as legitimate when Biden enumerated the quid and the quo along with the specific timeframe for compliance and the fact that the quid – the firing of Prosecutor General Shokin – was provided.

Consistent with the *"corrupt politics"*, we learned that Biden was excused because his actions were "Administration Policy" that would have been set by the POTUS – in that case, Obama, without Trump, as his successor, having the right to set or continue the same policy. Under that government policy, the Vice President had the right to demand a foreign country fire its chief legal representative or threaten the very survival of that nation if the termination failed to occur on a schedule set by the American Vice President.

As we know, all who supported the impeachment held that, if the Federal Administration is run by a Democrat, America has the right to demand the termination of foreign government officials; no subsequent Republican Administration has the right to investigate or even question the facts related the exercise of that authority.

That the termination appears to have served nothing related to the national interest, but did bring about relief for the chief executive and owner of a Ukraine firm under investigation, and ensure the continued million dollars a year income being paid to the Vice President's son as a member of the board of directors of that firm engaged in criminal activities, is of no consequence. The crime or impropriety lay in the request for facts associated with the firing.

It would seem that nothing has changed since 1912. Criminal activities and the *"unholy alliance between corrupt business and corrupt politics"* is still supported by the voters. The calls for M4A are no different than contained in the 7 August 1912 platform which Teddy

Roosevelt ran on and is fundamentally no different than the things Bernie Sanders had promoted throughout his political career.

In 1912, Progressives declared that *"This country belongs to the people who inhabit it. Its resources, its business, its institutions and its laws should be utilized, maintained or altered in whatever manner will best promote the general interest."*

In the Wuhan virus age, it would be nice to determine what changes would be in the best long-term *"general interest."* It would appear, based on those programs deemed necessary in the stimulus packages, that the *"general interest"* is well served by free medical examinations and care; that it is also served by ensuring a minimum income for all citizens – a UBI.

We hear the cynics scream about "socialism" while also being critical of the cost of public assistance programs – it is a fantastic example to the cognitive dissonance which prevents society from achieving its full potential while maintaining those last vestiges of a slave culture cynics also denounce.

Traditionally, though many deny the facts, slaves were paid and supported by their masters. But they were kept at levels which prevented advancement – where possible, education was denied; it was improper for a slave to have a skill that did not directly serve its master. A slave had to be kept sufficiently healthy to ensure their ability to perform productive work, or long enough to reproduce and provide replacement labor.

To this day, the poor reproduce at a higher rate than the rich or educated. The scholar and purveyors of wisdom have, throughout history, been loaners – people without spouses or with spouses and maybe children, but none that history has decided to speak of.

When we look at the Wuhan virus we see the worst outcome among the poor and those with existing medical conditions – most of whom are also elderly who are approaching or have lived beyond the national average lifespan and reside in high-density population areas.

Realities are ignored when people want to blame Trump for everything they can twist to that purpose.

This is a time for Existential Change – when we rethink our inherent traditional stupidity of playing the *Blame Game*.

On 22 January, while WHO was still denying any reason for travel-related concern over the Wuhan Virus, President Trump was in Davos, Switzerland and the media focused tightly on whatever 17-

year-old Greta Thunberg had to say about Climate Change and how she was reacting to seeing Trump.

The previous year, Greta had been chosen as TIME's '*Person of the Year*' after her '*school strike*' had garnered international attention and had served to transform vaguely defined anxieties over the future of the planet into a worldwide movement to finally focus on addressing the issue of Climate Change. It was an issue that had been around, as we know since Greta's relative postulated it in 1896 and one that has definitely been around since the formation of the 1988 formation of the Intergovernmental Panel on Climate Change.

But, as we know, warnings about disaster go ignored by the general public, media, and governments – at least until they become realities and '*Blame Game*' players invoke hindsight to target their favorite scapegoat.

On 23 June 2008, the New York Times ran an opinion piece entitled "*1988-2008: Climate Then and Now*" which detailed much of what we had been ignored over the eight decades since the first warning was issued about the dangers of climate gases and the need to cut air pollution.

In 1979, Jimmy Carter was ahead of the 1980's curve when he installed solar collectors on the White House. But it didn't matter, because, in 1981, Conservative Icon Ronald Reagan immediately ordered the collectors removed – when Trump raised doubts about the causes of Climate Change, he was speaking to Reagan's base. It was George W Bush who, in 2003, reinstalled solar to heat the pool and spa, and to provide them with hot water, but not for real energy to power the White House or address the environmental issues.

Barack Obama is the one who, in 2011, focused on the various environmental concerns and to underscore the commitment "*to lead and the promise and importance of renewable energy in the United States.*" Those panels provided six times the power of those Carter installed and, by the 2019 impeachment had paid for themselves – meaning the White House is basically operating on free energy, and it is important to recall that Trump suggested the "Border Wall' also carry solar collectors that would, very quickly, serve as a source of 'free' energy to border communities.

But the "Blame Game" requires the media to avoid or ignore the fact that those who have sought the impeachment of Trump since 8

November 2016 have not done anything – nothing at all – to address and promote strong action against the climate issue. That is significant in the context of COVID-19 when all the nations which have been infected and have had to go into some form of lock-down have reported a 30-percent drop in air pollution.

Because of the virus, the global industrial community has far exceeded the goals of the Paris Climate Accords. The real issue then became one of how does the world "open for business" and keep the pollution levels where they were in April 2020?

The media covered Greta and how she looked at Trump as he passed her during the 21-24 January annual meeting of The 50th World Economic Forum (WEF) in Davos-Klosters, Switzerland.

Even if COVID-19 was not addressed at all, which effectively represents the position expressed by Sweden on 10 April, when they revealed they were not going to order the closure of restaurants and bars, or playgrounds and schools. Instead, the Swedish government was relying on voluntary action to stem the spread of COVID-19 and Swedish state epidemiologist, Anders Tegnell, explained: *"I think Sweden is doing okay. It's producing quality results the same way it's always done. So far Swedish health care is handling this pandemic in a fantastic way."*

In Sweden, people were encouraged to properly wash their hands and, if they felt sick, stay home. They were also encouraged to avoid crowded restaurants, as opposed to mandating the closure of those businesses. As for keeping their schools open, Tegnell said: *"We know that closing down schools has a lot of effects on health care because a lot of people can't go to their work anymore. A lot of children are suffering when they can't go to school."*

By 13 April, Sweden had about 11,000 cases with about 920 deaths – about 8.36 percent. Neighboring Finland had about 3,065 cases with 60 deaths (1.95%) and Norway had 6605 cases, with 135 death (2.04%). In the United States, the toll approximated 682,620 cases and 23,530 deaths for a rate of 3.45 percent. Looked at in a slightly different way, Sweden's population is roughly the combined population of Finland and Norway. If we look south to Denmark where there were about 6,515 cases and 285 deaths (4.37%), we see a nation half the size of Sweden that's connected to Europe.

Looking at the fatality rates, Sweden might have made quite a serious mistake. And, if we consider the overall population and the number of total cases, it would appear Sweden has made a mistake, or that there is something else happening.

In Sweden the median age is 41.1; in Denmark, it's 42.3; for Finland, it's 43.1; for Norway 39.8. The highest risk is for those over 40, meaning Finland should have the highest fatality rate, yet it has the lowest. The United States has a median age around 38.5, so its fatality rate is extremely high – it is even higher when we consider that roughly half the deaths are in New York City, where the median age is two years lower than that of the nation.

But there is a distortion created by the fact that the minority population is a quarter of the population and comprise a third of the deaths.

When this pandemic comes to an end, there is going to be a serious demographic issue surrounding the numbers and a need to explain the racial disparities which existed long before Trump took office. There is a serious need for an Existential Change in the way healthcare is delivered and the environmental conditions which define racially defined residential area.

More than a decade before the emergence of a Wuhan virus, Harvard Professor Michael McElroy said of the climate issue: *"If we choose to take on this challenge, it appears that we can slow the rate of change substantially, giving us time to develop mechanisms so that the cost to society and the damage to ecosystems can be minimized. We could alternatively close your eyes, hope for the best, and pay the cost when the bill comes due."*

The Wuhan virus has presented the first installment of a bill that is predicated on the pollution levels in our cities.

If we look at pollution, on average, the air quality in Sweden is good, but higher pollution levels do occur during the cold winter period in which the pandemic arose. Air quality in Finland is also rated good and the impact from air pollutants is minor – though the nation does have 1,600 early deaths attributed to pollution, which should affect the numbers but doesn't seem to have. Denmark has about 2,600 pollution-related deaths. And this issue of pollution is apparently the key – despite having one of Europe's lowest levels of air pollution, in Sweden, about 7600 people a year die prematurely due to exposure to air pollutants which create respiratory distress.

On 28 June 2017, Harvard published *"Study of US seniors strengthens link between air pollution and premature death"* which was summarized as "*A new study of 60 million Americans – about 97 percent of people age 65 and older in the United States – shows that long-term exposure to airborne fine particulate matter (PM2.5) and ozone increases the risk of premature death, even when that exposure is at levels below the National Ambient Air Quality Standards.*"

That paper describes the basis of the respiratory distress caused by allegedly clean air which would explain why Sweden is more susceptible to the Wuhan virus than its immediate neighbors. In the United States, the Harvard study included the statement "*that although we think air quality in the United States is good enough to protect our citizens, in fact, we need to lower pollution levels even further.*"

Based on data from or before 2010, and funded by a grant to the New York City Department of Health and Mental Hygiene from the National Center for Environmental Health, Centers for Disease Control and Prevention. In February 2018, a formal study of effects of New York City air quality – entitled '*Air Pollution and the Health of New Yorkers: The Impact of Fine Particles and Ozone*' – stated:

"Among residents age 40 years and older, an estimated 920 annual hospitalizations for cardiovascular events are attributable to current PM2.5 levels in New York City. These rates vary much less (3-fold) across the city than rates of respiratory hospital admissions (7.5-fold); the highest rates occur in the Bronx, Northern Manhattan, North Central Brooklyn and parts of Southern Brooklyn Adults older than 65 years of age have rates 4.5 times higher than younger adults of PM2.5-attributable hospitalization for cardiovascular events; overall, an estimated 63% of PM2.5-attributed cases occur in older adults."

So, a year before the Wuhan virus struck New York, the very population segment which is the most likely to die from exposure to the pandemic was specifically identified. We, therefore, should ask what steps the governmental authorities of New York City and State were taking to address the issue?

This is not a Federal issue; it only becomes Federal when the problem crosses state lines and affects interstate commerce. But, if it affects interstate commerce the power of the POTUS and Congress is generally considered absolute (a possible exception would involve Native American reservations).

The health and welfare of New York City residents fall upon the Mayor and city officials – with any additional assistance that might be required to augment the need for ventilators falling on the State and therefore the Governor.

But then we also have issues related to the US Environmental Protection Agency and US clean air standards which New York was free to exceed, but certainly was required to comply with. A draft policy assessment from September 1919 addresses related issues.

The *"Review of the National Ambient Air Quality Standards for Particulate Matter"* was issued as a draft document that was *"being circulated to facilitate discussion with the Clean Air Scientific Advisory Committee (CASAC) and for public comment to inform the EPA's review of the National Ambient Air Quality Standards for Particulate Matter (PM)."* Thus, it would not have directly influenced environmental issues contributing to the virus mortality rates in New York City in the way the 2018 report should have. But the very fact that it could draw on available information means areas with the highest potential mortality due to respiratory distress were "on notice" and should have been prepared.

Based on a quick perusal of the charts, it would be anticipated that the top three highest COVID-19 mortality would be in areas the draft report shows as: *"New York-Newark-Jersey City, NY-NJ-PA"*, *"Los Angeles-Long Beach-Anaheim, CA"*, *"Philadelphia-Camden-Wilmington, PA-NJ-DE-MD"*, and *"Detroit-Warren-Dearborn, MI"* – where the first has twice the fatalities of the second; the third and fourth are roughly equal and are each half of the second. Compared to the combined total, these four metropolitan regions account for roughly half the national total.

Naturally, there are multiple variables involved, but in each of the tabulations, the New York and Los Angeles are the top two – in half the tabulations, *"Chicago-Naperville-Elgin, IL-IN-WI"* can be seen emerging in third place. When the pandemic has officially or formally been declared at an end, it will be interesting to see how these five metropolitan areas faired. As of 13 April 2020, the placing of New York first is consistent with it providing about 7,900 {31%} of the reported 25,160 deaths attributed to COVID-19.

Since we are in the *"Blame Game"* era, and these reports are dated within months of the Wuhan virus appearing in China, it is very important to note that the underlying research papers were all published early in the first Obama-Biden term and came on the heels of the H1N1 virus outbreak – dated from 12 April 2009 to 10 April 2010 – and involved a CDC estimated 60.8 million cases, with 274,304 hospitalizations, and 12,469 United States deaths.

By Obama's second term, there was certainly ample time for the initiation of the necessary preparation for a recurrent virus of the type presented by COVID-19. In accordance with the Strategic National Stockpile created in 1999, there should have been medical equipment and pharmaceuticals available to augment State reserves.

In a 26 March briefing on resources related to a pandemic, Trump stated, *"We took over an empty shelf. We took over a very depleted place, in a lot of ways."* And four days later he said, *"We started off with an empty shelf. We didn't have very much in terms of medical product ... and we built something really good."*

Of course, the *"empty shelf"* concept was standard Trump rhetoric. Rocco Casagrande, managing director of a consulting firm hired to evaluate government emergency readiness, stated: *"that across the variety of threats that we examined, the Strategic National Stockpile has the adequate amount of materials in it and by and large the right type of thing."* This tells us the stock meets some undefined and subjective *"adequate amount"* standard.

A former homeland security official, Dr. Tara O'Toole, is on record as having stated *"The SNS was definitely not an empty shell"* but also that, over the years, *"the SNS mission has expanded"* and *"one could argue resources did not expand commensurately."* She also said *"You can't stockpile your way out of a pandemic like this. What we need is not a big stockpile. We need a new strategy. We need to use the technologies we have now to create the capacity to respond to something in close to real-time. ...rapidly design and manufacture what we need, when we need it, and the quantities demanded."*

Obama-Biden administration failed to direct the appropriate agencies to create a new strategy and initiate the *Existential Change* – will Trump-Pence be allowed to initiate that change?

CHAPTER FOUR – Existential

"In an Impeachment, you can't use a work of fiction as the theory for the case, filling in gaps with presumptions against the President. It was a weak presentation, self-indulgent, & he didn't deliver the goods." ~ Robert Charles

What will be the existential change that eventually creates a cultural change? Will the culture change in 2021, or not until after the next World War or that Biblical Apocalypse that is supposed to occur sometime in this century?

When using currently popular term, Existential, it should be to talk about the continuity of human existence, in the context that it often appears, it refers to the foundation or fundamental element of a thing – without really concerning itself with humanity or reality.

In 1981, Ronald Reagan became the catalyst that allowed the nation to accept *"Voodoo Economics"* and the idea that debt was to become meaningless in a culture where double-digit inflation might have become a normal economic reality. It was an economy where minimum wages and the economic stability Social Security was to offer senior citizens were to be depleted so as to ensure both groups of recipients drifted into poverty, became dependent upon public assistance, and were systematically belittled for accepting it.

The COVID-19 pandemic triggered a $3.8 Trillion deficit that threatened to accelerate the economic decay and death Reagan had implemented in a manner that would see its culmination when the last of the Baby-Boomers achieved the age Reagan was when he left office. That would be about 2043; Sir Isaac Newton projected that the Biblical Apocalypse would occur in 2033. So it didn't matter – either way, the world ends.

This change began in December 2019, when Taiwan told the World Health Organization (WHO) of an undefined outbreak in Wuhan, China. Later WHO would assert that Taiwan had failed to mention human-to-human transmission of the Wuhan coronavirus was possible; for some perverse reason, WHO's director-general, Tedros Adhanom Ghebreyesus, accused Taiwan of *"racism."*

On 14 July, about five months before WHO's director-general made his assertion, Nancy Pelosi (@SpeakerPelosi) tweeted *"When @realDonaldTrump tells four American Congresswomen to go back to their countries, he reaffirms his plan to 'Make America Great Again' has always been about making America white again."*

That is, she called Trump – and by extension Ronald Reagan and all Reagan Republicans – *'racist'*.

Invoking racism or anti-Semitism is a very post-World War Two Hippy generation late *Silent Generation* to early *Baby-Boomer* Hippy knee-jerk Hippy fallback position thing to do.

Also in July, Alexandria Ocasio-Cortez (AOC) had used the racist attack against Pelosi – asserting she "*explicit singling out of newly elected women of color*" as a means of retaining control of the Democratic Party, and "*the persistent singling out ... it was just outright disrespectful ... the explicit singling out of newly elected women of color.*"

Everything in the 21st-century appears to revolve around or in some way devolve into accusations of bigotry, xenophobia, and racism. The "*racism*" associated with the Wuhan virus was seen in the way WHO reacted to the Taiwanese information.

On 11 April, the Central Epidemic Command Center (CECC) chief, Chen Shih-Chung, revealed the contents of the 31 December e-mail to WHO, enquiring about the emerging threat and apparently serving as notice of the emerging virus:

"News resources today indicate that at least seven atypical pneumonia cases were reported in Wuhan, CHINA. Their health authorities replied to the media that the cases were believed not SARS; however, the samples are still under examination, and cases have been isolated for treatment"

"I would greatly appreciate it if you have relevant information to share with us.

"Thank you very much in advance for your attention to this matter."

Based on this, WHO knew of the "*atypical pneumonia cases*" and, as has been established, did not perceive any threat for, at least, another month. It was 12 January, when Who acknowledged a novel coronavirus was the cause of respiratory illness.

As previously noted, Trump initiated his multiple travel bans on 31 January, these included temporarily suspending the entry into the United States of any foreign nationals who have been in China during the prior 14-day period. The main focus were citizens of six nations seeking 'green cards' immigrant visas – two, Kyrgyzstan and Myanmar (Burma), border China, and four Eritrea, Nigeria, Sudan, Tanzania are in Africa. Accordingly, because the nations were not "European white," Trump declared a racist xenophobe.

The focus on the travel ban was utilized by both Pelosi and media pundits to attack Trump while concealing the issuance of his *"Proclamation on Suspension of Entry as Immigrants and Nonimmigrants of Persons who Pose a Risk of Transmitting 2019 Novel Coronavirus"* on the same day. By doing so, they have been able to claim Trump did nothing to mitigate the transmission of COVID-19 beyond the two cases now known to have arrived in mid-January – one, a man in his 50s, had been to Wuhan and, on 26 February, died in King County, Washington. He and a woman in her 80s who died the same day are counted as the first two fatalities.

According to the CDC Coronavirus Disease 2019 (COVID-19) webpage, when Trump issued his 31 January *"Proclamation"* there were 38 King County, Washington confirmed cases and no deaths. The *"Proclamation"* states:

"The virus was discovered in China in December 2019. As of January 31, 2020, Chinese health officials have reported approximately 10,000 confirmed cases of 2019-nCoV in China, more than the number of confirmed cases of Severe Acute Respiratory Syndrome (SARS) during its 2003 outbreak. An additional 114 cases have been confirmed across 22 other countries; in several of these cases, the infected individuals had not visited China. More than 200 people have died from the virus, all in China."

According to popular lore, Trump *"delayed taking action"* to address the issue. When, on 11 April, he said *"Nobody knew there would be a pandemic or epidemic of this proportion,"* he was not telling the truth. However, on 19 February two Iranians died; on 21 February Italy had its first death; the first United States death was on 29 February; Syria had its first death on 29 March. And knowing that, who was stopping international travel before Trump?

The *"Proclamation"* states, *"Neighboring jurisdictions have taken swift action to protect their citizens by closing off travel between their territories and China. On January 30, 2020, the World Health Organization declared the 2019-nCoV outbreak a public health emergency of international concern."*

So we know Trump issued the proclamation within 24 hours of the state of emergency so, should we assume Trump's detractors believe his proclamation – which was deemed racist and xenophobic by his detractors – should have preceded the WHO declaration?

It should be noted the proclamation points out that, "*During Fiscal Year 2019, an average of more than 14,000 people traveled to the United States from China each day, via both direct and indirect flights. The United States Government is unable to effectively evaluate and monitor all of the travelers continuing to arrive from China.*"

Just as Pelosi was encouraging group congregations in San Francisco's Chinatown on 24 February, she and her ilk have argued that it was xenophobic for Trump to prevent 14,000 potential carries of the pandemic into America. What position was Joe Biden taking in January or early February 2020 – was he even paying attention?

On 27 January, an opinion piece by Joe Biden was published by USA Today which opened with: "*The possibility of a pandemic is a challenge Donald Trump is unqualified to handle as president.*"

Biden then stated: "*I remember how Trump sought to stoke fear and stigma during the 2014 Ebola epidemic. He called President Barack Obama a 'dope' and 'incompetent' and railed against the evidence-based response our administration put in place — which quelled the crisis and saved hundreds of thousands of lives — in favor of <u>reactionary travel bans that would only have made things worse</u>.*"

So Biden clearly saw the pandemic coming, but the last line seems to indicate he would have opposed the travel bans the rest of the world came to accept. The then gets into what many would recognize as ongoing talking-points utilized by Trump's detractors: "*Trump's demonstrated <u>failures of judgment</u> and his repeated <u>rejection of science</u> make him the <u>worst possible person to lead our country</u> through a global health challenge.*"

Remember, Bernie Sanders built his campaign on the simple assertion: "*We must come together to defeat the most dangerous president in modern history.*" However, he has never established why Trump deserves such an esteemed rank or distinction.

In his January article, Biden stated: "*The outbreak of a new coronavirus, which has already infected more than 2,700 people and killed over 80 in China, will get worse before it gets better. Cases have been confirmed in a dozen countries, with at least five in the United States."*

In terms of available data, the difference between the figures in Trump's proclamation and Biden's article represents less than a week – numerically four days, 7,300 reported cases, 120 dead, and ten countries. That difference indicates the severity of the pandemic – and its rapid spread – WHO was denying existed until the day before Trump issued the Travel Ban; for the chronology, we need to remember he had given airlines with Asian routes two weeks notice of the ban, meaning he was a week ahead of Biden and two weeks ahead of WHO.

In declaring the emergency, WHO Director-General Tedros stated: *"the main reason for the declaration is not because of what is happening in China but because of what is happening in other countries. ..."*

So all nations were on notice, and Trump had acted two weeks before that notice was given, and, three days earlier, Biden is on record asserting that it would be given. Then, on 4 February, we heard the State of the Union speech which Pelosi characterized with the words: *"That was not a State of the Union. That was his state of mind."* She also asserted, *"I tried to find one page I could spare that didn't have a lie on it."* That means the COVID-19 was, in her opinion, a lie. The case could be made that her statement referred to something else on that page, but until Pelosi specifies what it was, the fact remains, on 24 February, she dismissed the virus by inviting the Chinatown gatherings – so any new disease spread would have an explicitly Chinese context.

Of course, when the speech concluded, she made a show of ripping it up, and later would assert, *"I saw the compilation of falsehoods."* And, *"There has to be something that clearly indicates to the American people that this is not the truth."* Because *"He has shredded the truth in his speech, shredded the Constitution in his conduct. I shredded the address. ... Thank you all very much."*

And, apparently, the truth Trump shredded was: *"Protecting Americans' health also means fighting infectious diseases. We are coordinating with the Chinese government and working closely together on the coronavirus outbreak in China. My administration will take all necessary steps to safeguard our citizens from this threat."*

If we grant any credibility to Pelosi, then the 4-part tweet by Pennsylvania Congressman Dan Meuser on 14 April must be seen as false:

(1/4) Even on Easter Sunday, the mainstream media was trying to convince the public that @realDonaldTrump is to blame for #COVID19. The facts tell a different story. On 1/23, the @who said #COVID19 was "not a global health threat."

(2/4) On 1/30, they reversed that statement by declaring a global health emergency, meaning they expected the virus would expand beyond Chinese borders. On 1/31, @realDonaldTrump imposed travel restrictions from China. Later that day, @SpeakerPelosi called them "un-American."

(3/4) On 2/24, @realDonaldTrump called for emergency aid. That same day, @SpeakerPelosi told the public that San Francisco's Chinatown was safe. On 3/1, @NYGovCuomo said public risk remained "low."

(4/4) On 3/13, @NYCMayor reiterated that NYC Schools would remain open, the same day that @realDonaldTrump declared a national emergency. Enough Orwellian deception already, this is serious. If you're not part of the solution, you're part of the problem.

Is Pelosi part of the solution, or is it more likely that since she entered Congress in 1987 she has evolved into the type of politician who thrives on being a pervasive part of the problem?

The words or attitude exhibited by Pelosi appear to be merely a variation on Sander's *"most dangerous president"* propagandist phraseology.

Historian Don P. Levy, director of the Siena College Research Institute, has established criteria where *"The presidents at the bottom were the ones who failed to safeguard us and adequately lead us during periods of crisis or tainted the office through scandal and incompetence. Andrew Johnson, James Buchanan, Warren G. Harding – they earned their spots at the bottom."* Om 18 March, it was reported that Levy and his wife Jane had become COVID-19 cases.

Unfortunately, the criteria deal with the *Best and Worst*, but not with the Sanders' related concept of *Most and Least Dangerous*. The Pennsylvania-born single-term Democratic President James Buchanan is generally deemed the "worst" – based on his acceptance of slavery and various legal decisions that helped support its spread into the western territories acquired by the Louisiana Purchase and the Mexican War.

In terms of *"dangerous"*, what can be more dangerous than a president who initiates the longest military conflict in the nation's history? Or the president who violated a promise made during the Second World War and initiated the Vietnam War?

In October 2017, Hillary Clinton was asked about Trump and responded, *"I think he is [the most dangerous president]. He is impulsive, he lacks self-control, he is totally consumed by how he is viewed and what people think of him, he is vindictive."*

But is Trump more dangerous than a president and Congress that encouraged outsourcing of basic or critical industries so that we could be in the position of having – as reported by the Wall Street Journal on 16 April 2020 – *"Over a million coronavirus test kits As and other urgently needed medical items bound for the U.S. … sitting in Chinese warehouses because suppliers don't have the necessary new export clearances from officials in Beijing."*

In the article, there is mention of a memo sent from the U.S. State Department, a few days before, which said China's policies *"disrupted established supply chains for medical products just as these products were most needed."* This means that those who, in previous administrations, encouraged outsourcing have jeopardized the health and wellbeing of the nation.

We can add the guilt of those Presidents and Congressional members the ongoing threat I have written about over the decades that have passed since the Nixon-era. With the depletion of liquid oil reserves and the necessity to turn to fracking, America persists in remaining oil-dependent.

We hear nonsense about Trump profiting, and yet, nobody pointed out, or became upset, over the fact that George W Bush was in the oil business with the Saudis and his wealth was derived from making America dependent on the Saudis for energy, even as they were moving to meet their own needs with extensive installations of solar and wind technology.

Trump is alleged *"the most dangerous president"*, but it was Bush-43 who lied to begin a war which, as of the 2020 election, will have spanned nearly nineteen years and cost the nation multi-trillions of dollars that could have provided universal health, or created sufficient solar and wind installation to render the nation energy independent – while also addressing Climate Change.

Still, the nation is holding to the ideas put forward by Bernie Sanders while he was campaigning: "*We are going to defeat Donald Trump because the American people know that he is running a corrupt administration... that not only is he a liar, he is a fraud.*"

But again, there are no specifics.

But the nation and planet were playing with the COVID-19 virus, and that was both specific and very real. More important, there was a reality people wanted to avoid as they kept their anti-Trump rhetoric going – Climate Change related pollution emerged as a key factor in the death rate; it was the driving force behind the culling and was also contributing to a rapid cleaning of the air.

n January, the U.S. House of Representatives Committee on Energy & Commerce issued its preliminary version of the CLEAN Future Act, which was intended to transition the United States into a fully clean energy economy by 2050. However, the bill would not actually clean the air, it would simply provide a basis for emissions trading, with standards that were sufficiently lax to retain the use of fossil fuels.

Apart from not actually helping clean the air, the bill would ensure a primary problem being exposed by the COVID-19 lockdown and budging oil surplus which made fracking uneconomical. More important, in the event of a war in the three decades between 2020 and 2050, reliance on fossils in the military or any civilian industry that provides for military needs, means the United States would be dependent on nations like Russia, Saudis Arabia, and Venezuela for its national defense needs. That is, America would be where Nazi Germany was when the Allies cut off its access to Middle Eastern oil supply lines.

America must face the existential reality that its very survival depends on Green Energy and keeping pollution levels near or below the pollution levels that appeared during the COVID-19 lockdown. If nothing else, they need to retain that level so that the respiratory distress which underlies the deaths will be mitigated.

Evangelicals must take their heads out of Elmer Gantry sands and see the wisdom within the Old Testament and the other ancient texts that speak of caring for the planet – or a pandemic will do it in a way that was being reported during its first four months.

In my February 2014 book, *"Biblical Prophecy: Are we in the Revelation era?"*, I showed the timeline determining method that is confirmed by historic events that comport well with the existential symbolism that defines the continuity of human existence after a third of life dies or becomes extinct.

Fortunately, when dealing with Prophets – those gifted in the projecting events based on know recurrent cycles or event patterns and making predictions based on those projections – the symbolic nature of their work allows for interpretations that have nothing to do with what is actually being said.

Humans like to take things out of their proper context and insert them into something that suits their political needs. We saw it in the Obama Birther Movement; now we are seeing it as *"Trump Derangement Syndrome."* Yet the traditional cycles continue to be as functional as they have always been, and the predictions fall in line. Coronavirus is a culling virus and fits the prediction for this era. Think about this:

Which deaths count toward the COVID-19 death toll?

The knee-jerk response is that someone with COVID-19 died of COVID-19. But is that true or is it the contradictory double meaning rhetoric that we see applied to Trump's statements? It could be a rhetorical distinction for determining the mortality rate that distorts the statistical basis.

In April, while the infection-death curve was turning down, the CDC was determining the validity of counting cases was tainted by the lack of confirming tests. Other investigators were beginning to raise questions about the "cause of death" in those contracting COVID-19 while being treated for known fatal diseases – nursing home patients.

As such interesting statistical anomalies have been observed with regard to the deaths normally attributed to pneumonia, which appear to have fallen in a manner consistent with the increase in COVID-19 deaths. In China, the number of COVID-19 deaths was increased by simply assuming it to either be the cause of death or because death had been reattributed to the pre-existing condition in those who contracted the virus.

Bill Maher, satirist-comedian host of HBO's "REAL TIME" talk show, has challenged "politically correct" complaints or outrage over calling COVID-19 the Chinese or Wuhan virus when represents the traditional mode of naming diseases by their point of origin. In a show episode {S18: E11} on 17 April, the outspoken liberal said:

"Enough with 'the life will never be the same' headlines, and stop showing us this, you know everything looks scary when you magnified it a thousand times. We need the news to calm down and treat us like adults. Trump calls you fake news, don't make him be right."

Maher ripped into the media over what he termed as their persistent '*Panic Porn*' – his rhetoric term for *"If It Bleeds It Leads"* journalism that can only focus on the negative because the public loves to see the suffering of others. The Good Samaritan parable has no meaning unless there are people standing around watching the merchant's suffering and doing nothing – much like Nancy Pelosi on vacation while small businesses need stimulus assistance.

On 11 April, POLITICO wrote, *"Just two weeks after the largest economic relief bill in U.S. history failed to arrest the economic collapse, Trump needs another rescue package far more than Democrats do. The economy he loves to brag about has shed more than 16 million jobs. The stock market that he obsessively tweets about has plunged 20 percent. Trump doesn't want to run for reelection during a full-blown depression, so he desperately needs more legislation."*

Later in the article, they mentioned that *"Pelosi and her partner in the Senate, Minority Leader Chuck Schumer, blocked Senator Majority Leader Mitch McConnell's $250 billion power play for small business owners,..."* Allowing for her normal political positioning, Pelosi is conducting business as usual – undermine the national wellbeing for political gain in the next November election.

But during his closing monologue, without realizing it, Maher described the reality of COVID-19 as a culling virus. The reference in question was to the number of deaths among those under age-50.

On 8 April, it was reported that *"at least 759 people under age 50 across the United States who have perished amid the deepening pandemic, according to a Washington Post analysis of state data."*

Maher referenced that article and then said he looked up how many under fifty died of the flu in 2019, and found it was almost three thousand, adding that, *"hospital-acquired infections may very well kill more than Coronavirus. Ninety-nine thousand last year. Fifty thousand die of nephritis every year..."*

Maher chuckled, *"And I don't even know what that is."*

I Googled *nephritis* and discovered it is a kidney problem, *"an inflammation, which is also known as glomerulonephritis, can adversely affect kidney function."* It appears that inflamed kidneys kill more people than the virus. Does Congress care?

Maher looked at the growing unemployment numbers and he pointed out they also lost their medical coverage when they lost their jobs. He then stated what should be well known, *"Studies show that lacking health insurance kills people."*

Of course, those who have read this book series know that there is ample evidence Trump was a fan of PT Barnum and might recall in Book One, "NO TRUMP CARD," you were made aware of the fact you would see Barnum in Trump's approach to his new managerial responsibilities. Thus it would be no surprise that, on page 90, you read:

"Of course, Trump would know PT Barnum's book, *"Golden Rules for Making Money"*, which opens with the sentence: 'In the United States, where we have more land than people, it is not at all difficult for persons in good health to make money.'

"Barnum explained that reality in terms which reflect upon the reality behind *The American Health Care Repeal Act of 2017*: *'The foundation of success in life is good health: that is the substratum fortune; it is also the basis of happiness. A person cannot accumulate a fortune very well when he is sick.'"*

Barnum published this business thesis in 1880, Otto von Bismarck's social legislation, the *Health Insurance Bill of 1883*, was introduced three years later. Despite have about 20% of the number of reported cases in America, when Maher's gave his presentation, Germany had 11.50% of the fatalities – their 140-year-old healthcare system works.

Health is the basis of both happiness and wealth. Thus, we know the Swamp Denizens will do all in their power to ensure any who might prove to be competition will remain sick. That means we have a weak and ineffectual Obamacare and no Medicare for All – even as Trump says when he referred to the Australian system, he would like to see America have the best medical care in the world.

Maher also referenced INSIDE EDITION which said: "76,000 have died, so some make comparisons to the Apocalypse." And he laughed at the stupidity of the analogy embodied with the worldwide death toll. However, the Revelation Prophecy does say this era will see a third of life die – evangelicals could term it an "Angel of Death" and with Maher including in his presentation an article published on the first day of Passover, we should not that *"Shelter in place"* was the exact strategy used by the ancient Hebrews, and that they were "social distancing" from the non-chosen – or unblessed – peoples of the surrounding culture. It seems to follow that the media would then report, on Good Friday (in 2020, the second day of Passover), those who are the true butt of *Saint Paul's Joke* attended in-person services.

Were the churchgoers actually believers, they might have recognized the parallels between the Wuhan virus and Passover. It is not necessary to focus on them, we need only point out they can be seen by those with *"eyes to see and ears to hear."*

Since Wuhan virus deaths are related to existing respiratory distress, it would appear that many Wuhan fatalities are actually people who would have died in the absence of the pandemic. That means the virus is not actually "killing", rather hastened what was an inevitable demise and should result in the overall deaths for 2020 being statistically indistinguishable from normal expectations.

Over the coming months, tests that can identify antibodies in the blood of people who were unwittingly exposed to the virus will allow for a closer approximation of total infections in different populations. One such set of tests was being performed in California – it's anecdotal in terms of an actual study, but 32% of 200 Chelsea, Massachusetts residents who gave a drop of blood to researchers in a random street sample tested positive for antibodies linked to COVID-19, indicating possible widespread asymptomatic infections within the densely populated city.

Even with testing more widely available for Americans with COVID-19 symptoms, the proportion of people infected by the virus who do not feel appreciably sick is unknown, including in places with some of the highest deaths per 100,000 people: New York (55), Spain (40), Belgium (36), Italy (35), New Jersey (32), France (23) and Louisiana (22).

While great *'Panic Porn'*, the Wuhan virus is insignificant.

CHAPTER FIVE – Cultural Change

"And I find it kinda funny, I find it kinda sad
The dreams in which I'm dying
are the best I've ever had
I find it hard to tell you, I find it hard to take
When people run in circles it's a very very
Mad world, mad world"
~ Roland Orzabal, "Mad World"

While Wuhan virus is proving to be statistically insignificant in terms of annual death rates, it is gaining significant importance for those looking at the accompanying changes – these can be seen as the focus of the stimulus packages on guaranteed income and the specific healthcare access associated with the pandemic, or it can be the changes in air pollution that have been documented wherever the virus has hit the hardest.

The only real issue is whether or not the media proves honest enough to intensely alert voters of the realities being exposed. Will the media end its "Panic Porn" attacks on Trump and focus on what is needed to make a strong, healthy, prosperous 21st-century nation for our children, grandchildren, and great-grandchildren?

As you saw in the previous chapter and were told in the first book in this series – published 16 April 2017, fully three years before the linkage between the pandemic and indisputable nomination of Joseph Biden as Trump's political competition in November 2020 – health is the criteria for wealth. PT Barnum spoke in terms of monetary wealth, Donald J. Trump has been termed a germaphobe who has managed to amass a few pennies; in 1860, Ralph Waldo Emerson wrote, in philosophical terms, *"The first wealth is health."*

Those who honestly want America to prosper are those who promote Medicare for All and ensure that no citizen who can be kept healthy is allowed to become sick. But, those who hate America will encourage illness and seek to deprive citizens of free medical care. If they wish to speak of elective care – cosmetic surgery that was not forced upon people by an accident of disease – that's different. And there is no reason for non-citizens to be given the same level of free care unless the lack of it threatens the health and welfare of citizens.

In terms of work and cultural importance, the virus revealed what many have long known – in terms of female employment, a third of essential jobs are held by women, a fact confirmed when the federal essential worker guidelines were cross-referenced to census data. Plus, essential jobs are more likely to be the responsibility of nonwhite women who seem to constitute an underpaid unseen labor force responsible for keeping the nation operational under normal circumstances and more so during a pandemic emergency.

We know of the wage disparity between men and women, it is, to a large extent, created by the Minimum Wage Laws and their disregard for keeping people out of a costly public assistance system.

As mentioned in my previous books, we have a group that is devoted to *"The Most Harm to the Most People"*; in recent decades it has been connected with the Right-wing Conservatives, but now it is emerging as a baseline Left-wing doctrine at war with the Bernie Sanders Progressives within the Democratic Party.

As was seen, it took a global pandemic to explode the myth of government spending needing to be "paid for." Federal government spending can always be exercised or afforded when it buys what is denominated for sale in its currency – the currency in which it will be "paid for." This has long been recognized in terms of Modern Money Theory and is actually the basis for asserting – as was done in the case of what became Reagan's Voodoo Economics – that debt did not matter. For Reagan, there was an assumption of prevailing inflation rates continuing and therefore monetization of debt would be inevitable.

Monetization of debt simply means funds are borrowed at the purchasing power they hold when the debt is acquired, but are later paid back after inflation as reduced the purchasing power of those funds. If we look to Bernie Sanders equating 2020 wages with those of 1965, we see that the purchasing power of the dollar is one-tenth of what it was 55-years ago. That being the case, it followed that the gallon of gas that was 27-cents in 1965, in 2020 would sell for $2.70 in 2020.

But, a Russia-Saudis price manipulation combined with the Wuhan pandemic suppressed the petroleum market – in late April the gasoline pump price fell to $1.53 – about 15 cents in 1965. And the continued declining demand promised lower prices in May.

The value of a dollar still declined, just not as much.

Monetization of debt has an inherent problem created when the debt is refinanced rather than repaid. The theory is solid when dealing with a mortgage or loan secured by an asset that accrues value because of inflation and at the end of a fixed period is debt-free. That's the beauty of Real Estate or any "hard asset" business and one of the ways those – like the Trump family – amass wealth.

It is not an economic model that works for governments – in the history of America, only Andrew Jackson paid off the National debt and had a debt-free nation. All others add to the debt and roll-over the debts they inherited from their predecessors.

So, in real terms, beyond trying not to accrue more, forget about the debt. But recognize that what we might label as "the Trump method" is sound – restructure expenses so that the same work and outcome is achieved without amassing new debt. And that is done by consolidating departments to reduce redundancy.

And this brings us to something else revealed by the Wuhan pandemic – the nation can both afford and benefit from Universal Basic Income.

It has a beauty which has gone unmentioned. It replaces unemployment insurance and public assistance subsidies; in terms of income taxes, it would eliminate the *"personal deduction"* and might well serve to eliminate the need for many other deductions on business-related tax forms. Toss in *Medicare for All* (M4A) and that line item also vanishes – as well as the medical cost deductions that appear on the taxes of those who are sick.

Tax forms become simplified, while real costs are decreased.

The Covid-19 crisis has clearly demonstrated what should have been obvious already: provisioning society – whether with food, disinfecting wipes, toilet paper, or medical supplies – is not a financial issue. If we can't produce enough masks, ventilators, or food, finance will not help. Society's capacity to produce real output is what limits its ability to provision itself. And this is precisely what the virus threatens, as workers stay home, supply chains break down and businesses shut their doors.

For three years, Trump has emphasized something he again pointed to as a result of the pandemic. As part of a daily briefing on 20 April, he said: *"This pandemic has reaffirmed the importance of keeping vital supply chains at home. We cannot outsource our independence, we cannot be reliant on foreign nations. I've been saying this for a long time. If we've learned one thing it's let's do it here, let's build it here, let's make it here."*

When the US government needs more ventilators or masks, finance cannot be an impediment, and if it says it cannot afford to help its people, it has become a slave master tightening the chains of disposing of slaves.

By buying into the deficit myth, generations of Americans were forced to live below "our" means – paralyzed by the belief that finance is a fixed constraint. Prolonged periods of jobless recoveries disincentivize investment, further hurting productive capacity and labor productivity.

Once this pandemic passes, the deficit scolds will be back at it again; they will strive to put roadblocks in front of the progressive policies that defined the stimulus packages. We will hear that we cannot afford *"for All"*: Medicare, Jobs, College, or halting climate change – the latter being a side effect of the pandemic clean air results. There is this warped idea of "normal" in which America's economy demands we leave most people behind and then pollute those areas where our blue-collar and minorities are concentrated.

The pandemic has created an opportunity for the Democrats and Progressives to promote a different kind of economy through a Green New Deal – a program that can repatriate production and so provide Donald Trump with the thing he has called for well before he became POTUS.

We need to distinguish between myth and constraints that are basic reality – that which is technically feasible versus that which is financially possible for a sovereign democratic republic. Affording the Green New Deal is about utilizing resources and technology that already exists. Financing them is simply a matter of encouraging the jobs that will be created.

The original New Deal faced the same screams or concerns about "excessive" spending. Then the Second World War eliminated that obstacle, unleashing the type of national economic mobilization the nation has always been capable of – after all, immigrants came to America because its streets are paved with gold. FDR unleashed that gold fever and the Baby-Boomers were raised amid decades of prosperity. Hopefully, as a culling virus, COVID-19 will not prove to be as destructive as the Great Depression, but it has destroyed, the deficit myth while revealing the wisdom of the Green New Deal.

People – slave master wannabee types – yell about inflation, but inflation is exactly what Ronald Reagan planned to use to erase the National Debt – if people prosper, through improvements in their health, welfare, and lifestyle, inflation becomes an accounting adjustment similar to that applied to Social security, but which could also be applied to the UBI and Minimum Wage.

Reagan's Voodoo economics failed because he relied upon and hoped for the very thing people do not want and right now there is no inflation, so the budget deficits are disnerving, while the same lack of inflation means lower long-term interest rates on both the National Debit and home mortgages.

In the third week of April, ten-year Federal bonds carried a 0.65% interest rate – for perspective, after the Second World War, Baby-Boomer economics was defined by roughly 3% inflation, and mortgage interest was 8%. Now, a thirty-year mortgage is 3%, with a projected 2.9% for 2021.

The greatest housing boom in American history – drawing people moved from crowded city tenements, or apartments of the type that initially funded the Trump fortune, to suburban housing developments. This was achieved with interest rates twice the 2020 levels. Business expanded and a generation went to college – their parents might never have finished high school. Of course, a need for space to house the boomer children contributed, and now families are shrinking – there is a baby-bust – people are moving back to the cities. The low interest will make it easier to own a Condo or Co-op. It will also make it cheaper to fund new (Green) industries – if this is promoted by the 2020 candidates.

In the third week of April, the price of Benchmark Crude oil actually went negative – producers needed to pay buyers to take the stuff. If Americans were not devoted to making their neighbors into slaves, things would be great. The reduction in oil use explains the virus associated decline in air pollution – the same pollution that is a driving force behind the culling deaths of a virus that would prefer its hosts to live and contaminate others.

In April, Harvard economist Jason Furman said: *"In some sense, the market is telling us now loud and clear don't worry about the debt. I think there are limits. I think whatever we need we should do, but I don't think you should be doing five times more than you need just in case."*

Furman estimated that resupplying the small business rescue program would require $1 trillion in 2020 to extend unemployment benefits and provide additional household funds. And, should the unemployment rate remain it would then take another $1 trillion in 2021. And low-interest rates mean it can be done, and also show that soaring US spending, has not scared investors, so they are not demanding higher interest rates. However, if either Congress or the President decides to they can scare the hell out of investors.

The investment community has confidence in America and in Trump. If we look at the economic picture in August 2020, after Biden has been formally anointed as the Democratic nominee and has revealed his Vice Presidential choice, the markets will assess who the winner is likely to be and behave accordingly.

In 2016, when Hillary Clinton was the presumptive winner, the markets drifted downward – rebounding sharply, when Trump was formally declared the winner. In 2020, the winner will be the one who breaks with the old and embraces the new as defined by the COVID-19 stimulus package elements that can be made permanent – monthly payments in the form of UBI, healthcare access that is not dependent on an employer, a solid economic foundation for all.

In terms of amounts, it would be logical to set UBI payments at the current public assistance standard of 140-150% of poverty. It would allow the idiots who enjoy having costly slaves to argue they are paying people not to work. But, in fact, the money would allow the elimination of Federal, State, and Local bureaus that normally oversee welfare qualification and payment. The IRS would issue the checks by direct deposit to every citizen with a valid Social Security Number (SSN).

As for Social Security, rather than being an elderly or disabled support system, it would become a reward for those who work – one that enhances their UBI when they retire. Social Security benefits income would remain a pay-as-you-go system that is represented on the Federal books as an accounting entry attached to the National Debt. But, in reality, it is one that is reduced with the death of each beneficiary, making it an accrued liability to be reduced as negative population accelerates.

However, with a pay-as-you-go system, negative population growth also imposes serious cash flow constraints. But that can be addressed using the method suggested by Bernie Sanders – remove the cap on income subject to constitutions. Immediately the payroll tax system would generate a cash surplus for the general budget.

In terms of the general budget, Military Expenditures need to be reduced so that they are no more than a third of revenues. This could be done with a more intelligent approach to national defense where the first response is the total annihilation of an enemy. You might call it "genocide" – which is what war is all about, either the extermination of an enemy or they exterminate you.

As mentioned in earlier books in this series, there was once a "Queens Schoolyard Rule" for fighting: You never throw the first punch. If knocked down, get up; knock down the one who attacked you – but make damned sure they do not get up. Much of this rule can be seen in Trump's use of the MOAB in Afghanistan or his use of tactical strikes in Syria.

On 25 September 2001 Defense Secretary Donald Rumsfeld announced the onset of "Operation Enduring Freedom." That was the start of what, in 2020, became a 19-year undeclared war that, in Afghanistan, cost: the lives of over 38,000 Afghan civilians; $2 trillion that could have improved America; plus the lives of 2,400 American soldiers. And it was because a "rag-head" named Osama Ben Laden convinced 19 Saudis to commit suicide by destroying the New York's World Trade Center and murdering 2,996 people.

Bin Laden knocked us down, but instead of getting up and then knocking Bin Laden down, Bush declared him "irrelevant" and attacked Afghanistan and Iraq – about whom he lied so as to justify the murder of Saddam Hussein and trigger the disruption that has come to defined the Middle East and give Russia the basis for its intrusion there. Bush also contributed to creating the 2007-2009 Great Recession.

Queens rules would have made Bin Laden the target, and the whole thing might have been over in months. Troops under Obama nailed Bin Laden while Obama initiated an economic recovery that, when continued by Trump, became the longest in history.

When the Swamp fought back it enlisted Democratic Swamp Denizens who knew that impeachments crash financial markets – headed by Pelosi, Nadler, Schiff, and Schumer – to finish the work begun by Maxine Waters and Al Green, who had spent three years pursuing ways to fabricate justifications for Articles of Impeachment against Trump. They failed – they might begin anew in 2021.

While the Swamp Denizens failed in their impeachment in the same way their Republican kin failed with the Birther Movement against Obama, they were not about to turn their backs on benefits derived from the "panic porn" associated with COVID-19 and its detrimental effect on the markets.

But, as Jason Furman – who served 8-years as an economic advisor to Obama – pointed out, the financial markets trust Donald Trump's leadership. It was extremely doubtful those markets would extend the same level of trust to Biden – but, as the Impeachment House Managers knew, Biden was exactly the candidate the Swamp Denizens would welcome. Therefore, they manipulated the process to filter out Tulsi Gabbard; they then allowed non-POTUS Cousins to delete themselves, and finally, Warren fell by the boards, to leave only Bernie Sanders – a non-POTUS Cousin, whose personality and insight was that of a classic wise and personable Jewish grandfather.

Pelosi delayed advancing the Articles of Impeachment to the Senate – trapping Warren and Sanders in Washington and keeping them away from the campaign trail that was now exclusively Biden's to control. At the same time, Schiff pushed for the Senate to gather evidence call witnesses – which threatened to block campaigning for another eight weeks (into April). But, McConnell was not about to acknowledge the validity of an impeachment in search of a statutory crime – where the only "evidence" was the persistent Schiff lie about there being "overwhelming evidence" that, if it really existed, would have negated the need for additional investigation by the Senate.

Trump Derangement Syndrome allowed Schiff's lies to gain the little traction they had. And subsequently, it allowed the lies about Trump not taking action early enough – the timeframe illustrates he was ahead of the World Health Organization, Italy, Spain, France, and Britain and all the nations with far higher fatality rates. Some will point to known cases, but that only reflects a combined effect of massive testing within the world's largest economy – where travelers (domestic and foreign) arrive and depart in massive numbers.

Trump Derangement Syndrome has prevented people from realizing the enormous opportunity that COVID-19 has presented those who are supporters of a Green Economy.

Senator Bernie Sanders proposed a "Green New Deal" which would see the United States eliminate fossil fuel use by 2050. It was said to carry an estimated cost of $16 Trillion. But, if we look at the reduced use of fossil fuels that accompanied the virus, and if we also envision the potential for social changes that can be instituted now, so America is not decimated by the next, and far more serious, pandemic there is no real cost – only the benefit of millions of Green jobs to replace those lost with the shutdown of the highly polluting Fracking industry.

Trump has routinely said it – we have one such quote above – We have outsourced our freedom and independence. The reliance on foreign oil that has been demonstrated so pervasively by the fall in oil prices caused by the pandemic has underscored the need to go to Green Energy – and there is the perverse reality that even Saudis Arabia are going Green.

You have a nation with only 33.4 million people, that controls proven reserves of 267 Billion barrels of crude oil and 9,069 billion cubic meters natural gas reserves, is shifting to solar power for its electrical needs. As of 21 April, Saudi Arabia had 11,631 confirmed COVID-19 cases with only 110 deaths (0.9% fatality rate versus 5.4% in the USA, which is a somewhat meaningless aside).

The point is the world is going Green, even where there is an abundance of liquid petroleum. The Saudis have no real production and so they are dependent on other nations – and that is not about to change. For the United States, which has always been relatively independent, that reality is different.

As Trump has said:

"We've got to start bringing our supply chains back. Somebody years ago got this crazy idea: 'Let's build all over the place and let's have parts, let's have a screw for a car delivered and made in a country that's far away. And let's have a fender made someplace else and let's do this, and let's do that and let's put it all together.' I like making it right here in the U.S.A. and I think we've learned a lot about that and especially maybe when it comes to pharmaceutical products."

When those suffering from Trump Derangement Syndrome blindly assert things like the idea he didn't act early enough, they are blinding themselves to the real threat from those who support the outsourcing of basic industries.

It's one thing to move a factory across a border into Canada or Mexico, but another to move it to the other side of the planet.

Bernie Sanders' Green New Deal effectively declares climate change a national emergency; it envisions building new solar, wind, and geothermal power sources across the country; and commits $200 billion to help poor nations cope with climate change. Trump has a vision that simply excludes giving money to other nations before we have gotten our own straightened out.

The cost of Sander's program, assuming that his detractors' estimates were accurate, would be the COVID-19 stimulus package spread of the first seven years of the initiative. The difference being on the other side – the stimulus has nobody working; the Green New Deal would create millions of jobs. Those jobs would be filled by people who were working the Fracking Oil Fields – and making the planet dirty – and many others who would be creating self-sustaining jobs that could span multiple generations.

Our culture must change. We cannot continue to be Luddites opposing the emergence of the Industrial Revolution. Rather we are the ones creating the new age revolution – in 1969 Hippy speak, this is the *"drawing of the age of Aquarius."* We stand on the threshold to the future.

In "mystic" terms expressed in the books connected with this administration, with Obama we cross the boundary that separated or defined the transition from a 56th to 57th quadrennial which we can then equate to Stonehenge, the Metonic calendar systems of the Hebrews and Chinese, and year one of our common calendar – which, in the Hebrew calendar, is the 198th Metonic cycle or 66th full circle at Stonehenge reset to one.

Trump entered office at the critical "mystical" transition point and, as such, it has enormous significance to all those professing to adhere to the Bible and Biblical prophecy. It also has meaning for Hippies and those following eastern spiritual doctrines. For those who deny all "luck" and have never said "Thank God" the symbolic significance can be blow-off. In no way will change the astronomy or alter historical patterns of the universe, but it does assure the prophecies based on the recurring patterns can be fully fulfilled without disruption.

Since my books have been written to ensure very few readers; it follows that only historians might be reviewing these pages, and reflecting on "what if" events so critical part to all second-guessing hindsight, will have something contemporary to reference.

We can do the "What if" games and engage in all the usual second-guessing nonsense. But, the next day we are likely to learn of events that reveal just how nonsensical those second guesses are.

"What if" Trump were to look at the stimulus packages and realize that many aspects of them could become a sound economic practice that would glorify his presidential legacy?

"What if" he realized he could assure himself the re-election and destroy Biden by adopting his version of those policies phrased in terms of the Progressives supporting Bernie Sanders?

"What if" Trump promoted Universal Basic Income as the only rational substitute for the complex system of unemployment and public assistance welfare that traps people in poverty?

UBI would also end the stimulus package disparity created by cash dispersals which have those on unemployment receiving more cash than *essential workers* making less than $20/hour.

"What if" Trump proved true to his stated desire to have a healthcare system better than Australia's and instituted calls for a Medicare for All system – maybe calling it the "Pandemic Readiness Program"? Then it would no longer be a "socialist" idea, but rather a means of addressing the observed breakdown at VA hospitals and ensuring the necessary supplies are available on both the Federal and State levels. The fact that it would also reduce costs and free-up those funds going to meaningless private insurance. Those funds could go to the Federal Government as payroll taxes and still place additional disposable income into the hands of minimum wage and middle-class workers who constitute the foundation of the economy.

But "What if" has no meaning beyond its use to attack actions already taken. The use of hindsight can weaponize "What if" as a tool for baseless accusation – accusing people of doing things wrong or delaying actions that, if they had been taken, "might", in theory. have resulted in a different outcome. We see this with the persistent claims that Trump delayed his response – even though the factual timeline does not support that accusation; to the contrary, it refutes it.

On 22 April, having finally thrown his support behind Biden, Barack Obama tweeted: *"While we continue to wait for a coherent national plan to navigate this pandemic, states like Massachusetts are beginning to adopt their own public health plans to combat this virus – before it's too late."*

Of course, there is the rational problem that, after the 2003 SARS pandemic there were things Bush could have done to create "*a coherent national plan to navigate* [the next] *pandemic*"; and that would have made things easier for Obama when he had to address the 2009 H1N1 Pandemic.

Obama lucked out, because "*nearly one-third of people over 60 years old had antibodies against this virus*" – his administration and the pandemic coincided with Baby-Boomers turning 65 in 2010; their Generation X (Baby Bust) successors turned 50 in 2015, and Wuhan virus targets them, their parents, and remaining members of their grandparents' Silent Generation.

Did Obama create "*a coherent national plan to navigate* [the current] *pandemic*" or in any way address the future pandemic that Climate Change scientists have, for decades, stated would devastate the planet around the year 2030?

If the American culture is to survive, its citizens must change their way of thinking. We have seen how nature defends itself when, in response to Global Warming, it triggered attacks on those who were creating the problem – a problem that became meaningful with the 1910 Great Manchurian Plague that coincided with the run-up in global temperatures. The 1st World War cooled things down, but the post-war warming brought the 1918 influenza epidemic. And, in the 2nd World War pattern the repeated – but the Polio epidemic replaced the flu.

The pattern infers wars cool the planet, and nuclear war is seen as potentially causing a "Nuclear Winter" – which would put an end to "Global Warming" (and possibly the human race). Those who accept The Book of Revelation should realize the apocalypse, with its associated horseman of war and disease, is due around the same 2030 timeframe associated with major arctic melting and the periodic flooding of many well-populated areas, as-well-as disease equatorial regions appearing those regions now being struck by the COVID-19.

In 2019, the average global temperatures were exceeded by about 3.4 degrees – and, due to fossil fuel pollution, continue to rise, while COVID-19 has had the effect of reducing air pollution. There is now a choice between keeping the pollution low or returning to the practices that have accelerated it over the past century.

For the U.S.A., November 2020 decides our decision.

CHAPTER 06 – BIDEN

"The nation has suffered through a grinding campaign against its norms and institutions from the same people who keep shouting that our norms and institutions need defending." ~ Senator Mitch McConnell

"In the multitude of words sin is not lacking, but he who restrains his lips is wise."~ Proverbs 10:19

None of the quotes seem to apply to Biden, though – if he is to be POTUS-46 – he will become the last America Chief Executive to have the power to determine the probability of America's survival beyond that period when, as the Book of Revelation predicted, about a third of life shall perish.

Whether it is Biden or Trump who is elected, there is a reality embodied in the fact that neither is going to run in 2024. Donald J Trump will have completed his two Constitutionally defined terms; Joseph R Biden Jr. would, at age 82, simply be too old and too out of touch with the culture to survive the renomination and election process. Having made all the noise we've heard throughout 2016 to 2020, the "Silent Generation" of Pelosi, Waters, Sanders, and Biden will finally be silenced, either by voters, senility, or death.

On May Day, the nation dealt with propaganda exchanges surrounding COVID-19 and the emerging face-off between Joseph Robinette Biden Jr (born 20 November 1942) and President Donald John Trump (born 14 June 1946). In many ways, it was a conflict between the Silent Generation and Baby-Boomers, where the former built a career living off the nation or public treasury, and the latter belonged to the third generation of the multi-generational family whose livelihood was derived from their economic contribution that was based on providing people with places to live.

When we study the presentation styles of Trump and Biden, it becomes clear that Biden is disoriented or unable to conceptualize even scripted material; Trump generalizes concepts in the manner observed in many creative and highly intelligent individuals. This comparison and the latter statement is very disturbing to all those suffering from _Trump Derangement Syndrome [TDS]_.

A derangement sample is associated with Trump's statement on 23 April, as a prelude to introducing Dr. William N. Bryan:

"With each passing day, we're learning more and more about this enemy. The scientists at DHS have released a report offering a number of insights about how the virus reacts to different temperatures, climates, and surfaces. The findings confirm that the virus survives better in cold or in drier environments and does less well in warmer and more humid environments.

..., we're going to have somebody up; Bill will be up in just a little while. It was a great report you gave. And he's going to be talking about how the virus reacts in sunlight. Wait until you hear the numbers. You won't even believe them."

Afterwords on the states of the pandemic by Vice President Mike Pence, Dr. Bryan introduced and said:

My name is Bill Bryan and I lead the Science and Technology Directorate at the U.S. Department of Homeland Security. ...

...Yesterday, I shared the emerging results of our work that we're doing now with the Coronavirus Task Force. And today, I would like to share certain trends that we believe are important...

..., our most striking observation to date is the powerful effect that solar light appears to have on killing the virus – both surfaces and in the air. We've seen a similar effect with both temperature and humidity as well, where increasing the temperature and humidity or both is generally less favorable to the virus. ...

We're also testing disinfectants readily available. We've tested bleach, we've tested isopropyl alcohol on the virus, specifically in saliva or in respiratory fluids. ..."

So Bryan introducers "*disinfectants*" ... "*specifically in saliva or respiratory fluids*" – triggering a concept.

Trump referred to a discussion before the press conference:

"So I asked Bill a question that probably some of you are thinking of, if you're totally into that world, which I find to be very interesting. So, supposing we hit the body with a tremendous – whether it's ultraviolet or just very powerful light – and I think you said that that hasn't been checked, but you're going to test it. And then I said, supposing you brought the light inside the body, which you can do either through the skin or in some other way, and I think you said you're going to test that too. It sounds interesting.

[Bryan interjects: *We'll get to the right folks who could.*]

Right. And then I see the disinfectant, where it knocks it out in a minute. One minute. And is there a way we can do something like that, by injection inside or almost a cleaning. Because you see it gets in the lungs and it does a tremendous number on the lungs. So it would be interesting to check that. So, that, you're going to have to use medical doctors with. But it sounds – it sounds interesting to me.

On Friday, 24 April, House Speaker Nancy Pelosi asserts a false claim that, in the above statements, President Donald Trump had said people should *"inject Lysol into your lungs."* Social media had also made that assertion, possibly based on the Pelosi comment, that Trump said Lysol and Clorox should be ingested or injected.

However, video from the briefing clear shows that Trump was talking about something he had discussed with Bryan and that it was in the context of *"you're going to have to use medical doctors with."*

MSM made it a point to disregard scientific research of the type reported in *"CORNEL CHRONICLE"* on 7 April: *"Researchers seek universal treatments to impede coronavirus."* In that article is mentioned a research paper published on 6 April: *"Coronavirus membrane fusion mechanism offers a potential target for antiviral development"* which postulated there exists a *"CoV replication cycle that may be vulnerable to inhibition by broad-spectrum or specific antiviral agents."*

Basically, the article is focusing on a *"disinfectant"* – which in this context means a way *"to remove infection"* and not some off the shelf house cleaning or laundry agent. Of course, those suffering from TDS behave like Pelosi.

It should be noted, Pelosi has a history of second-generation political behavior that could be termed "Machiavellian" and serves to define almost all her disruptive actions. With the emergence of her "inject Lysol' interpretation of Trump's musings, Biden concedes Coronavirus related topics to Pelosi and Schumer.

Radical voices like Alexandria Ocasio Cortez, Rashida Tlaib, and Ilhan Omar are Sanders surrogates who, along with the terms of the stimulus packages, given Democrats an opening to accept the policy platform based on a combination of M4A and UBI, along with free college tuition. However, the stimulus also made it possible for Trump to initiate a platform that incorporates the stimulus basics as part of a preventative measure that will serve to prepare the nation for the next pandemic – effectively cutting the Progressives off at the knees.

At the same time, Biden is in the rather difficult position of having to appease demands of radical left-wing voters, who make up a highly vocal and significant portion of the younger Democrats, or face the equivalent of losing support which has been said to rely on "hold your nose and vote for Biden, the Democratic nominee."

Democrats have already expressed a voter apathy triggered by having to choose between a president who said, *"There's nothing in the world like first-rate pussy."* And, speaking as a one who was in the entertainment industry, rather than politics, has said, *"You know I'm automatically attracted to beautiful — I just start kissing them. It's like a magnet. Just kiss. I don't even wait. And when you're a star, they let you do it. You can do anything. Grab them by the pussy. You can do anything."* With the alternative being the well documented handsy-kissy character professional politician Joe Biden who has been charged with improper conduct toward women.

The handsy-kissy assertions against the former vice president are accompanied by an assault allegation dating to 1993 – which was documented, on the 11 August 1993 broadcast of the CNN talk show, *"Larry King Live"*, when the victim's mother alluding to "problems" her daughter faced while working as a staffer for the Senator from Delaware. A transcript from that broadcast has been published:

"San Luis Obispo, California, hello," King begins.

"Yes, hello. I'm wondering what a staffer would do besides go to the press in Washington? My daughter has just left there, after working for a prominent senator, and could not get through with her problems at all, and the only thing she could have done was go to the press, and she chose not to do it out of respect for him," the caller says.

"In other words, she had a story to tell but, out of respect for the person she worked for, she didn't tell it?" King inquires.

"That's true," the woman responds before King cuts away to a panel to discuss her claim.

Even though the statute of limitations had expired, in order to ensure there was an appropriate record, in 2020, the victim, Tara Reade, filed a criminal complaint with the Washington Metropolitan Police Department. She is also on record describing the event as one where, *"We were alone, and it was the strangest thing. There was no, like, exchange really, he just had me up against the wall. His hands were on me and underneath my clothes. "He went down my skirt, but then up inside. He penetrated me with his fingers."*

Subsequent to the formal charges, it appears CNN deleted the "Larry King Live" Episode 155, entitled *"Washington: The Cruelest City on Earth?"*, with subsequent episodes renumbered to conceal the deletion.

It is noteworthy to recognize that this was the same period in which Clinton was having 'Oral in the Oval' *"because he could"*, and House Speaker Newt Gingrich was having an affair with Callista Bisek, an aide in the office of Wisconsin Rep. Steve Gunderson. Joe Biden had been married to his current wife for about 15-years when he molested Tara Reade.

What was being established with the nomination of Joe Biden was effectively an attack on *#MeToo* movement standards opposing sexual harassment and sexual assault of women.

Actress Alyssa Milano tweeted {4:21 PM – Oct 15, 2017}: *"If you've been sexually harassed or assaulted write 'me too' as a reply to this tweet."* The tweet included an image that said: *"Me Too. / Suggested by a friend: 'If all the women who have been sexually harassed or assaulted wrote 'Me too.' as a status, we might give people a sense of the magnitude of the problem.'"*

In December 2017, Minnesota Senator Al Franken was placed in the position where he had to resign amid accusations of sexual impropriety – when the event was the rehearsal of a comic skit whose script called for a man to "surprise" a woman with a kiss, in a *"sort of sudden"* way.

But, as with Biden's boast of violating Federal law, which was documented by C-SPAN – in which he detailed his extortion against Ukraine's government and people to have the Prosecutor General fired, with a defined demand, timeline, and consequence against a Ukraine – there is a clear double standard being displayed. The Harvard educated Franken was broadly attacked by his fellow Democrats for scripted actions, but Biden gets a pass on events that were objected to at the time and involved *"physical penetration"*.

Hypocrisy has consumed a once honorable Party.

They are, as we shall learn, the Party once denounced – in 1845, by a Springfield, Illinois lawyer – has reemerged to be taken over by a class of disrupters who believe the route to victory lays in outdoing that which they assert defines Donald Trump.

In March, Bernie Sanders tweeted a definition of a *"return to normal"* called for by Biden, asserting it meant there would be 87 million without proper medical insurance; that fossil fuel companies would be free to destroy the planet; that the poor would become poorer while the rich became richer – with an inference that Hunter Biden would gain access to more "do-nothing employment."

The same day, Trump's campaign asserted that *"The Biden campaign is scared as hell that voters will see the flood of unedited and embarrassing verbal stumbles that will continue go viral if 'Status Quo Joe' is the nominee."*

With those words, it appeared that both the Sanders' and Trump campaigns viewed Biden in the same light – though, four weeks later, Sanders would endorse Biden, and then the New York Board of Elections saw no reason to hold a Democratic primary.

As we know, in November 2019, Adam Schiff asserted: *"The basic allegations against the president are that he sought foreign interference in a U.S. election, that he conditioned official acts on the performance of these political favors."* And referring to Joe and Hunter Biden, he is on record saying: *"Here you have the president of the United States seeking help from Ukraine in his reelection campaign in the form of two investigations that he thought were politically advantageous, including one of his primary rival."*

So, Schiff made it clear, as the basis for impeachment that, on 25 July 2019, Joe Biden was already Trump's *"primary rival"* in the 2020 election. What is interesting is that it was 25 April – or exactly three months earlier – that Biden announced would be seeking the nomination. Bernie Sanders had announced on 19 February 2019, and despite an established strong base was already being dismissed.

Since 1984, Joseph Biden had made multiple attempts to win the nomination – voting results: 1984, 0.03%; 1988, 0.03%. Then, in 2008, he received 0.18% against Barack Obama (49.03%) and Hillary Clinton (47.66%). Bernie Sanders ran for the nomination in 2016 and received 43.12% support against Clinton's 55.23% and yet, Schiff was saying Biden – who had never gotten even a full percent of the primary vote – would defeat Sanders.

Now, apart from the fact that Biden is a POTUS Cousin and Sanders is not, what rational or historical basis would there be for

Schiff to assert Biden would be Trump's *"primary rival"* – could it be that the game was rigged from the beginning? That none of the twenty-plus opposing candidates had any possible chance of gaining the nomination? That the Swamp had picked someone they knew they could bribe or otherwise control?

For Trump, it came down to simple polling and the idea that presumptive nominee Biden held the lead. As Trump was reported to have declared in a phone call which gave him the late April polling results, *"I am not fucking losing to Joe Biden!"*

But, that was April, Bernie Sanders had just endorsed Biden and the pandemic was leveling out; the American death toll had just passed that of the Vietnam War, and was not quite seen in a relative perspective that reflected the reality of the American population as equal to the total combined population of France, Germany, Spain, Italy, and the United Kingdom – where 108,710 had died, versus the 60,875 in the United States.

Think about this: Bernie Sanders was a man with a plan – one that has been consistent throughout his many decades in politics. If we look at that plan, we see, as soon as the nation was faced with a major pandemic threat, it was immediately implemented as a basis for the stimulus packages. The Universal Base Income [UBI] is the checks and additional unemployment payments that were issued; a look at the government paying all COVID-19 related medical costs is a virus targeted Medicare for All [M4A]. Because the virus attacks those with other conditions that compromise the immune system, any medical treatment targeting COVID-19 would, of necessity, need to also address the related conditions – pandemic M4A.

Bernie has been sidelined but refuses to stay quiet, his life of advocating for a rational economic foundation has come to the fore. He has the pandemic to thank. But other things must be addressed.

In 2015, a quote attributed to Thomas Jefferson appeared on Social Media; there is no apparent basis for the attribution, but the words most certainly fit the 57-quadrennial election cycle and the current transitional point in America's history:

"The government will one day be corrupt and filled with liars, and the people will flock to the one who tells the truth."

Oh, if only the quote attribution were real.

Image the wonder of the Declaration of Independence's creator, the third President of the nation it gave birth to, describing the reality that seems to have befallen the beginning of the nation's 2nd 57-quadrennial cycle. But is there "*one who tells the truth*"?

A well-versed student of PT Barnum occupies the Oval; liars attempted to impeach him; he is blamed for doing what his rival was praised for bragging of doing – extortion for personal gain. The last POTUS impeach had committed Oral in the Oval, the current one has been yelled at for making "vulgar comments," such as the one on 8 October 2016, when he was exchanging comments with Billy Bush – or, more formally, William Hall Bush, the nephew of George W Bush, POTUS-41 – six days before his whose 45th birthday. Their repartee was caught on tape, and we can start with Bush's comment:

Billy Bush: *Sheesh, your girl's hot as shit. In the purple.*

Trump: *Whoa! Whoa!*

Bush: *Yes! The Donald has scored. Whoa, my man!*

[Crosstalk]

Trump: *Look at you, you are a pussy.*

[Crosstalk]

Trump: *All right, you and I will walk out.*

[Silence]

Trump: *Maybe it's a different one.*

Bush: *It better not be the publicist. No, it's, it's her, it's —*

Trump: *Yeah, that's her. With the gold. I better use some Tic Tacs just in case I start kissing her. You know, I'm automatically attracted to beautiful — I just start kissing them. It's like a magnet. Just kiss. I don't even wait. And when you're a star, they let you do it. You can do anything.*

Bush: *Whatever you want?*

Trump: Grab 'em by the pussy. You can do anything.

It seems comical that, as '*a star that can do anything*' he would need 'tic tacs' because he's concerned about his breath. It is also interesting the those suffering from TDS chose to focus on the obviously exaggerated extreme example of "*Grab 'em by the pussy.*"

It also seems a bit comical that, exactly one month after the open-mic recording, Donald John Trump was the President Elect.

Nobody seems to care that it was Billy Bush who set the tone with the comment about Melania "*Sheesh, your girl's hot as shit.*" Or that the hot-mic recording was basically "guy talk" about a reality of the show-biz and fashion industry – where everyone kisses, and doing more is normal. After all, how many actors end up marrying, or just having an affair with, a co-star or someone on the crew?

It might also, for context, be relevant that, on 19 September, Billy and his wife had announced their separation. So just 18-days before the guy talk, Billy was en route to becoming a free agent and, effectively, Trump was telling him that, as a TV host and nephew of a former president, Billy was a star who had his pick of the available ladies.

But, as what promised to become a campaign issue, Joe Biden was accused – as a Senator in 1993, and again as a 2020 candidate – by Tara Reade of actually grabbing her pussy and inserting his fingers.

At least eight women have publicly stated Biden had touched them in ways that made them feel "uncomfortable." Yet, both the Democratic Party and the anti-Trump media have actively distracted from the charges leveled against Biden – a practice that was also seen with the Ukraine extortion which resulted in the firing of their Prosecutor General, and has since given rise to his filing a criminal complaint against Biden for violation of Ukraine law. There does seem to be an emerging pattern in which Biden fulfills the Trump assertion about being able to shoot someone on Fifth Avenue and not lose support – TDS has reached a point where its suffers allow Biden to do things forbidden to others.

Former Biden opponents Bernie Sanders and Amy Klobuchar commented on the Reade accusation, reiterated that all women have the right to be heard, and Michigan Governor Gretchen Whitmer, a survivor of sexual assault, also expressed a belief women should tell their stories – but rejected the evidence to accept Biden's word.

The tone of response to the accusation supported by witness statements, and the 1993 call to Larry King, clearly established that Democrat Party bosses got the candidate they wanted and everyone else was falling into place behind the Party line; at the same time, the average voter was demonstrating a lack of enthusiasm for Biden but was also ecstatic about the prospect of changes in the Oval.

By throwing her endorsement support behind Biden, Hillary Clinton managed to keep herself in the public eye while displaying the same level of cognitive dissonance displayed as one who opposes sexual misconduct but yet supported her own husband's Oral in the Oval infidelity – she revealed herself as a classic enabler.

Speaking to Dan Rather on 13 June 2004, Bill Clinton used these words to explain his actions: "*I think I did something for the worst possible reason – just because I could. ... I've thought about it a lot. And there are lots of more sophisticated explanations, more complicated psychological explanations. ... Only a fool does not look to explain his mistakes.*" And given Biden's touchy-feely habit, it would seem he too does things, "*just because I could,*" and either deny or find "*sophisticated explanations*" such as a claimed "*Administration Policy*" justification for the Ukraine extortion.

Alyssa Milano, promoter of the #MeToo movement, turned her back on reality to assert: "*It's not up to women to admonish or absolve perpetrators, or be regarded as complicit when we don't denounce them. Nothing makes this clearer than the women who are still supporting Joe Biden even with these accusations. Hillary Clinton, Kamala Harris, Stacey Abrams, Amy Klobuchar, Nancy Pelosi, and Elizabeth Warren have all endorsed Biden and like me, continue to support him. Because it's an impossible choice.*"

In contrast, Alexandria Ocasio-Cortez says silencing Biden's sexual assault accuser is "*gaslighting.*" And explains: "*If we again want to have integrity, you can't say, you know, both believe women, support all of this, until it inconveniences you. *"*I find this kind of silencing of all dissent to be a form of gaslighting... A lot of us are survivors, and it's really, really hard and uncomfortable.*"

As seen in book 3, "*The Swamp Fights Back*", having lost control of the Right-wing, the Swamp Denizens immediately turned and revealed that they also controlled the Democratic leadership – in a way, they revealed themselves to be "the deep state."

As a deep state protégée, Biden's Deputy Campaign Manager and Communications Director, Kate Bedingfield, promoted his cover story: "*Vice President Biden has dedicated his public life to changing the culture and the laws around violence against women. He authored and fought for the passage and reauthorization of the landmark Violence Against Women Act. He firmly believes that women have a right to be heard—and heard respectfully. Such claims should also be diligently reviewed by an independent press. What is clear about this claim: It is untrue. This absolutely did not happen.*"

Interestingly, there might be evidence of the complaint in the documents Biden deposited with the University of Delaware in 2012.

In theory, those records – 1,875 boxes of "photographs, documents, videotapes, and files" and 415 gigabytes of electronic records – were to be opened to the public either on 31 December 2019 or two years after Biden *"retires from public life"* whichever comes later. With his candidacy and then the de facto securing of the nomination, it would appear those records will be sealed until either the November election results are posted or until January 2025, when his successor assumes office and the then 82-year-old is no longer fit for office.

On 1 May, in an MSNBC "Morning Joe" video interview from his basement, Biden said: *"The idea that they would be made public while I was running for public office, they could be taken out of context ... they could be fodder."* Supposedly, there were speeches, interviews, meetings conducted overseas – which would include the extortion episode – as well as position papers, and meetings with Putin and others that could be detrimentally spun against him in the campaign.

Biden was then asked since there were no personnel records in the University of Delaware, why not approve a search of those records for her name? To which he responded, *"There is nothing, they wouldn't, they're not there. And if [*he stutters and stumbles nervously trying to get word out*] I - I - I - I don't understand what the point you're trying to make. ... There are no personnel records – by definition."*

Biden then asserts that it is necessary to keep those records sealed because of various confidential conversations – conversations that were, had he not sought a 2020 nomination, to have been made public in 2019 – inferring the information is exclusively detrimental to him and not to anyone else. Yet he is saying a name search for Tara Reade cannot be done – without anything else being released – and that infers seriously detrimental contents that he cannot risk having "leaked."

"This is an open book. There's nothing for me to hide," Biden said in the interview, conducted from his home in Delaware where he is self-isolating during the coronavirus outbreak. Nothing to hide, other than University of Delaware records covering the period when he was a Senator – when the assault occurred, he was known as "the Senator from MBNA" because of Hunter Biden working for the Delaware firm while daddy Joe pushed legislation beneficial to the credit card company, but which harmed the average worker.

On 24 April, Pelosi said: "*Elections are about the future. Now more than ever, we need a forward-looking, battle-tested leader who will fight For The People: a President with the values, experience, and the strategic thinking to bring our nation together and build a better, fairer world for our children.*"

But, if Biden is afraid of what might be leaked from a search of the University of Delaware records, we must seriously question his core values during the period when his son was a "consultant" for the firm Biden legislated on behalf of, an then how he boasted of committing extortion to fire a prosecutor looking into a firm that was paying his son a million dollars a year for similar "consulting."

One thing we are learning from the Biden candidacy, America has returned to the days of the "Yellow Dog Democrat' – one who will support any Democratic Party candidate, regardless of their personal qualities or political ethical morality. It's a term that dates to an 1848 speech by Republican [Progressive] Abraham Lincoln to describe Andrew Jackson's popularity among Democrats: *Like a horde of hungry ticks you have stuck to the tail of the Hermitage lion to the end of his life; and you are still sticking to it, and drawing a loathsome sustenance from it, after he is dead— A fellow once advertised that he had made a discovery by which he could make a new man out of an old one, and have enough of the stuff left to make a little yellow dog.*" Then Lincoln said: "*You not only twice made President of him out of it, but you have had enough of the stuff left to make Presidents of several comparatively small men since; and it is your chief reliance now to make still another.*"

In 2020, the only issue – is it Trump or Biden who shall draw the *"horde of hungry ticks"*?

CHAPTER 07 – CYCLES

"'If they would rather die,' said Scrooge, 'they had better do it, and decrease the surplus population.'"
~ Charles Dickens' A Christmas Carol"

"Silence is Gold because whatever you say will come back against you; only if it is good, will it come back to your advantage." ~ "Saying of the Fathers"

America has reentered an embryotic stage in its evolution. Its first birth occurrent in 1789; 2017 saw a transition into what will be its second birth and, if the "child" survives, it will carry the nation forward until the year 2245.

As with any birth, there is pain, and the pandemic has shown areas of weakness, points of pain that are tender, and serve as the umbilical cord connecting the baby to its parent. Many see that cord as "normal" because the grew and developed relying upon it for the substance that supported them and gave them nourishment. But it is not something to remain attached to.

But it is worth knowing, and certainly worth remembering, plague and pandemic are a part of human history and the history of the nation. In 2020, COVID-19 brought Italy to the fore as the place where the most people died; when the American nation was being born, the pilgrims were finally settling in, with some thinking about founding Harvard, Italy was experiencing the Great Plague of Milan which, between 1629 and 1631 killed around a million people.

But, because Central Europe was consumed by a Thirty Years' War (1618–1648), while all of Europe found diversion in periodic but ongoing witch-hunts or trials, historians don't find much profit in writing about something killing Italians. It's only when Italians, like the Mafia, are killing others that it gains entertainment value.

As much as we know about the birth of America, and hear about George Washington, how often have you heard about the 1793 yellow fever epidemic in Philadelphia which killed fifteen-percent of the city's population between 1 August and 9 November?

Why didn't they blame Washington? Imagine how they'd yell at Trump if 250,000 Philadelphians died of Wuhan flu today – it's roughly a fifteen-percent equivalent and apparently, the epidemic was brought in from another country. So it's about "the same."

At the time, publisher and economist Matthew Carey wrote something that has significance in the modern age of the "elbow bump": *The old custom of shaking hands fell into such general disuse, that many shrank back with affright at even the offer of the hand.* So there are some similarities.

The handshake is a means of disease transfer that changes what was once a sign of being unarmed and a friend into the threat of deadly aggression – it changes the political 'meet and greet.'

On 6 October 1999, NBC news-anchor Stone Phillips brought up the issue with known germaphobe Donald Trump, who declared what is now a fundamental COVID-19 reality: "*I am not a big fan of the handshake. I think it's barbaric. ... Shaking hands, you catch colds, you catch the flu, you catch it, you catch all sorts of things. Who knows what you don't catch?*"

Two decades later, at his 2020 State of the Union address, the media reacted to what appeared to be President Donald John Trump rejecting House Speaker Nancy Pelosi's attempt at a handshake just prior to the speech she would call lies, and among those "lies" was mention of the threat from the COVID-19 virus.

But then, some things never change – a quarter-century ago, on 27 October 1996, Trump was quoted saying, "*Everybody wants to shoot at me because it's me.*" And then five years later, on 1 April 2004, he observed, "*Nobody has gotten more bad publicity over the years than Donald Trump.*" To which we can now add, the title "President" and recognize that the "*bad publicity*" is simply a rhetorical variation on being "*shot at*" – this is the world of Trump which he defined, on 4 December 2001, as one that gives him a chance to do what he loved – "*I loved coming back from adversity.*"

As a warning to those attacking him now, back on 23 March 1992, Business Week quoted him predicting: "*You'll never see me sitting in the corner sucking my thumb. The name Trump will be hotter than ever.*" And finally, we can roll back the clock to 7 April 1985, when the Los Angeles Times quoted him saying, "*It was easier for me ten years ago. Nobody knew who I was and nobody cared. Then, I wasn't the guy everyone was trying to stop.*"

As of 8 November 2016, Trump truly became a man everyone wanted to stop. And his reaction to adversity, the fact he thrives on it, made him the right man for the right job arriving at precisely the right point in history – Franklin Delano Roosevelt, in 1933.

Readers of my more recent books are aware I've been playing with Metonic cycles (19-year) that form a basis for the patriarch ages in the Book of Genesis and is also the basis of both the Hebrew and Chinese calendars – year one of our western calendar is based on or derived from the 198th Metonic cycle of the Hebrew calendar. Our western calendar is actually the Hebrew calendar reset to one.

Evangelicals should love this. It contributes to fulfilling the Biblical Messianic Prophecy whereby the ancient Hebrew laws are universally accepted – as has been done with the washing and other hygiene laws that are taking on importance in this pandemic age.

The prediction also carries the loss of a third of life – an event consistent with elderly Silent Generation and sickly Baby-Boomers who are due to die over the course of the next decade; doing so in a context of Climate Change related extinctions. For the evangelical, this could serve to validate the premise of their beliefs. As shown in my book, *"Biblical Prophecy: Are we in the Revelation Era,"* the 57-cycle defines one means of dating the prophecies that the Bible said could not be dated [because they do not provide the starting date].

The circle at Stonehenge is composed of 56-upright stones, and if we count each stone, the 1st and 57th stone are the same. This gives us the observed 56th and 57th quadrennial election cycle fall in the second Obama term (2013) and the start of Trump's first-term (2017). Obviously, if we were playing with Stonehenge astronomy or wished to be "mystical", the transition between the historic act of a true African-American being elected POTUS, and a non-politician international businessman is monumental.

Hebrew had a unit of measurement, called an Omar, which is composed of 49-units. Some might recognize it as the numerical representation of the folklore *"seventh son of a seventh son"* who has "special powers"; it is also seven calendar weeks of the period that establishes Shavuot thru the Counting of the Omer that begins on the second day of Passover – in 2020, this fell between 8 and 16 April. And, of course, Passover celebrates the Hebrews "sheltering-in-place" as pandemic which killed the first-born of Egypt pass over the homes of those Hebrews who had marked their doors and were followers of Moses.

In 2020, we even have the Metonic 19 presented in the form of the Covid-19 pandemic, and the coincidence of the start of the Omar count falling on Easter's Good Friday – bringing the two days together had been the intention of Pope St. John I who, in 525, requested a calendar that would align Easter and Passover and was presented with the one we now identify as the Western Calendar. As those familiar with history and the New Testament know – detailed in my Vatican approved book, *Saint Paul's Joke* – Herod died four years before the calendar starts, and Jesus had been in Egypt two years, so was born about three years earlier, so the idea that our year one is the year of his "*incarnation*' is a lie Christianity has promoted for about 1500 years. Jesus was born around our year 7BCE.

We are a culture constructed on mathematical coincidence and lies. When the lie benefits the culture is brushed aside, when it hurts those who would cheat the cultural changes they object to and yell "Lie" about everything – even the truth.

As seen in the Trump Card series and "*Jonathon's POTUS Cousins*" historical cycles are given significance. The Wuhan Flu has occurred 57-quadrennia from the start of Washington's second term and it is also two Omar after the Spanish Flu of 1918-1921.

It was estimated that the worldwide death toll from Spanish Flu was exceeded 50 million, with 675,000 occurring in the United States. Seven years earlier, the Manchurian plague was responsible for approximately 60,000 Chinese deaths. The primary difference between then and now is transportation – global travel. A disease can evolve and spread even before it has begun to show it exists.

Modern discoveries have revealed the Spanish Flu had been circulating among soldiers long before it was recognized – for it to spread, those soldiers needed to finish fighting and return to their homes.

On 23 March 2014, the World Health Organization reported cases of Ebola Virus Disease (EVD) in southeastern Guinea's rural forest region was later defined as the West Africa Ebola epidemic. The epidemic was later traced back to multiple cases reported on 24 January – on the date of the WHO report, there were 49 confirmed cases.

The CDC confirmed the first travel-associated case of EVD on 30 September 2014 – a man who had traveled from West Africa to Dallas, Texas. WHO had declared the Public Health Emergency of International Concern (PHEIC) status on 8 August 2014, and lifted it on 29 March 2016.

Ebola provides the basis to analyze CDC or WHO responses.

Of course, March had begun with both Trump and Clinton each winning seven primary elections, and a week later the EU recognized a migrant problem that resulted in Macedonia, Croatia and Slovenia closed their borders to migrants seeking entry into Northern Europe.

March 2016 also saw Barack and Michelle Obama visiting Cuba – establishing a change in diplomatic relations with Cuba since 1957 that can be equated to Trump stepping across the border into North Korea.

Moving forward to 11 July 2016, Ambassador Susan E. Rice received a memo entitled, *"NSC Lessons Learned Study on Ebola,"* which warned: *"Because the way the world is developing makes epidemics more likely to occur and spread rapidly in the future, epidemics must be considered one of the most pressing threats to global security."*

The memo also cited a reality about WHO that existed under Obama and we observed in a COVID-19 context:

"Built into the U.S. government approach to the containment of infectious diseases abroad was the assumption of a level of capability and competence in the WHO that turned out not to exist. By August 2014 it was clear the WHO had lost control of the epidemic and that the U.S. must rush resources into West Africa to avoid a global catastrophe."

The WHO had screwed-up in 2014 and again in 2020, yet it came as a surprise that Trump – who likes things to run smooth – had, on 14 April, announced his decision to cut funding to the group that had repeatedly failed to perform its job responsible and professional manner. Trump was attacked for stating the obvious reality when he accused the organization of *"severely mismanaging and covering up the spread of the coronavirus."*

Trump went on to say:

"America and the world have chosen to rely on the WHO for accurate, timely, and independent information to make important public health recommendations and decisions. If we cannot trust that this is what we will receive from the WHO, our country will be forced to find other ways to work with other nations to achieve public health goals."

Recall, on 14 January, WHO had Tweeted: *"investigations conducted by the Chinese authorities have found no clear evidence of human-to-human transmission,"* and note, there is a recurring use of the "*no clear evidence*" justification or excuse used whenever WHO or other politically motivated groups want to act in a manner that is inconsistent with scientific principles that dictate you must prove a fact-based hypothesis wrong.

That principle is actually seen in the American justice system where innocence is the accepted fact that must be disproved – a reality ignore by House Impeachment Managers who had repeatedly asserted they had "*Overwhelming evidence*" of a Constitutionally impeachable "*High Crime*," when they could not even define a basic statutory crime to include in their Articles of Impeachment.

The memo and House logic are interesting because Trump was called a xenophobic racist for instituting his Travel ban.

The 2016 memo clearly stated that: "*Management of the risk of disease spread by international travelers is essential.*" But then, the memo also stated that "*New mechanisms are needed to harness better the potential contributions of the private sector, foundations, and the digital humanitarian community.*" And this is combined with "*Greater study of population behavior change and social mobilization is needed.*"

As we saw on page 34, one example to the related studies was the February 2018 study of effects of New York City air quality that identified the epicenter and population that would be most affected by a future pandemic virus: '*Air Pollution and the Health of New Yorkers: The Impact of Fine Particles and Ozone*'

We can leave it to Biden supporters to address the facts noted in the memo observation stating: "*The Ebola epidemic showcased substantial gaps of global preparedness and capacity in infectious disease response. When the U.S. mobilized after the WHO failed to contain the epidemic, gaps in preparedness and capacity surfaced in every major agency tasked with health and security in the U.S. government.*"

We do know that Trump has repeated stated, and on 6 May told ABC News' David Muir: "*The cupboard was bare. The other administration, the last administration, left us nothing. We didn't have ventilators. We didn't have medical equipment. The tests were broken — you saw that. We had broken tests. They left us nothing. We've taken it and we've built an incredible stockpile, a stockpile like we've never had before.*"

And, while alleged "fact Checkers" might assert his statement to be false, Trump's statement is fully consistent with the Obama Administration Memo and the faults it reported four-months before the election. Thus, if the cupboard was filled, there would be an appropriations bill and related record of it having been filled before 20 January 2017. Former Vice President Joseph R. Biden should be able to enlighten the nation as to the newly installed "*stockpile*" that had to have been created in the last six months of the Obama-Biden administration.

Those seeking to attack Trump would, quite logically, want the inventory records for the Obama Administration. Without them, Trump's statement would seem to comply with the memo referring to the Ebola era "*gaps in preparedness*" still existing under Obama.

But the Ebola issue was 23 March 2014 to 1 June 2016, and we know, in terms of the Metonic and quadrennial cycles that 2016 is the point of importance. In 2013, in my book "*President Ted Cruz and the 2016 Election*" I both dismissed Cruz as a viable candidate and the birther movement ridiculous – yet, it was stated that the events dictated a Republican would win the Oval in 2016.

Let's look at the numbers, years, and a bit of history.

If we count the first election or inaugural as one, in 2008/09 we have our 56th and 2012/13 presents the 57th quadrennial. If we count the cycles the way we do birthdays than the start of Obama's second term (2012/13) becomes the 56th quadrennial and Trumps first-term (2016/17) becomes the 57th anniversary of the first cycle and the start of the 1st quadrennial of the second set of 57 terms – the modern or next version of the history begun in 1789.

Taking a quick glance at the Metonic quadrennial cycles, we discover the first, the 19th-quadrennial, is the one that encompasses Abraham Lincoln (1860-1865), while the second (38th-quadrennial) is defined by the second term of Franklin Delano Roosevelt, (FDR, 1936-1941). Clearly, after Washington, they are the most famous of all the 45 POTUS and share the common element of association to a "War" that changed the course of the nation and, in many ways, history. Donald J. Trump could be designated a "Metonic POTUS" engaged in a war that, on 19 March 2020, he termed "*our big war*" against what is an invisible enemy named COVID-19.

By the same token, Barack H. Obama Jr. could be designated a "Metonic POTUS" and his war would resemble that confronting FDR

– rather than inheriting a *"Great Depression,"* Obama received both the *"Great Recession,"* and the war resulting from 9/11, rather than a 12/7 Bombing of Pearl Harbor.

As shown in my 2016 book, *"Jonathon's POTUS Cousins,"* in times of national stress, a strong POTUS Cousin will always emerge – in 1939, the Allies had FDR, Churchill, Eisenhower, and numerous other POTUS Cousins (descendants of the 4-Sisters also tied to the founding of America) in command positions.

Only Britain is still ruled by descendants of the 4-Sisters, so few other nations compare to the United States, though the same players are still in the comparative historic cycle game. They share the beliefs that define America and those beliefs control our actions – even though there have been significant modifications.

Before there was a defined Democratic Candidate who has a presumptive status as the 2020 nominee, Polls asked: "*Who would you vote for, Donald Trump or someone else?*"

Both the phrasing and reality were that they were offering a propaganda based choice between *"Trump or anyone but Trump."* There was no issue of qualifications, platform, or any other normal basis for judgment – the intent was to initiate or enforce a mindset bias against Trump.

By doing so, they open those they are "polling" to acceptance of impeachment – resulting in POTUS Pence – or accepting anyone else who makes it through the vetting that should be the nomination process, but which House Managers had already determined would be Joseph R Biden.

The polling process was being utilized to both reenforce and spawn new TDS sufferers – in some cases, it was accompanied by questions that would undermine Bernie Sanders or any other threat to the Biden nomination. It also served to allow Trump's alleged lies to amplified without fact-checking, while negating examination of the history of lies associated with Biden – a factor which contributed to his repeatedly failing to achieve nominee status throughout all his attempts since 1987.

The pollsters rely on the fact that people will accept a huge lie much more readily than they do a minor distortion. It was an idea that Hitler explained in "Mein Kampf":

"...in the big lie there is always a certain force of credibility; because the broad masses of a nation are always more easily

corrupted in the deeper strata of their emotional nature than consciously or voluntarily; and thus in the primitive simplicity of their minds they more readily fall victims to the big lie than the small lie, since they themselves often tell small lies in little matters but would be ashamed to resort to large-scale falsehoods."

Discussion of Biden's acts of extortion were explained by the use of "*Government Policy*" because to question it would require too much time and thought for the short attention span associated with "*the broad masses of a nation.*"

But the "Big Lie" idea was that was associated with the base justification for our Western or Christian calendar.

Fifteen hundred years ago, Roman Christians accepted a calendar that had Jesus born when he was seven, and time travel back to interact with Herod. They accepted a birth on 25 December because that was the time of their traditional Saturnalia holiday, and the idea he was an only begotten son of God agreed with their traditional deities and the "men of renown" who died in Noah's Flood.

We believe what we are conditioned to believe by our parents and the dominant culture whose belief system they either reinforce or refute. When there is an evolutionary step, everything remains the same, we just change the name (the gift-giving happy holiday of Saturnalia becomes Christmas) – designating the old name as wrong and cherry-picking accepted or loved elements to apply to the new name or application of an old concept. The idea of Socialism, or the things now referred to as Progressive ideas, are only the Biblical "*do unto others*" combined with the "*Good Samaritan*" – and are rejected because the society is subliminally biased against religion.

If we believe in reincarnation, then there is a limited number of souls who are either alive or awaiting an available body. And in that regard, I'm reminded of a poster on a NYC subway car during the 1960's hippy era which declared: "*Half the people who ever lived are alive today.*"

Was the posted comment about some emerging concerns over the size of the population – concerns which gave rise to the 1968 book, "*Population Bomb?*" At the time, the global population was 3,551,599,127; in 2020 it is recorded as 7,794,798,739 or 2.2 times as large. And while there are issues of hunger, people are being fed.

As we know, with global population growth at 1.05%, we are in a population bust. In 1963, growth peaked at 2.2% and it was believed population growth would be exponential. That exponential growth assumption was the premise behind the *"Population Bomb."*

LOL, it would also seem that now, ALL the people who have ever lived are alive today – if you believe in reincarnation and accept the estimates of ancient population numbers then we are faced with a possible reality that we are in the Biblical transition era.

In terms of both reincarnation, and in terms of the Biblical prediction of a judgment day when all the souls shall be brought together, we are almost there. I say almost because we will be there when there are no longer souls who can occupy bodies and therefore every birth would have a matching death. Judgement Day happens we have a numerically true and accurate zero population growth.

Of course, we need only end this century without a world war or the loss of a third of life. We are long past the idea that people are ignorant of Hebrew law – there is no undoing of that prophecy.

Are we headed to the fictional STAR TREK UNIVERSE type of United Earth government? That is what the Bible says is due in this century – roughly two thousand years after Jesus but before the year 2100. If that is where we are going then we are very likely to have a World War bring it about.

It's silly to talk about religion and mystical prophecy.

When we acknowledge beliefs yield *"self-fulfilling prophecy,"* we must also acknowledge that the "war" that is now beginning its 19th-year comports well with being a prelude to the global war. The numbers are coming together – either as reality or coincidence. For America, there is no evidence that the cycles DO NOT apply – and until that evidence appears, it is worth functioning as if it is reality. What does it hurt?

Do we reject or utilize belief? The calendar, which works in a very real and consistent manner, came about because people had a belief system predicated on the idea *"Grandpa Was A Deity"* and all the leaders or *"men of renown"* were the sons of "his sons" and mortal women. That evolved with the various cultural traditions and were eventually combined into the western idea of the divinity of Jesus. In advanced cultures, the religious differences are little more than an emphasis on one element of the common foundation belief system that evolved as humanity did.

It's a belief like that of the symbolism of 57, Omar, or Metonic cycles – if we remove their astronomy, archaeological, and proven scientific value as buried within the mythology that was acceptable to the masses. Hitler's *"Big Lie"* as a cultural reality.

Obviously, I enjoy the references and the effects they have had on history and the way humanity works to deny reality. That which defines history is defining our current point in time, and our attitudes toward Trump or Obama.

We know the Swamp Denizens are making a last-ditch effort to harm the nation in the misguided belief they will benefit. We saw the same irrationality among those who crashed the hijacked planes into the World Trade Center and attempted to do the same with the Pentagon.

You have those who would kill themselves in order to harm others. The Muslim terrorists were under the delusional belief that they were furthering some religious mandate by actively violating their religion and its prohibition against the harming of innocents. We also see it when they use innocent children to carry their suicide bombs into marketplaces or to kill those on pilgrimage to holy sites.

Those who attack the idea of *Medicare For All* and *Uniform Basic Income* for all citizens are no better than the suicide terrorists who kill themselves for the sole purpose of murdering or harming others. Not addressing the warped thinking can affect our current situation and future history.

Of course, the beauty of my books comes in the fact that only a very select group – a self-selecting population that wants a good future for their families, friends, and even those who might someday fit that description – can read and think about the ideas and facts presented.

When dealing with ancient texts and wisdom, researchers have been know to refer to it in terms of *"wisdom influence"* such as forms, vocabulary, and themes. Or be seen in the form of *"wisdom contact"* which involves rhetorical questions and quotations. These are embodied in the idea that the spirit lies in "Wisdom, Knowledge, and Understanding."

The spirit is that of the wise, those who can see through the mythology – who can see behind "the curtain" and see or know the "Wizard of Oz" and the root of his "magic." The curtain is being pulled back and humanity has the choice to see reality or ignore it.

Ignoring the Wizard is what we tend to do. In 1939, when the movie "The Wizard of Oz" was released, ignoring the Wizard defined the Great Depression-era; when the original children's story was first published, in 1900, it was drawn from the author's experience with the droughts in South Dakota and the theater – which provided us the showmen's curtain concealing reality from an audience or population that flocks to any place that allows them an opportunity for fantasy and an escape from reality.

Of course, as one might suspect, Wizard author Lyman Frank Baum was, through his mother's line, a descendant of the 4-Sisters. And, consistent with the politics of the Trump era, he was connected to both New York (birth) and California (death). Baum was also a strong supporter of Woman's Suffrage and he advocated for Native American genocide based on a rather convoluted logic:

"The Pioneer has before declared that our only safety depends upon the total extermination of the Indians. Having wronged them for centuries, we had better, in order to protect our civilization, follow it up by one more wrong and wipe these untamed and untamable creatures from the face of the earth." [Saturday Pioneer, January 3, 1891]

There was a comedy in his little peace, which went on to say:

"In this lies future safety for our settlers and the soldiers who are under incompetent commands. Otherwise, we may expect future years to be as full of trouble with the redskins as those have been in the past.

An eastern contemporary, with a grain of wisdom in its wit, says that 'when the whites win a fight, it is a victory, and when the Indians win it, it is a massacre.'"

The first part advocates genocide that is inconsistent with the idea of women's equality, or the expressed idea of fairness to those who have been *"wronged...for centuries."* And, interestingly, that the soldiers are *"under incompetent commands."*

Taken "out of context" he is a Nazis advocating genocide, in context he is sarcastically attacking those who would kill the Indians and showing the hypocrisy of those writing the description of an event. Can you, the reader, comprehend the relationship to Trump and his TDS or CNN attacker presentations?

CHAPTER 08 – Swamp

"And were it left to me to decide whether we should have a government without newspapers, or newspapers without a government, I should not hesitate a moment to prefer the latter. But I should mean that every man should receive those papers and be capable of reading them."
~ Thomas Jefferson to Edward Carrington in 1787

There seems to be a history with the media that predates the nation. And apparently, Jefferson preferred to trust the media over the government.

But that was a year before the 1st quadrennial election began the cyclical process the came to an end with Barack Obama and his Vice President, Joe Biden.

Newspapers? Reading? This is the age of the internet, a time when everything has gone visual and personal. The visual network news is skewed to the political and commercial benefit of the media – there is no need to read.

Then there is cellphone texting, social media, and Twitter – with its typed character limitations that reinforce a limited attention span. Yes, people can read. To use web-based media or text, you do need to read a little – often paying a lot for the privilege.

Jefferson thought *"every man should receive those papers."* And, since he was writing in a period in history when only adult men were deemed worthy to vote, was he also thinking that only men should be taught to read? And, since they should all *"receive those papers,"* did he envision *"those papers"* should be free?

Could Jefferson – who existed in a period when so few people could read that future-president Andrew Jackson had to be taught by his wife – could Jefferson have envisioned the type of widespread media we now have? Or, could he have projected there would be a fakenews – yellow journalism based upon sensationalism and crude exaggeration – or level of media propaganda Hitler would denounce in *Mein Kampf* and then utilize secure his place in history while fulfilling Revelation's White Horsemen Four Horsemen parameters?

In his 2014 book, *"Duty: Memoirs of a Secretary at War,"* we find the Defense secretary for the Obama administration, Robert Gates, saying of Joe Biden: *"He's a man of integrity, incapable of hiding what he really thinks, and one of those rare people you know you could turn to for help in a personal crisis. Still, I think he's been wrong on nearly every major foreign policy and national security issue over the past four decades."*

Gates pointed out a problem which manifested itself again on 13 May 2020, when it was reported that Joe Biden supported rent and mortgage forgiveness during the period dominated by COVID-19.

Journalist Peter Hamby had asked if it was possible for there to be *"some kind of federal rent bailout,"* Biden replied: *"Absolutely. There is. And we should. We should. ... There should be rent forgiveness and there should be mortgage forgiveness now in the middle of this crisis. Forgiveness. Not paid later, forgiveness. It's critically important to people who are in the lower-income strata."*

Biden's position sounds *"something for nothin'"* great and it might attract a few votes, but only among those who do not grasp the reality of the economic process deemed Gross Domestic Product (GDP) creation and growth. His statement reveals his destructive ignorance of economics.

GDP is defined as "total value of goods produced and services provided" – usually for a period of one fiscal or calendar year, and applied on the national level, though it can be utilized to compare any economic community, city, county, or state.

The GDP is tied to another metric, an *"economic Multiplier"* which equates to the number of times a unit of currency circulates within an economic community before it leaves and circulates in a different economic community – or removed from circulation. The idea of *"Not paid later, forgiveness"* denotes a form of removal for the purpose of destruction.

Assume the residence building carries a mortgage. If the rent is not paid because it is *"forgiven"*, those funds cease being available to pay a mortgage, do basic repairs, provide heat, or even pay the building superintendent's wages. If we focus on the mortgage, then, since the borrower receives no rent they cannot pay the mortgage.

When the mortgage is unpaid, the bank has no funds to pay its staff, pay monthly interest on savings accounts, or even pay its staff. Without their salaries, the staff cannot shop for food, demand falls and now the grocery stores cannot pay their staff; and then there is the problem that neither the bank nor grocery employees are going to be able to pay their rent or mortgage.

As we can see, there is a ripple or butterfly effect that, in this scenario grows into a negatively compounding economic multiplier that is the mirror image of the stimulus effect created by providing funds to the poorest segment of the economy.

The traditional positives stimulus is to provide some form of unemployment insurance that will allow them time to find new work or, failing that, to provide public assistance (welfare) that will keep money entering the economic stream where it will create economic demand and provide jobs. Andrew Yang had proposed a Universal Basic Income (UBI) as part of his candidacy platform, specifically because it would create a reliable and secure economic foundation that would ensure the stability of the economy in times such as those seen with the lockdowns necessitated by the COVID-19 pandemic.

Biden's *"Forgiveness. Not paid later,"* proposal serves only one purpose – one which proved inherent in Reaganomics *"Trickle Down"* theories – it undermines whatever economic foundation we might see functioning through the crisis period. For the economic multiplier to have maximum effectiveness, money must be injected at the lowest level possible, In general, this means a minimum wage that is, in FY2020-dollars, at least $15/hour and ideally $20/hour.

Since COVID-19 mitigation requires that individuals are not working, the government would need to provide the mortgage and rent money throughout the lockdown period.

With Biden we also have the problem that he has no ideas that are his own, and that he lacks the mental acuity to grasp any of the inherent ramifications of his words or deeds.

In this case, the idea of debt forgiveness can be attributed to members of *"The Squad"* whose progressive ideas have crossed over into the realm of the failed Communist Socialism ideologies and do not reflect either Biblical or Marxist ideas of utilizing any "surplus capital" for a common basic good of all members of society. Marx held that the individual was entitled to and should benefit from the fruits of their labors – that which remained would help others.

Of course, the Progressive or Marxist focus was on helping to ensure your neighbor was in good health and had basic shelter from which to begin their efforts to generate surplus capital. This would mean UBI and M4A are mandataries for any society that wishes to survive through the current Climate Change era in which pandemics will become a normal occurrence.

Were we thinking in terms of the Evangelical "End of Times", nothing would change. A third of life is going to die within the next two decades – mass species extinctions have already begun and the Baby-Boom generation, currently the 10% of the population over 65-years-old, will be deceased by 2035. If we add wars, accidents, and pandemic or plague deaths, we can account for another 25%. As the back cover chart shows, reproductive rates are 1.0% falling to 0.8% and adjust for mathematical variances among that third of humanity who are contributing to the Revelation prophecy.

If our leaders can be attacked rather than guided, we ensure the prophecies can be fulfilled with the maximum detrimental effect so desired by the religious or conspiracy fanatics. Attacks make for media profits – *if it bleeds it leads*, so they strive to create as much blood as is humanly possible.

The day before the Senate impeachment trial against Trump began, the Bernie Sanders campaign circulates this op-ed attack on Joe Biden.

On 12 March, the nation was informed that Joe Biden was to make a speech against the background of the COVID-19 pandemic taking the lives of 800 in Italy and only 67 in South Korea, with it yet to spread in America: *"Today's speech will be presidential, not political. It will be clear-eyed about the challenges we face and offer thoughtful ideas on the path forward. It will offer a view into how Biden will lead in times of crisis as president."*

When he finally gave that speech, he acknowledged that *"this is going to require a national response. Not just from our elected leaders or our public health officials, but from all of us."* But also fell back on the contradictory talking points with inaudible portions represented here as *"[??]"* :

"The world [??], officially declared COVID-19 a pandemic. [??] Being overly dismissive or [??] is only going to hurt us and further advance the spread of the disease, but neither should we panic or fall back on xenophobia labeling COVID-19 a foreign virus does not displace accountability for the misjudgments that have taken thus far by the Trump administration."

Yes, WHO finally acknowledged a pandemic existed, after having basically denied there was a basis for international concern. He also invoked *"xenophobia labeling COVID-19 a foreign virus"* in an apparent denial of the reality that COVID-19 is of foreign origin.

And then there is the idea of Trump's *'misjudgments"* – which are never specified or defined in any way.

Though, we do know, it was less than two months earlier that Biden labeled Trump's Travel Bans as *"hysterical xenophobia"* – apparently because Trump exhibited a level of foresight to act before WHO formally contradicted its own public statements and reversed itself to acknowledge the virus was both a threat to other nations and involved the human-to-human transmission it had previously denied.

Of course, Trump is a liar, and Biden is honest – unless you look back to 22 September 1987 when a fact check article looked a statement Biden had made the previous April while he making a campaign appearance in New Hampshire. Apparently triggered when a questioner challenged his academic credentials, in a video tapped response Biden stated: "*I think I probably have a much higher IQ than you do, I suspect. I went to law school on a full academic scholarship, the only one in my class to have a full academic scholarship. In the first year in the law, I decided I didn't want to be in law school and ended up the bottom two-thirds of my class and then decided I wanted to stay, went back to law school, and in fact ended up in the top half of my class.*"

According to the Syracuse Law School records, Biden "*ranked 80th in a class of 100 his first year in law school, 79th of 87 at the end of his second year, and 76 of 85 the final year.*" As for the full scholarship, it was only a partial one. Only the IQ claim is possible – the average law school graduate has an average IQ of 135. But that would mean Biden should have been in the top 25 of his class and might explain why he lied about ranking there.

Note, Biden is consistent – he lies on video. He lied in 1987 and in 2018 when he confessed to the "Obama approved" extortion.

As we know, Biden also lied in asserting that Trump's actions – since duplicated globally – were based on *"hysterical xenophobia"* rather than a rational, *Obama Pandemic Playbook* response to the emerging global pandemic. On 18 May, Biden chose to return to the assertion and interject his support for Nancy Pelosi attempting to do on 24 February when she attempted to promote Chinatown tourism by declaring *"what we're trying to do today is to say everything is fine here."* It was an action she took just twenty-days after she tore up the SOTU speech and called it a pack of lies – including a stated fact: "*Protecting Americans' health also means fighting infectious diseases. [referring to COVID-19] My administration will take all necessary steps to safeguard our citizens from this threat."*

Obviously, Speaker Pelosi had intentionally sought to create conditions which would increase the spread of the disease that was making New York City its epicenter. It was just another example of *the Most Harm to the Most People* agenda which had defined the far Right-wing and Tea Party before Trump took office – it was Pelosi revealing she was part of the swamp that needed draining. And with his May support of her actions, we began to have evidence that Joe Biden was also one of the swamp denizens occupying the Left-wing.

Blame Trump was a pattern defining the pandemic election.

Ignoring realities seen in the July 2016 Rice memo, where the problems begin *"When … the WHO failed to contain the epidemic, gaps in preparedness and capacity surfaced in every major agency tasked with health and security in the U.S. government."*

Rice was talking about a United Nations (UN) agency that receives fifteen percent of its funding from the Federal Government – it is supposed to spearhead international public health efforts and their failures appear to have been mirrored by Obama and Biden. The *Obama Pandemic Playbook* prepared nothing, it only provided a series of questions to guide responses, such as:

"Is there sufficient personal protective equipment for healthcare workers who are providing medical care?

"If YES: What are the triggers to signal exhaustion of supplies? Are additional supplies available?

"If NO: Should the Strategic National Stockpile release PPE to states?"

It seems rather straight forward if it were only a domestic playbook. But it's not. The domestic element falls under the Office of the Assistant Secretary for Preparedness and Response (ASPR) which was formed in 2006. The FY 2016 requested a total of $170 million allocated to costs relative to Pandemic Influenza. It is of note that all the federal level documents cite primary responsibility is vested in State, Local, Tribal, and Territorial Governments.

The SLTT health departments are to be assisted, the federal government does not, as such, have mitigation responsibility beyond those things that are Constitutionally under Federal jurisdiction. If we look at the FY 2016 budget, and recognize that ventilators were a primary focus with Covid-19, we note mention of project *"Aura, a next-generation portable ventilator for adults"* which had just been licensed by the FDA.

A New York Times article on 29 March 2020, *"The U.S. Tried to Build a New Fleet of Ventilators. The Mission Failed"* reported the shortage of ventilators was an issue dating back thirteen years, making it one of the first issues to be addressed by ASPR in the era when Bush-43 was POTUS and Barack Obama was a Senator. As the Times relates:

> *"Money was budgeted. A federal contract was signed. Work got underway.*
>
> *"And then things suddenly veered off course. A multibillion-dollar maker of medical devices bought the small California company that had been hired to design the new machines. The project ultimately produced zero ventilators.*
>
> *"That failure <u>delayed the development of an affordable ventilator by at least half a decade</u>, depriving hospitals, states, and the federal government of the ability to stock up."*

We then learn that a new manufacturer was obtained in 2014 and that their *"ventilator was approved only [in 2019] and whose products have not yet been delivered."* Furthermore, on the date of the Times article, *"the nation's emergency response stockpile is still waiting on its first shipment."*

On 6 April, President Trump stated: *"But they also gave us empty cupboards. The cupboard was bare. You've heard the expression, 'the cupboard was bare.' So we took over a stockpile with a cupboard that was bare."* And based on the New York Times assertion, it is clear that Trump's statement was accurate; it is also clear that the Obama Administration was not at fault. Nor could we hold SLTT responsible for their shortages.

Biden ignored reality and lied to the American people when he attempted to sell the idea there were no problems handed over to Trump and then said *"unfortunately this virus laid bear the severe shortcomings of the current administration."* What *"shortcomings"* could be assigned to Trump based on private sector issues?

And, it must be noted that the problems occurred during the last two years of the Obama-Biden Administration. So we have a pattern of behavior that is akin to that of Biden's Ukraine extortion in which he bragged or boasted in a way that implicated Obama and gave to Obama the primary responsibility for threats to the survival of the

Ukrainian nation. And again, we must note that Obama has never accepted that liability – nor has he ever stated he approved the extortion or in any way explained the "National Interest" justifying threatening the survival of a free nation to achieve the replacement of a qualified attorney with an ex-felon engineer as the Prosecutor General.

Biden is setting up Obama to take the blame for his actions as Vice President. And while those suffering TDS live in denial of the factual reality Biden continues to lie. We saw an example on 22 May, when Biden told his audience to *"Take a look at my record. I extended the Voting Rights Act for 25 years. I have a record that is second to none. The NAACP's endorsed me every time I've run. Take a look at the record."*

That claim resulted in a prompt repudiation from the NAACP president and CEO Derrick Johnson: *"We want to clarify that the NAACP is a non-partisan organization and does not endorse candidates for political office at any level. ... The NAACP has one mission and that is fighting for and advancing our Black communities towards an equitable reality."*

But of course, even if they did endorse candidates, they would reject any suggestion that such a person would be Joe Biden – Biden has said, *"Poor kids are just as bright and just as talented as white kids."* So we know, instinctively, Biden sees the poor as non-white. And, during an interview with Charlemagne tha God, co-host of '*The Breakfast Club*', Biden declared: *"I tell you if you have a problem figuring out whether you're for me or Trump, then you ain't black."* It would appear that Biden believes the African-American votes as a monolith dedicated to whoever the Democrats nominate.

When Trump was elected, did the previous administration advise him of the *"gaps in preparedness and capacity"* he was being gifted with? Or did they sweep it under the nearest rug and act like all was well?

On 12 March, Biden gave a speech dealing with the COVID-19 in which he claimed the Obama Administration created the White House security council directorate for global health security and biodefense *"to better respond to future global threats after the Ebola crisis of 2014. It was designed for exactly this scenario, but for some reason I still don't understand President Trump eliminated that office two years ago."*

The White House National Security Council directorate Biden was referring to had been charged with preparing for the next time a pandemic hit the nation. In May 2018, the team was disbanded, its leader exited the Trump Administration, while the staff merged into other areas of NSC. The former NSC director for biodefense, Tim Morrison, said, *"It is true that the Trump administration has seen fit to shrink the NSC staff. But the bloat that occurred under the previous administration clearly needed a correction."*

Biden took pride in being party to a curious enhancement to America's bureaucracy whose claim to fame is being involved with the outbreak of Ebola Virus Disease (EVD) in the rural forest region of southeastern Guinea which came to the attention of the WHO in December 2013, when it manifested in 18-month-old boy – the first medically defined cases appeared on 24 January 2014, the Ministry of Health Guinea defined an unidentified illness in the capital on 13 and March; at that point, WHO officially declared an EVD outbreak based on 49 confirmed cases and 29 deaths.

By September 2014, the United States had brought seven medically evacuated cases into the country – two nurses who treated an Ebola patient subsequently contracted the disease. Individuals were also infected as passengers on airlines transporting medical evacuees. Anyone wishing to take credit for the handling of Ebola must also take full responsibility for those nurses and passengers who died due to the incompetence associated with protecting them.

But there was nothing they could have done that Trump did not do better – though they had been watching the rise of flu strains in China and yellow fever in Angola.

However, as we know, Rice's memo criticized the Ebola team. And we also know that the travel bans which would aid in keeping the spread low were met with charges Trump was a racist and hysterical xenophobe.

Biden was, at best, invoking selective 20-20 hindsight vision when he describes the era he was helping to oversee. But that seems to be a common Biden trait which results in him changing his wrong policy decisions or stances into hindsight assertions that he was on the opposite or right side of the issue.

There is a beauty to the political blame-game. Biden knows, if elected, he has set the stage to blame Trump for incompetence and any subsequent or ongoing economic or national health problems. The

Republicans understand the game and know that, if Biden wins the blame game will not work – rather it will give them a chance at victory in the midterm elections and then yield control of the Oval back to them.

However, if Trump wins the election, Biden goes down in history as a loser; he might be indicted by Ukraine for the extortion boast; Republicans seeking related details in Obama Administration documents might add to the Ukraine case while gaining the added benefit of being able to tarnish Obama – which would make the far right-wing happy.

Politically, the Republicans would need to tarnish Obama and attack Biden in order to discredit the Democrats. If they fail to do that, in January 2025, the Democrats take possession of the Oval Office.

Readers of this series, or my earlier books – dating back to the 1970s – are familiar with a variation on a quote, which appears on the Official Biden Campaign web page: *"Champ, when you get knocked down, you get back up."* In speeches, he attributed it to his father.

In this series, you know it as the line my father taught me: *"If they knock you down, get up, knock them down, and make sure they do not get up."* {Bk-4, "The Victor The Spoils", page 106, 2017} Is it possible Biden has been reading the Trump Card series in an attempt to get a handle on dealing with Trump?

Unfortunately for Biden, he's not Trump. Biden lacks all the skills necessary to knock down an opponent and ensure they cannot get up. Or, alternatively, allow them to get up onto their knees and become useful supplicants and servants.

Biden also introduces an age issue, even though he is only a presidential term, older than trump. Trump was born 14 June 1946 and Biden 20 November 1942. Symbolically, it is interesting that, in both 1942 and 2020, Election Day fell on 3 November.

And in keeping with the '56 and 57' symbolism mentioned in this series the ages at which presidents assumed office takes on an interesting element – since 1789, 44 different men have served as President of the United States; their average age when taking office for the first time was approximately 56 years and 146 days; Biden would raise that average by about a month. There is another 56 which has emerged.

On 23 May, Dr. Birx gave a press briefing, citing a decline in hospitalizations, in addition, she provided a graphic presentation that showed various types of Flu and influenza-like illness (which includes Covid-19) had fallen below the baseline. Another graphic, a map, showed that, in week-18, two states including Maryland had active spreading – Biden is hiding in his Delaware basement. The other state, Wisconsin, was still active in Week-19.

While Trump played golf, the number of cases was steadily declining. National testing in each state had exceeded 4% of their population, where 2% had been the recommended criteria level. She also pointed out that Los Angeles County accounts for 56 percent of Californian deaths, with a 12 percent decrease in deaths during the previous week and a 15 percent decrease in hospitalizations.

So we have the mystical that conspiracy theorists might love, the home territory for Biden is one of the last hotspots in the nation, and Los Angeles – which includes California's 28th congressional district represented by Adam Schiff – accounts for the bulk of that states deaths. The 'conspiracy' element? We know swamps are hotbeds for disease, so it would follow that the residence place for a Swamp denizen would be where the disease would most likely be abundant.

CHAPTER 09 – BIDENGATE
"Be ungrateful and complain about trivia,
Ignore the meaningful.
Tomorrow, Today becomes the Yesterday you regret."

A week before the 2016 election, FBI Director James Comey released his letter inferring Hillary Clinton was under investigation. At the time, this book series wondered about his intention – was he in the process of scuttling her election?

On 12 May 2020, the events unfolding around the decision not to prosecute General Michael Thomas Flynn, and the revelation that the FBI had attempted to blackmail or coerce him into acting against Trump, resulted in something President Trump would name "Obamagate."

Blackmail, coercion, extortion, bribery, are all things which, in the House Impeach testimony, were associated with the actions of Joseph Biden – which he asserted were approved by Obama – to have the Ukrainian Prosecutor General removed and replaced with a recently released convicted felon, who was an engineer and not a lawyer.

As asserted in the multiple witness testimony, there was nothing wrong with Biden's actions, since they were *Government Policy*" – they were Official Obama Policy. And, as of 12 May 2020, former President Obama has never denied he knew of and approved of the extortion – the same crime the Democratic House Managers attempted to fabricate Trump was guilty of.

As is known, with the 8 November 2016 announcement of Trump's Electoral College victory, there was an immediate call for Impeachment – without any specified crime or evidence of wrong-doing – and it is therefore not much of a surprise that, two days after the inauguration, on 22 January 2017, *The Wall Street Journal* reported an investigation was initiated by U.S. counterintelligence agents into communications which supposedly occurred between General Flynn and Russian officials.

The next day, Democrat Flynn became the 25th United States National Security Advisor under Republican Trump. The ties to the Trump had emerged during the campaign when Flynn served as a senior Trump advisor – Flynn is a Democrat.

We are faced with the possibility the attacks on Flynn were a form of political retaliation, using law enforcement welding as the courts as their weapon of choice. Flynn's crime? He was working for Hillary's Republican opponent and therefore had been branded a turncoat, a traitor. That Federal Prosecutors would be a weapon involved echos the firing of Shokin – where we saw Biden declare a convicted felon and engineer to be a "solid" Prosecutor General – an act which was approved by Obama to neutralize the effectiveness of Ukraine's judiciary. A different use of the same weapon.

Trump ran on a "Drain the Swamp" platform that recognized both Republican and Democratic camps were infested with Swamp Denizens. As we know, in *"The Swamp Fights Back"* (book three of this series), early in the process Trump had tamed or destroyed the Right-wing denizens. But then the Left-wing branch of the swamp family emerged from politically correct mud that camouflaged their disruptive objectives.

These are the same left-wing denizens who have refused to enact legislation to protect and grant legal status to DACA children and who use illegal migrants to gerrymander representative counts in their state and federal districts.

Was there a self-protection motivation behind the attack on Flynn in connection with the false claim of Russian collusion that would form the basis for the Mueller investigation?

Two weeks after the WSJ article (8 February), it was revealed that Flynn was being accused of having a December 2016 discussion with Russian Ambassador Sergey Kislyak which included the Obama administration sanctions placed on Russia.

Flynn denied that topic was discussed, and his spokesman stated "*... that while he had no recollection of discussing sanctions, he couldn't be certain that the topic never came up.*"

In late 2017, Flynn pleaded guilty to lying to FBI agents about two contacts with then-Russian Ambassador Sergey Kislyak. It was later asserted that the prosecutors violated his rights and tricked him into accepting a plea agreement. In January 2018, he had a new legal team who, based on the prosecutors' illegal actions, sought to change his plea.

Upon internal review, the Justice Department determined it would drop the charges against Michael Flynn, and Representative Devin Nunes determined it would be wise to focus his attention on the conduct or approach of the special counsel Robert Mueller who had been appointed after Trump fired FBI Director Comey. Apart from any improper actions regarding Flynn, Comey distinguished himself with his attempt to derail Hillary Clinton when, just days before the 2016 election, on 28 October 2016 he issued an "open" letter numerous committee chairmen which inferred Clinton emails were again being investigated: *"I agreed that the FBI should take appropriate investigative steps designed to allow investigators to review these emails to determine whether they contain classified information."*

Having impacted the pre-election news cycle, on Sunday 6 November, just two days before the election, Comey covered himself by issuing a second letter in which he said: *"with respect to former Secretary of State Clinton's use of a personal email server. Since my letter, the FBI investigative team has been working around the clock to process and review a large volume of emails from a device obtained in connection with an unrelated criminal investigation."*

Obviously, the *"unrelated criminal investigation"* nuance is easily missed or can be misconstrued to infer there was yet another investigation involving illegal actions by Clinton. The timing of the letters was ideal to influence and bias some voters toward Trump – Comey was involved in the Swamp's defensive actions, which would then involve the immediate post-election initiation of the impeach Trump movement on 9 November 2016.

In connection with the impeachment movement, in 2018 or 2019, the Swamp determined it would promote Joseph Biden – the one candidate that it knew it could easily own and control. So it was that, on Memorial Day 2020, the #NOJOE Movement was formally initiated to prevent Biden's nomination.

Given that the "Deep State" has determined to do all it can to elect Biden, those who want the nation to change have little choice but to support Trump – and somehow convince him that his legacy will benefit from taking elements of the Stimulus and making them permanent. Those elements include a Paycheck Protection Program (PPP) in the form of a Universal Basic Income that would allow the elimination of public assistance programs.

A *"CRS Report: Welfare Spending The Largest Item In The Federal Budget"* based on 2011 data placed the *"total amount spent on …federal welfare programs amounts to roughly $1.03 trillion."*

At the time, the report stated the expenditure amounted to "*21 percent of federal outlays*" and exceeded the cost of Medicare, defense, or Social Security. Since Social Security is a dedicated pay-as-you-go tax system, it is not a true budget item but does serve to provide a cash surplus that is deposited as Federal Bonds which then becomes a debt that supplements the budget expenditures.

The failure to increase Social Security benefits – diversion of funds to the general budget – has actually forced an increase in the public assistance welfare budget to compensate as the population ages. Under Reagan, Reaganomics involved increasing the age of full retirement from 65 to 66 for those born between 1943 and 1954; those born between 1955 and 1961 had two months is added for each year of birth until full retirement was vested with age 67. The law also created an incentive to delay retirement until age 70 or later, when the retiree would receive 132.0% of their basic benefit. From an actuarial perspective, the delayed retirement actually eliminated many from collecting anything at all or decreased the total payout.

The problem remains one of low benefits requiring subsidies based on the existence or performance of retirement portfolios. The recessions of July 1990–March 1991, March 2001–November 2001, December 2007–June 2009, and now the COVID-19 market decline of 2020, have all damaged retirement portfolios and pension plans.

We can focus on Obamagate or salacious assertions regarding the behavior of our politicians and political leaders – they form the type of tabloid media distraction which has become mainstream for the twenty-first-century remnants of nineteen-century mentality – it does serve the best interests of the Swamp Denizens. But, there is a reality that the best interest of the nation is found within the basic fundamentals of economics. That is why, when the COVID-19 arrived in America the response was to ensure money whet to the citizens who had to stay at home and experience lockdown reality.

Because so many issues point to the Obama Administration, it becomes easy to call it Obamagate. But the common element is Joe Biden. And, because of the Ukraine extortion and Burisma, that rates a Bidengate designation – at least until such time as it can be proved that Obama was directing the operations and had given his blessing for the Ukraine Extortion, framing of General Flynn, or any of the numerous issues that were emerging during the pandemic.

Bidengate would, of necessity, explore Hunter Biden.

Hunter Biden is connected to the Ukraine extortion that now has Ukraine exploring criminal charges against Joe Biden and any possible facts connecting him to Burisma and any investigation of the Burisma founder that might have been going on at the time of the extortion. Then there is the billion-dollar China deal which saw Hunter using Air Force Two to conduct private business – some might see that as illegal, and if it were, it would be a proven basis for impeachment.

But we also have the costs associated with Hunter – there was a media report on 16 March 2020 which cited a Washington Free Beacon report of 16 March that claimed: *"taxpayers paid $193,696 for Hunter Biden's Secret Service entourage."* Then it claimed that *"the Secret Service detail for all of Trump's children combined is recorded to have cost about $40,000."* And, naturally, there were other "expenses" covered by taxpayers – all of which could play into any Bidengate investigation.

They would also examine the Biden aspect of those things being said about President Trump. Biden exhibits senility related gaffes and memory issues consistent with his age – an age Trump is not going to achieve until 2025. Biden's lies and misrepresentations are well documented and date back to the start of his political career in 1969/70; they are far more substantial than anything attributed to Trump.

For a POTUS, there are also issues of courage and cowardice. We discussed an aspect of this in earlier books in this series – Trump, who had a 1A draft status right up to point where the draft was being wound down and he had attained the age where he would not be drafted – at that point he was diagnosed with temporary bone spurs. Biden complied completely with the scams and schemes that comprised the lyrics of *"The Draft Dodger Rag."* Without a doubt, Joseph Robinette Biden Jr. was an intentional draft dodger.

An individual who shirks responsibility for their own actions is a coward and undeserving of a role where they are responsible for the lives of others; those who accept responsibility and move on are brave. Then there are those who are stupid and reveal that stupidity by boasting of their dishonesty or cowardice – the Joe Biden's of the world.

Prior to the 2016 election, a parody account tweeted what was intended to present a derogatory fascist comparison.

The tweet related Trump with fascism by quoting Mussolini: "*It is better to live one day as a lion than 100 years as a sheep.*"

But rational educated individuals recognize the lion-sheep is also a traditional master-slave association. It's no different than the assertion: "*I'd rather die on my feet, than live on my knees.*"

The Mussolini quote dates to 1922, and when asked about it, Trump stated: "*I know who said it. But what difference does it make if it's Mussolini or anybody else?*"

Trump's response raised an interesting problem of cogitative dissonance being demonstrated by those who would reject a rational thought because it was expressed by someone who leads his nation for 21-years, and in his youth had studied Nietzsche.

Friedrich Nietzsche has produced many lines worth quoting – consider: "*To live is to suffer, to survive is to find some meaning in the suffering.*" Or the famous, "*That which does not kill us makes us stronger.*"

Of course, Biden has said we should accept truth over facts; from Nietzsche, we have "*There are no facts, only interpretations.*" Or something that seems to either define or plague TDS sufferers: "*Sometimes people don't want to hear the truth because they don't want their illusions destroyed.*"

But, as for the Mussolini quote, Trump would accept the quote because it is "*interesting*" and it makes sense to all those who would not spend their lives as slaves.

And in that context, Nietzsche might be relevant: "*The snake which cannot cast its skin has to die. As well the minds which are prevented from changing their opinions; they cease to be mind.*"

Biden is a skin that must be shed; those mindless attacks on Trump, which are devoid of tangible facts, cannot continue – not if the nation can expect to survive a period in history when everything is changing. Again, we can turn to Nietzsche: "*Today as always, men fall into two groups: slaves and free men. Whoever does not have two-thirds of his day for himself, is a slave, whatever he may be: a statesman, a businessman, an official, or a scholar.*"

You must ask yourself whether or not you are a slave. Is your mind defined by hate?

Are you a puppet whose strings are the popular social media platforms and mainstream media propaganda?

The dynamics of the affected population, those voters whose November decision will determine the path America will take, are an interesting demographic.

It is believed Biden has older generations firmly committed to being part of his base demographic – those we designate either as Silent and Baby-Boomer. The older generations encompass World War and its immediate aftermath. The Boomers know of Korea and had the disruption of Vietnam to deal with at a time when there was also the need for fairness and equality which still reverberates in the assertions that "Black Lives Matter."

That family history or experience presents a real existential difference from the defined reality and experiences of those known by the designation of Gen X or Millennials. The older generations knew Depression and War; their lives were shaped by their ability to overcome hardships that are unknown to the younger generations.

Curiously, that created a fit of jealousy or a misguided belief that hardship is necessary – it appears to be a subliminal belief that has evolved from the internalization of their life-experience. This had the effect of making them vicariously relive their youth through their children – by forcing the children to unnecessarily experience many of the same experiences.

Reagan experienced the poverty of the Great depression and so he created programs to ensure Americans would experience that poverty again. He ensured debt, kept Social Security and minimum wages low, introduced workfare to disqualify people from any public assistance benefits, while also creating free workers for charities or non-profits.

Another aspect of Reaganomics is to make higher education excessively expensive so it will create insurmountable debt during their working life – but, in accordance with a monetization of debt, educational debt is irrelevant. If the economy experiences runaway inflation – something approaching hyperinflation levels experience in Venezuela in 2018 – the debt vanishes because it is in fixed value dollars that depreciate against current dollars.

Reagan also promoted open borders and amnesty for illegals who would then provide cheap labor and also allow gerrymandering of the population to enhance representation for California without adding any actual voters. House Speaker Nancy Pelosi promoted the same agenda. A culling coronavirus assists in their objectives.

There is also the effect of lowering the educational levels for a brief period. This is augmented by the temporary discouragement of higher education created by the prospect of excessive debt which would then align the demographics with the Silent Generation.

A Pew Report from 27 May compared the comparative family life for each generation as they approached forty. Keep in mind that the pandemic attacks the Silent and Boomer generations whose way of life was distinguished by their educational level.

Only 28% of the Silent generation went to college (only half received a degree) and 30% never graduated high school; among the Boomers, 45% attended college, while only 13% lacked a high school diploma. As working adults, 85% of Silent Generation and 69% of Boomers were living with a family of their own – a spouse and their children. So there is a basic family identification which drives them to think in terms of their grandchildren or great-grandchildren – even if they do not have any.

When we look at the Gen Xers we find on 13% lack their high school diploma, 57% have some college – half of them have at least one degree. Only 8% of the Millennials, have failed to achieve high school and 67% have some college – 39% have one or more degrees, and 55% of those are women. Female graduates exceeding males is something first seen in Gen X and appears to be increasing further with the current younger Gen Z who have been identified as Bernie Sanders and AOC groupies.

So we have life-experience versus education providing one of the dynamics of the 59th-election to begin the 59th-administration. It's a massive change from the first event which came about through revolution – after numerous colonial regions began to emphasize the importance of education.

That drive and importance of education became codified in numerous forms, including the 1778 *"A Bill for the More General Diffusion of Knowledge,"* authored by Thomas Jefferson, which, as with Bernie Sanders and the Progressives today, denounced the accident of birth bestowed upon those born into wealth resources to educate their children, while *"disabling them from so educating, at their own expense, those of their children whom nature hath fitly formed and disposed to become useful instruments for the public, it is better that such should be sought for and educated at the common expense of all, than that the happiness of all should be confided to the weak or wicked."*

After the nation came into existence, the colonial Bill became *"An Act to Establish Public Education,"* in 1796. As the data shows, the educational goal did not really take root for two centuries. Since the nation has always been run by the educated, its government has remained consistent with the cycles. And, as seen in the campaign calls for some means of addressing student debt, Jefferson's issue is still a factor in defining the future of the nation, and other issues are also consistent with the conflicts that defined the birth of the nation.

In 1787, the Northwest Ordinance provided for an American expansion which would ban slavery in the new states. It also had a provision which stipulated that every township set aside a section of land dedicated to the support of education, because, *"morality, and knowledge, being necessary to good government and the happiness of mankind, schools and the means of education shall forever be encouraged."*

As we know, slavery was recognized in the Constitution, while education was omitted; slave states, it was even outlawed because it was the working poor and slaves who would be excluded. That exclusion became socially accepted and can be seen reflected in the Silent Generation figures. If we look at Biden, we see someone who wants to own the colored-minority vote without offering them any justification to believe he would improve their lot – and now they are the ones who receive the lowest pay, provide "essential services," have the highest pandemic exposure, and the lowest access to what has emerged as "remote learning" – due to a lack of computers and internet access.

In 1787, it was a matter of land, building, and "schoolmarms"; in 2020, it is all about bandwidth, tablets, and virtual-teachers. In 2002, Maine's Governor, now Senator, Angus King stated, *"I think we're going to demonstrate the power of one-to-one computer access that's going to transform education...the economic future will belong to the technologically adept."*

He followed up on his remarks with a program that gave Maine students an Apple laptop computer. His successor, Governor John E. Baldacci built on the Maine Learning Technology Initiative (MLTI) and could honestly say it produced a technology generation ideally suited for tech companies seeking tech-savvy areas in which to expand

and relocate. MLTI had its original roots in an editorial, on the emerging internet (The Bangor Daily News), which caught the eye of John E. Baldacci as he was beginning his 1992 Congressional campaign.

Internet social media groups like Twitter have pointed out that Biden has trouble using a cellphone – a reality that raises issues about him being the one to lead the United States into the 5G and then 6G would where Trump seems so comfortable. Arguably, it can be said that Trump gave life and significance to Twitter and all the other platforms which allow direct communication to the electorate – those who in the days of FDR and his fireside chats found a reason to purchase a television that might, possibly, receive one station.

Trump changes society, he has exposed the hidden denizens of the proverbial swamp, while Biden bungles his words and hides in a cellar. He does have writers who can present platitudes seeming to be coherent statements.

On 31 May, his campaign released a statement he had written on the issue of the protests over the death of George Floyd: "*The act of protesting should never be allowed to overshadow the reason we protest. It should not drive people away from the just cause that protest is meant to advance.*"

The statement addresses a high concept but ignores a reality that accompanies anger released as violence. At the point where the violence erupts the "bad actors" have taken control, reason has been overshadowed.

On 20 June, a press release issued by the Trump campaign opened with a summary of Biden's apparent position on the Floyd Protest rioters:

"*Joe Biden's campaign made it clear that they stand with the rioters, the people burning businesses in minority communities and causing mayhem, by donating to post bail for those arrested. He has obviously made the crass political calculation that unrest in America is a benefit to his candidacy. Biden has a history of cozying up to notorious racists in the Senate, he attempted to inflame race relations by claiming Republicans want to put Black Americans 'back in chains,' and told a Black radio host that Blacks who didn't support him 'ain't Black.'...*"

Biden offers platitudes, but he never provides solutions. His historic positions are of importance in the current environment.

For the past 40-years, Biden has consistently advocated the cutting of Social Security. As Bernie Sanders claimed in the debates, "*Joe Biden has been on the floor of the Senate talking about the need to cut Social Security or Medicare or Medicaid.*" Sanders also pointed out that Biden pushed "*a bankruptcy bill that has caused enormous problems for working families.*"

But to be fair to Biden, he did say those "*...who are relying on Social Security when they retire. I don't know a lot of them. Maybe you guys do. So we need a pro-growth, progressive tax code that treats workers as job creators, as well, not just investors; that gets rid of unprotective loopholes like stepped-up basis; and it raises enough revenue to make sure that the Social Security and Medicare can stay, it still needs adjustments, but can stay; and pay for the things we all acknowledge will grow the country.*"

Thus, Biden advocates a "*progressive tax code*", but not the change in the payroll tax cap which causes the problems denounced in the current Social Security system. Sanders has addressed that problem with a simple fix – eliminate the cap on income subject to the payroll tax, and by doing so Social Security revenues would pour into the Treasury to increase Social Security benefits and relieve the need to borrow funds which increase the national debt.

During his current campaign, Biden has focused on acts that "*prevent cuts to American retirees.*" But current benefits are not at levels which negate the need for welfare subsidies for those who rely on Social Security.

While defending a proposed balanced budget amendment in January 1995, Biden assured his fellow Senators: "*When I argued that we should freeze federal spending, I meant Social Security as well. I meant Medicare and Medicaid. I meant veterans' benefits. I meant every single solitary thing in the government.*" His words foretold a direct attack on Baby-Boomers who would be collecting benefits and the Silent Generation collecting their earned benefits.

Speaking on the floor of the Senate, on 25 April 1984, Biden offered no pretense about the fact that while he was addressing a budget freeze, he was also advocating freezing funds related to the pay-as-you-go Social Security which is outside of the Budget. This is in the context of an economy he categorized as "*what may have been the worst recession since the 1930s, but we have emerged with incredible major economic weaknesses.*"

In the same context, Biden rejected Supply-side economics and spoke of spending by the folks in the gallery in terms that showed his support for demand-side economics while his cognitive dissonance could not make the connection between the inflation he pointed to and the cost of living adjustment he wanted to freeze for a year or more. He could not grasp he was attacking the financial basis for demand-side economics – people need money or a line of credit they can repay, to buy products.

Since we have a record of his approach to the 1984 recession, we know how he would address what is, in fact, *"the worst recession since the 1930s."* He would destroy any chance of a 2021 recovery and return to the record economic numbers which prevailed on 12 February 2020.

There is another cognitive dissonance made manifest by the pandemic. It is based on good or *"very fine people"* to be found in the company of those who are inherently destructive.

On 15 August 2017, President Trump made a statement about the violent protests in Charlottesville, Virginia. He was attacked for saying that "*you also had people that were very fine people, on both sides.*"

When Joe Biden announced his campaign on 25 April 2019 he referred to the Trump statement, asserting: "*With those words, the president of the United States assigned a moral equivalence between those spreading hate and those with the courage to stand against it.*"

Trump responded to the Biden summary by stating: "*If you look at what I said, you will see that that question was answered perfectly. And I was talking about people that went because they felt very strongly about the monument to Robert E. Lee, a great general. Whether you like it or not, he was one of the great generals.*"

But then, thirteen months later, the nation experienced the George Floyd protest riots and the media was suddenly praising the right to protest over the obvious violence and looting which has resulted in multiple police being shot. Meanwhile, nothing is being done to show that "Black Lives Matter," since businesses providing the livelihood to Black neighborhoods are being destroyed.

With the narrative role reversal we have Donald Trump Jr. tweeting (2 Jun 2020): "*Must watch video destroying the media's BS narrative that those rioting, looting and burning down communities are 'mostly peaceful protesters.' The MSM refuses to accept reality*

& will do anything to protect Democrats and defend the lawlessness we're seeing from the radical left!"

On 5 June, the media reported the results of a May poll that reflected the stress over the economy, race issues, and the pandemic which resulted in the international protests surrounding the death of George Floyd – this was the same day the May Jobs Report was released. According to the Monmouth University poll, *"The number of Americans who feel the country is on the wrong track is moving up - and posing a serious threat to President Trump's chances of reelection. ...74 percent of respondents asserting that the nation is headed in the wrong direction. Other recent polls have registered figures in the high 60s on that same question."*

Two days earlier, Trump had tweeted, *"I feel more and more confident that our economy is in the early stages of coming back very strong. Not everyone agrees with me, but I have little doubt. Watch for September, October, November. Next year will be one of the best ever, and look at the Stock Market NOW!"*

Republican pollster David Winston provided a context for the Monmouth University results, by referencing the 2012 Election Day exit polls which also showed a majority of voters believed the nation was on the wrong track and yet, *"A majority of the country thought the country was on the wrong track - and Obama still won."*

Trump had been castigated for placing an emphasis on the economy rather than the pandemic. But on 5 June, the number of new Covid-19 cases had leveled off, and the fatality rate had fallen. And the May job numbers proved interesting.

Protesters had inflicted an estimated $11 million in damage to predominately minority-owned businesses – Joe Biden tweeted this gloating comment: *"Black employment went up this month. Latino employment jumped to over 37%."* In the expectation that the jobs report would show overall unemployment at 19.8% – which would devalue the Dollar and damage American markets – Global stocks and euro surged ahead of U.S. jobs data. But then the actual numbers were released – revealing 2.5 million jobs that marked the start of the economic recovery and the largest monthly jobs increase in history. But, so long as social distancing measures remained in place, the unemployment level was expected to remain elevated.

CHAPTER 10 – It's 1984

" ...the hero of my book is condemned because he does not play the game."

~ French author Albert Camus, on "L'Étranger"

"The most effective way to destroy people is to deny and obliterate their own understanding of their history."

~ George Orwell

This is the problem so many have with Trump, *"he does not play the game"* that they are accustomed to. In many ways, we can say either trump or his opponents are absurd – meaningless to the point of having no discernable or predictable external justification for their existence.

At the same time, we might see the cyclical nature of events as an apparent continuity throughout history rendering to humanity a justification for existence in the form of catalyst for both change and evolution.

There are always those who oppose change and deny reality; in the Trump era, Joe Biden stands out – a fact he displayed at Biden said at the historically black school Delaware State University when he told his audience: *"Donald Trump still doesn't get it. He's out there spiking the ball completely oblivious to the tens of millions of people who are facing the greatest struggle of their lives. These folks aren't feeling any less pain today than they were yesterday."*

Biden views the negative and chooses to live in its realm. But well before the May employment figures were created, Trump was focused on the positive and the fact that the economy would quickly recover – if the naysayers didn't strive to prevent it.

The "Experts," that Trump was supposed to accept, were all saying the numbers would reach 20%. But, when the real numbers came out, May unemployment had fallen to 13.3% in May – it had been 14.7% in April – the economy gained 2.5 million jobs, while April had shown a loss of 20.5 million. In June, the Fed predicted the 2020 GDP finish down 6.5%, with unemployment at 9.3% – a reality that would require the economy to add another ten million jobs.

If the Fed "experts" are correct, Trump would have more to crow about and all the naysayers would have a problem – a POTUS Biden would need to sustain the employment trend, and then repeat or improve upon the record 3.5% unemployment rate which defined 2019 an introduced 2020.

Since the arrival of the first Massachusetts colonists, America has lived in the shadow of biblical Israel – the colonials held it was and would be the New Israel. Over the centuries, it has suffered witch trials, evangelicals, and atheists – the search for meaning and acceptance in a world defined by two extremely diverse or opposing perspectives.

For two and a half centuries, until the Trump administration, those who would destroy history have been seriously constrained or controlled by Constitution, which butts heads with those promoting warped biblical interpretations while also enforcing biblical law.

Why did God or the founders (via the electoral college) give us Donald John Trump?

Maybe the answer lies in the internal conflict we experience and all know as some form of the feel of 'buyers remorse' or second-guessing – the regret that comes from subsequent experience. Some experience it as a sense of being forced in a direction they want to go and yet are overcome by the anger derived from being compelled to do what they are included to do anyway.

The wise propagandist or salesman knows that the best way to get others to do your biding is to make them believe it was their idea. Even better, you must get them to force you to accept their will and go "kicking and screaming" where you wanted them to take you.

Maybe that was an element of the reality George Orwell was referring to when he wrote, *"The past was erased, the erasure was forgotten, the lie became the truth."* It certainly defines a great deal of human history.

Orwell might well have also defined Trump, when he wrote, *"There are occasions when it pays better to fight and be beaten than not to fight at all."* {Homage to Catalonia} But, even without Orwell's words, you know Trump's approach from the previous books in this series.

Everyone enters this world with two allegorical bags.

In one we find the challenges of birth, parents/ancestry, environment, and all those things which form of a circumstance of birth which we will carry throughout our lifetime – it is a sack so full that we might need to dispose of some of its contents as we journey through life.

The other bag is also something we are born with – it is only partially filled – ad contains the basis of our talents and many of the strengths necessary to withstand life's challenges. The space in the second is there so you can add things that will eventually serve to define yourself and your place in a society where everyone is dealing with their personal baggage.

Your mission or purpose is to use that second bag wisely, to add to it or pull from it, the tools to turn pain or frustration into joy and a realistically positive attitude.

It is your openness and willingness to share your experiences that inspire others, that guides your children nieces, nephews, and grandchildren. And if you have none of them, the children of others around you. It is your responsibility to bring hope and light to those who have not found those things in their bag.

It is up to you to show them the best way to approach the reality they are experiencing – so they can achieve more through the focus of the abilities they have, or gain a new ability to carry them forward. But you have a responsibility to yourself to be open to the positive reality they present to you – you are not obligated to accept their positive, though you are obligated to reject anything negative.

You bring understanding through any insight into where your experiences overlap and learn invaluable lessons from the sharing of positive perspectives as approaches to shared issues.

The hardest thing in life is silence, it allows the negative to move freely and destroy life. Yet, as those who meditate know, it can also be rewarding – it allows you to hear yourself, to find that thing in your bag that you didn't know was there but is exactly what you now have use for.

Sharing can help you find that unknown item, or provide a different perspective on the use of items you are accustomed to utilizing differently.

Those who are negative do not share, they attack and belittle. They get upset when someone like Trump speaks I'm the affirmative while surrounded or confronted by dangers. At one level, that is easily understood, it's a glass that is either half-full or half-empty.

But what if the glass that is three-quarters I'm one direction of the other?

The goal should determine attitude. If you intended to fill the glass, then a quarter full is a quarter of the way to your goal, and you are twice as close when it's half full. If your goal is to empty the glass, your perspective is different but still positive.

Trump "spike the ball" when employment moved up – those who are poor leaders or failures in life immediately pointed to the remaining unemployed. But when filling a glass, do you cry about how much space is left, or feel happy the glass is filling and soon be ready to drink from – perversely, that means to purposefully empty it and in the process positive spin on the glass being half-empty.

It seems silly that we will cry over spilled milk, but rejoice in spilling the contents on purpose; being silly, we are admonished not to "cry over spilled milk." Half-empty or half-full doesn't matter in any real-world context – only the intent that brought it to that state has any meaning. If you do not know the intent, a half-a-glass is just a half-a-glass.

Some people behave according to opinion polls and whatever is trending in the media; when the media says be negative, they feel stigmatized by being positive; because the media tells them to, they find joy in crying over the spilled milk – in the process, they often are the only ones spilling it.

As mentioned previously in this series, it is a matter of "the Emperor's New Clothes." Almost exactly a century after Anderson's Fairy tale collection was published, George Orwell summarized the same idea in more modern terms: *The people will believe what the media tells them they believe.*" And today the people believe what social media declares to be true, and they accept as true that which is a logical possibility and accept as logical any "conspiracy theory' that is consistent with any alleged "foregone conclusion" the fantasy media dictates.

God, nature, local or global society, and governing bodies are all part of a pattern of event cycles. Throughout history, every living entity must face those forces that manipulate it within the overall constant which defines the pattern of existence. Understanding the pattern, seeing it for what it is, and recognizing that it is your job to adapt to it is, is what evolutionary survival is all about.

Always be positive and reject the unfounded negative.

We are playing with the idea that 57-election-quadrennia can define that nation; 2016 was the 58th-Presidential election.

Based on that concept, Obama defined the end and beginning of two consecutive cycles; Donald John Trump, a man who held no prior political office, now defines the beginning of the new cycle. It took 228-years to achieve a dramatic change from a young nation building ships for its Triangular Trade whose concept was captured in the musical, "1776," and the words: *"Molasses to rum to slaves / Who sail the ships back to Boston / Ladened with gold, see it gleam / Whose fortunes are made in the triangle trade / Hail slavery, the New England dream!"*

Obama's family were never American slaves; never a party to New England profits, though both he and his father benefitted from studies at the University founded 150-years before the nation. Still, in a real sense, Obama was an African-American – the American half being the same bloodline as the founding fathers.

As revealed in my January 2017 book, "Jonathon's POTUS Cousins," Obama assumed an office first held by his 3rd-cousin 10x-removed. In the context of emancipation, his wife Michelle is a 3rd-cousin to President Zachary Taylor – the father-in-law of Jefferson Davis, the President of the Confederacy – and Obama is 5th-cousin 8x-removed to Confederate General Robert E Lee and a 6th-cousin 6x-removed to Union General and 18th-POTUS Ulysses S. Grant. But then, Obama is also 6th-cousin 6x-removed to Abraham Lincoln. And Lee is a 3rd cousin to Taylor and 4th cousin to Lincoln.

Everything is connected and seeks a conclusion. It seems the first cycle was logically concluded. Now we need to understand the second and the challenges presented that will need to be addressed at this point in history.

We have the remnants of challenges that emerged during the Hippy-era. Do we want mindless undeclared wars? With the 2020 election America is immersed in an OMAR length undeclared war of no significance beyond the death and disruption that is the legacy of George W. Bush – it is a proper companion to his Great recession.

In 2016 we acquired a PT Barnum personality, whose way of doing things is "outside the box" and a complete change from that which the institutional media is accustomed to. The conventional is no longer the dominant force; accordingly, the push is for Joseph Biden to restore criminality to the political realm. We are seeing an age when people require a unique strength of character to confront and adapt to the current challenges. As an alternative, we face the Luddite option of more traditional professional politicians whose perspective leans to the glass being empty or made empty while you stand by – thirsty – the traditional establishment enjoys the benefit of full kegs and, apparently self-filling, tankards of gold or silver.

In reality, the tankards fill because they drain resources, steal from the common folk through the manipulation of the law.

It is how it has always been, and those who struggle to erase and deny history ensure it will continue.

POTUS Cousins are the ancient nobility that came into being with Charlemagne the Great and have a lineage that passes through William the Conqueror. If we look at the history they want to bury, we find that nations rise to power under their leadership. The more directly linked they are, the more powerful the nation – Russia was always on the edge and its limited power was based on the fact they weren't worth the effort because they fought like Scythians – they never attacked and, when attacked, they withdraw.

Traditionally, Russia obeys the most basic of independence and power: Never throw the first punch; when hit, strike back with equal force; do not stand and fight, draw your enemy into your territory, so their supply lines (in commerce, their supply chain) are extended and thus become vulnerable to the slightest disruption.

In earlier Trump Card books, you read the rule my father taught me and Trump's father taught him. You don't start the fight, don't throw the first punch; if their punch knocks you down, get-up, knock them down, and make damned sure they don't get up.

When we look at Trump, he hits – as he did in Afghanistan and Syria – and then calls those he hit his friends. Of course, when he did this with Russia, China, and North Korea, he was called their puppet; it was said they had beaten him, but they struggled while he was playing golf or tweeting some silly nickname for a minor would-be opponent.

We hear about Trump's bankruptcies – where, ultimately, he walked away with millions in tax losses to shelter and render tax free even more millions. In Atlantic City, he made money from casinos while the city profited, filed bankruptcy, and sold the properties – if he had been a poor businessman, he would not have had money flowing into his accounts; a few years later, Atlantic City itself would go bankrupt, and befit a comparison to the words of Joni Mitchell's song, Big Yellow Taxi, would apply:

"They paved paradise / And put up a parking lot"

To be Trump accurate, the buyers of the Trump Plaza casino and hotel in Atlantic City had to board it up since 2014, and in 2020 announced it was being torn down. In 1992, Trump realized that the growing number of Indian Casinos were undermining the only draw Atlantic City had to offer, and its days as the east coast Las Vegas had come to an end. Billionaire Carl Icahn didn't see it, and bought the structure – keeping the Trump name, after all, who would go to a building called the "Icahn casino and hotel?"

When we see how Trump uses the courts, we can again turn to Orwell, as in his 'Homage to Catalonia': *"There are occasions when it pays better to fight and be beaten than not to fight at all."*

Kim Jung-un understands; you might too if you ever read the 1955 satirical novel or saw the 1959 Peter Sellers movie, *"The Mouse that Roared."* Sometimes individuals and nations initiate wars for the sole purpose of losing them; they are caught off-guard when they win. This was the premise of "No Trump Card," the first book in this series.

Trump had accepted the probability that Hillary would win and therefore was thrown somewhat off-balance when the electoral college produced his victory. We saw the signs in the fact Melania was not ready for the move; that there was no contingency plan for Baron to change schools; it was also in oft mentioned distancing we saw exhibited by Melania, born out of her lack of preparation for the FLOTUS role. As was seen, both did adapt rather quickly and the lack of hand-holding reported in the first 56-days vanished by the second cycle, and by the time the pandemic struck, the hand-holding was again a normal reflex behavior.

Since the start of the Cold War, the United States has adopted an Orwellian approach to fighting and war that is alien to the Trump philosophy. From Orwell's 1984 viewpoint, *"...the object of waging a war is always to be in a better position in which to wage another war."*

However, unlike his predecessors, Trump avoids the use of conflict as prelude or stepping stone to further conflict; instead, any conflict serves as the means to establish clear lines of demarcation where previously only vague references exist; his detractors point to cases lost when Trump has obeyed an Orwellian concept: *"The quickest way of ending a war is to lose it."*

In Korea, the north and south are technically still at war and a "demilitarized zone" defined and separated their claimed territory. his obedience to that construct is derived from the fact that a clearly defined line had been defined – a symbolic act of stepping across the line defining North and South Korea creates a border.

By symbolically crossing into the North, Trump defined the border. But on mid-June, with the pandemic and attacks on him tell the North Koreans he's weak or lacks support, North Korea moved troops to that border, possibly to symbolically threaten the south – or, maybe, to ensure the pandemic doesn't come north after South Korea reported a new wave of cases.

It's also possible, as was observed by Victor Cha and Tobias Harris of the Washington-based consultancy, Teneo Intelligence, postulated: *"It is possible that Pyongyang could be trying to regain Donald Trump's attention, as the president has been otherwise preoccupied with Covid-19, mass protests, and his reelection prospects."*

In that context, we have a former US diplomat for East Asia, Daniel Russel's tactical assessment: *"Ramping up pressure through escalating provocations is how Kim makes the point that without sanctions relief, sooner or later he will also blow up Trump's claim to have 'ended the threat' from North Korea."*

If inducing pressure is the goal, it is possible Kim Jong-un is seeking to manipulate the emotional environment created by the BLM protesters and thereby influenced things to promote Joe Biden's election – which raises the issue of the concurrent action by China on its border with India.

Biden is the Manchurian Candidate, and, interestingly, China choose the middle of June to resurrect a border dispute with India.

The North and South Korea problems date to the Cold War related division of the nation and resulted in the yet to be resolved 'Korean War' that came to a haul with the 1954 cease-fire.

China and India have had a Himalayan border dispute which manifested in October-November 1962 as the Sino-Indian Border Conflict that grew out of the March 1959 Tibetan rebellion Early in May 2020, this dispute again came into focus in disputed territories along their respective Line of Actual Control (LAC).

In 2017, a LAC military action and standoff came as Trump was in the process of instituting trade negotiations with China that then became a restricted trade war. Now, we see Trump dealing with the reality of a medical supply chain tied to and fully dependent upon

China – so naturally, China institutes a military distraction with the nation tied to much of our outsourced corporate support services.

If we toss in Vietnam, which was partitioned in 1954 under an agreement where the United States support for Ngo Dinh Diem had included opposition to democratically free elections in the South – because the South would have voted for unity with the Communist North – it appears the problems of the last 70-years are all keyed to the handling or mishandling of the aftermath of World War Two.

In effect, we see a pattern that persists, fear over the probable outcome of a free election has America opposing the Democratic will of the people. If we look at the opposition to Trump that has existed since 9 November 2016 – when the election results were announced and both Southern California and New York City lost their POTUS choice because the rest of the nation (as determined by an Electoral College vote representing a 4.5 million vote majority when those two locations are excluded from the count) objected to the Democratic process when doesn't favor them – we see the same anti-democracy bias that caused the Vietnam War.

In June 2020, the same people who have consistently oppose and sought to overthrow the outcome of a Constitutional election are yelling that Trump will not accept the outcome if Biden wins. It is truly a time of Orwellian dystopian thought where an imagined state of being revolving around great suffering or injustice is being created so that those doing the imagining can claim they are sane – as opposed to insane and self-destructive.

Curiously, even the Wuhan virus plays a dystopian role. As is easily observed by the number of asymptomatic cases, the virus is a culling one and not anywhere near a truly deadly plaque or event. It has infected about one-percent of the global population and only kills those who have life-threatening existing medical issues – about five-percent of those infected. In 2022/23/24 we will see reported numbers of medical deaths spiked in 2020 and then fell sharply to levels well below the expected numbers. We might even see that the 78.8 average life expectancy in the United States has gotten longer and will probably become 80-years or more.

In Sweden, they decided to ignore the pandemic; therefore, the number of infections and deaths is rather large. But Sweden had a life expectancy of 82.31 years – men live an average of 80.3 years and women live an average of 84.3 years. In the United States, the expectancy was 78.87 years – men live two years below the average and women three years beyond it.

The openness and older population combine to create more Swedish fatalities; the rejection of lockdowns ensured the economy remained stable. In terms of one metric, at the beginning of June, Sweden had 36 fatalities per 100,000, and the United States only 27 – but a third of the United States total is in New York City where the ratio was approximately 210 per 100,000.

The Sweden-NYC comparison has meaning when we realize that, during the average business day, they have a similar population (roughly 9 million people). There is a difference in the relative sizes of the locations – Sweden is roughly the size of California and about 575 times the size of NYC – it enjoys geographic social distancing.

Supposedly, Trump demonstrated incompetence in handling the pandemic but initially, NYC's Mayor Bill de Blasio was doing all he could to emulate Sweden. As we know, in 2018, NYC was warned by its own Health Department that its pandemic preparations were inadequate. Now, analysis by research groups at several University epidemiological research departments have indicated NYC accounts for 65% of the United States Covid-19 cases.

It's a logical finding. NYC is the national commerce hub and the primary transit point for European travel.

On 20 April, the Washington Post reported that NewYork-Presbyterian/Columbia University Irving Medical Center's labor and delivery unit tested patients and found 88% of those infected had no symptoms – this is consistent with subsequent studies that indicate roughly 80 of all cases are asymptomatic. In June it was reported that there appeared to be a link between blood type and fatalities.

On 18 June, JAMA published, *"Associations Between Built Environment, Neighborhood Socioeconomic Status, and SARS-CoV-2 Infection Among Pregnant Women in New York City."*

The article made a transmission connection of SARS-CoV-2 to *"neighborhood and building-level markers of large household membership, household crowding, and low socioeconomic status."*

Those neighborhoods also tend to be composed of minorities.

It appears physical proximity to large numbers of individuals is combined with Type-A blood to enhance the transmission of the virus. This explains both the lower infection rates and fatalities in nations where the Type-O and Type-B blood groups are dominant –

China and India, Africa and Russia, including the central Asian nations bordering it. Perversely it also explains the large number of cases in Sweden and NYC; it also infers both social distancing and lockdowns are not meaningful in non-urban environments.

If the blood type data proves accurate, the risk from Covid-19 can be reduced to those who are Type-A: In African-Americans 26%; in Asians 27.5%; Caucasian 40%; Latino-American 31%. In Sweden, 44% of the population is Type-A; the United States, Brazil, Italy, and the United Kingdom are 42%; Spain is 43%. In a few years, we can expect medical analysts to contrast and compare existing medical conditions with age and blood type; then, proximity environment is the controlling fact – how densely populated is the epicenter of each outbreak?

It's a matter of actually paying attention to the science in the context of the objective factual evidence. But, Biden defined it, *"we choose truth over facts."* When we speak of *"truth,"* it is whatever the *"Ministry of Truth"* declares it to be.

Since 2016, the overall context of events – disease, war, the debates over truth versus lies, and FakeNews – bring us back to the Orwellian world in which Social media provides: *"The Ministry of Peace concerns itself with war, the Ministry of Truth with lies, the Ministry of Love with torture and the Ministry of Plenty with starvation. These contradictions are not accidental, nor do they result from ordinary hypocrisy: they are deliberate exercises in doublethink."* {"1984", Part II: Chapter IX}

The Republicans, via The Lincoln Project, are supporting the Democratic candidate with a PAC {Political Action Committee} and opposing anything that passes as a Republican platform. And, as Biden hides in his cellar avoiding interviews, they are running commercials attacking in which we are told: *"We're not doctors, but we're not blind. It's time we talk about this: Trump is not well."*

The Lincoln Project is also promoting the John Bolton book, *"The Room Where It Happened"* – if it happened at all. But again, that is a matter for the *"Ministry of Truth."* Individuals who were actually in the room dispute the book.

Former national security adviser Bolton's book, whose new publication date was 23 June, is the same one House Managers had wanted to use in the Impeachment, but was delayed and, on 15 June, became the subject of a threatened lawsuit based on the assertion, *"I will consider every conversation with me as president highly classified. So that would mean that if he wrote a book and if the book gets out he's broken the law."*

When the Federal District Court of the District of Columbia ruled on the administration's motion to suppress publication of "the Room Where it Happened," District Judge Royce Lamberth allowed it to go forward, saying: *"With hundreds of thousands of copies around the globe – many in newsrooms – the damage is done. ... There is no restoring the status quo. ... The defendant Bolton has gambled with the national security of the United States has exposed his country to harm and himself to civil (and potentially criminal) liability. ... these facts do not control the motion before the Court. The government has failed to establish that an injunction will prevent irreparable harm."* Potentially, Bolton has taken on the role of Judas Iscariot – selling out his nation for an amount that is a bit more than thirty pieces of silver.

The curious thing about living out the storyline of '1984', it displays fiction becoming real; in the same vein, the March 17, 2015 – August 1, 2019 TV series, "iZOMBiE" seems to have been placing life into fiction, only to have the series end at a time when the fiction seems to have been reentering life.

We are all aware of Twitter, but who recalls the mentions it had in iZombie – such as when, in S2:E7 the primary character, Dr. Olivia "Liv" Moore, stated: *"Twitter, a vast collection of humanity's impetuous thought vomiting"* {17 November 2015}

Did life imitate fiction or fiction life, when the iZOMBiE virus appeared in Seattle, Washington – site of the first Covid-19 fatality. Then in another twist, the Zombie virus was spread using a variation of a deadly virus in from Europe – just as Covid-19 evolved from a SARS coronavirus identified in 2003; then the Zombie city of 2017 became the Seattle Capitol Hill Autonomous Zone (CHAZ) of 2020.

In an 1889 essay, 'The Decay of Lying', Oscar Wilde opined: *"Life imitates Art far more than Art imitates Life"* – we seem to be witnessing that reality. Is there more to see?

CHAPTER Eleven – Dippy Stuff

"Fear of the mob is a superstitious fear. It is based on the idea that there is some mysterious, fundamental difference between rich and poor, as though they were two different races, like Negroes and white men.

But in reality, there is no such difference. The mass of the rich and the poor are differentiated by their incomes and nothing else, and the average millionaire is only the average dishwasher dressed in a new suit. Change places, and handy dandy, which is the justice, which is the thief? Everyone who has mixed on equal terms with the poor knows this quite well.

But the trouble is that intelligent, cultivated people, the very people who might be expected to have liberal opinions, never do mix with the poor.

For what do the majority of educated people know about poverty?"

~ George Orwell, Down and Out in Paris and London

There is racism. As with all animals, humans are, by nature afraid or opposed to "the other." In evolutionary terms, without racism, no species could never evolve – as soon as a mutation occurs every creature is either attracted or repelled by it. Those creatures who are different from their ancestral line are drawn to those who share that difference.

The attack on "Gone With the Wind" – its removal from HBO Max – exposed the fact they were removing Hattie McDaniel, who, in 1939, was the first African American to win an Oscar, and would remain so, until Sidney Poitier won in 1963. "Gone With the Wind" was a landmark film that created an unsurpassed earnings record (when expressed in constant inflation adjusted dollars); it has had a massive audience.

It is in that film that we see and hear Clark Gable deliver the classic chillingly disdainful Rhet Butler line: "*Frankly, my dear, I don't give a damn.*" It's an historic line, delivered in an age when censorship rules on swearing almost had it removed. Of course, Scarlett O'Hara [Vivien Leigh] has what is the last word, "*After all, tomorrow is another day!*"

On some levels, the movie is a multi-level love story. Even that last positive line is delivered with the preface to handling many problems, because Scarlett has said, *"I'll go home, and I'll think of some way to get him back. After all, tomorrow is another day!"*

Tomorrow becomes today, only to quickly become yesterday, and yesterday is history. For "Gone with the Wind," HBO reversed itself and restored the movie to its rightful place on the viewer list.

As observed by George Orwell, *"The most effective way to destroy people is to deny and obliterate their own understanding of their history."*

In the case of the award-winning "Gone with the Wind," we are not looking at a story about southern slaves, rather, it is a love story set in the Antebellum South. More importantly, the depiction of the slaves' place in society was, in context, accurate. That some would prefer visions of a post-Civil War KKK murdering people because they were Black or Jewish or, maybe, Asian does not change the reality.

The bigotry and hatred of the KKK are little different from those demonstrated by those in the BLM movement. The true basis for attacking the film was because Hattie McDaniel, who played Mammy, a house servant, became the first African American to win an Oscar.

Many might object to their bigotry being exposed, but kook at the statues they are pulling down. As Trump would tweet on 24 June: *"They want to take down George Washington, how about that one?"*

But why not remove the first President, they also attacked the author of the Constitution, and third President, Thomas Jefferson.

If we recall the true history of the nation, we would know that Slavery was enshrined in the Constitution as a right for those states admitted to the Union as slave states. Abolitionists lacked the will or ability to write a Constitutional Amendment so slavery could be legally removed from the nation.

Factually, the Southern Confederacy was fighting to uphold its Constitutional Rights to own a class of "property." While modern minds find it abhorrent – putting aside the many who arrived as bond servants – many of those protesters would be Africans dealing with the brutality of the Boko Haram and enjoying the luxury that comes with living in nations like Nigeria – a region of origin for HIV. Do they really wish to be African – rather than American?

On 18 June, New York City's elected officials formally asked Mayor Bill de Blasio to remove the statue of Thomas Jefferson from City Hall. They ignored his words, 'all men are created equal', and the fact that after the death of his wife he began a life-partnership relationship with her half-sister – who was also her 'slave'; and he ensured their children would be free.

Look at the statues being attacked by protesters. You see people who were fighting for the Constitution – as written, subject to legal amendment; then there are the statues of those whose faces are commemorated on Mount Rushmore: Washington led the birth of the nation; Jefferson sparked its westward expansion; Lincoln preserved the union and emancipated slaves; Roosevelt championed industrial innovation.

And yes, the protestors are attacking Lincoln – destroying the statue of him issuing the Emancipation Proclamation. What would motivate them to destroy a statue symbolizing the end of slavery and a slave's rise to freedom?

Is it because the slave Lincoln has freed is depicted taking a knee then rising up as a freeman? Apparently, it's fine to take a knee if you are disrespecting the flag and national anthem, but not if you are gaining freedom – for that you can take the subservient posture to denote your voluntary acceptance that you are a willing slave to all who would destroy the nation and its laws.

This is not about race, it is, as it has been since 9 November 2016, about undermining and bringing down America.

Juneteenth, the celebration of emancipation coming to Texas, equates to justifying the destruction of statues in San Francisco's Golden Gate Park. Of course, these were not classic slave owners or those opposed to the 20th-century American way of life. The statues commemorated the Union Army General and 18th President of the United States Hiram Ulysses "S" Grant – whose initial "S" was an error by Congressman Thomas Hamer who recommended him for West Point.

Sometime after 14 April 1861, Grant wrote his father, *"My inclination is to whip the rebellion into submission, preserving all Constitutional rights. If it cannot be whipped any other way than through a war against slavery, let it come to that legitimately. If it is necessary that slavery should fall that the Republic may continue its existence, let slavery go."*

Grant did have a slave, William Jones, apparently received as a gift from his father-in-law, who he freed a year later.

The second statue was Francis Scott Key – whose 1814 poem became "The Star-Spangled Banner" which declared the nation to be *"the land of the free and the home of the brave."* It's a symbol of the American patriotism and goals that existed among those who could both oppose slavery and upheld the Constitution.

Perversely, Key was a slave-owner and attorney who, in 1836, would argue in United States v. Reuben Crandall apparently argued that the *"property rights of slaveholders outweighed the free speech rights of those arguing for slavery's abolishment."* It was a case argued in the aftermath of the 1835 race riots that shook the city of Washington – those riots provide the context, which focused on the distribution of the type of literature whose intent was *"to excite a discontented or insurrectionary spirit,..."*

In another phrasing, the literature incited another version of the Southampton Insurrection of 1831 (also known as Nat Turner's Rebellion) and was designed to incite civil unrest involving murder, looting, pillaging, and general social disruption. In terms of context, it should also be noted that 1835 was when Britain ended its slave trade and so ended a key aspect of the Triangle Trade.

Technically, Key was not defending slavery, he was defending Constitution – and the laws as they existed, which is the job of a state's attorney. Later, according to Smithsonian records, Key was the attorney of record for many slaves who were fighting for their freedom in the days before Lincoln. Key is on record as describing the general system of slavery was "a bed of torture" that was filled with sin, and he helped establish the American Colonization Society, whose goal was to facilitate return the African American slaves to their African homeland.

One of the Orwellian aspects of events as nailed by Trump in a 24 June Tweet: *"The radical left demands absolute conformity from every professor, researcher, reporter, journalist, corporation, entertainer, politician, campus speaker, and private citizen."*

Orwell wrote: *"Power is not a means; it is an end. One does not establish a dictatorship in order to safeguard a revolution; one makes the revolution in order to establish the dictatorship. The object of persecution is persecution. The object of torture is torture. The object of power is power."* To that we can add the destruction of statues and communities as representing the reality: "The object of destruction is destruction."

If the objective was to change the way society is run, the goal of protests would be to legislate equality through a guaranteed wage in the form of a Universal Minimum Wage, and improvements to health through Medicare for All. Destroying monuments to history and minority-owned businesses achieves nothing.

We're in the aftermath of the Reagan programs that initiated "1984" by expanding the National Debt and militarism, undermine the economy, and creating global instability – expanding the anti-democratic policies that gave us the Vietnam War and became the basis for regime change policies.

Curiously, on 14 September 1814, when Key wrote his poem it included these words: *"Then conquer we must, when our cause it is just, And this be our motto - 'In God is our trust.'"* The related musical composition became the American national anthem on 3 March 1931 {as 36USC § 301}, and it wouldn't be until 30 July 1956 that Eisenhower would sign the law placing *"In God We Trust"* on American currency.

Readers of "Biblical Prophecy: are we in the Revelation Era?" are aware that 1931 is mathematically flagged for the emergence of the White Horseman. Then, the nation's 32nd president was elected in 1932 and FDR – previously New York's Governor – and held that, as part of the Atlantic Charter, all people had the right *"to choose the form of government under which they will live."*

However, we can assert the existence of an implicit Cold War codicil, *"unless they are Communist, Marxist, or socialist,"* which negated the 14 August 1941 principle that *"no territorial changes that do not accord with the freely expressed wishes of the peoples concerned"* would be imposed.

The Atlantic Charter predates Pearl Harbor and might have contributed to it occurring. In asserting the false promise of rights to self-determination, the third principle also said the parties wished *"to see sovereign rights and self-government restored to those who have been forcibly deprived of them."* That meant the Vietnamese were entailed to evict France and China was entitled to evict the British; then too, it raises serious issues about the division of Korea – all of which was forcibly occupied by Japan.

The Atlantic Charter was between and signed by, Franklin Delano Roosevelt, and his 7th cousin 1x removed, Winston Spencer Churchill.

In accordance with the principles, on 2 September 1945, Ho Chi Minh declared Vietnam's independence and his Viet Minh began the process of forcibly evicting French colonialist forces. In his book, "Vietnam 1945: The Quest for Power", David G. Marr details the realities surrounding the origins of the modern Vietnam nation – deemed by objective observers to be a communist nation that is, as USA Today reported, in a 13 March 2015 article, *"one of the most pro-capitalist countries on Earth."*

This surprise anyone, Marxism was predicated on Capitalism producing "surplus capital' which would then be used to enforce Old Testament mandates requiring providing for those who could not provide for themselves; China is also a Capitalist nation generating many billionaires and an enormous tourist class – Trump's trade war and various supply chains, show the capitalist success of China has become a global one echoing its historic Mercantile stature.

Ho's declaration and assertion of freedom began with a quote Americans should know well: *"All men are created equal. They are endowed by their Creator with certain inalienable rights, among them are Life, Liberty, and the pursuit of Happiness."* But, as we are seeing with the riots, protests, and destruction of the historic American monuments to its past struggles to achieve freedom and equality, those are words without meaning to those supporting Joe Biden's campaign.

During Vietnam, Biden was a classic draft dodger – clearly a model for the Phil Ochs classic, "Draft Dodger Rag," where the youth claims, as Biden did, *"my asthma's getting worse, ... Besides, I ain't no fool, I'm a-goin' to school..."*

Biden's "asthma" – easily claimed, a lie hard to disprove.

Anti-Trump and Biden supporters yell about Trump, but as we saw in Book 8 eight, throughout the period of his eligibility, and up to the period when the draft was suspended prior to elimination, Trump was 1A. The infamous 'bone spurs' were a short-lived issue of the type that was physically documented by medical certification supported by x-rays or medical examination by military doctors.

Biden was a draft dodger, now loved by those who challenged the draft and Vietnam War as Hippies in the 1960s – meaning his natural base are the Baby-Boomers who began to turn 70 in 2015 and are now the 2020 elderly at most risk from Covid-19.

Biden represents a last hurrah for the 60's stoners.

The problem in 2020 is that the elderly are the focus of the Covid-19 pandemic and the age corresponding to the fictional world of iZOMBiE with its elbow bumps, lockdowns, and the brainless who separate from the country and isolate their a Seattle location. In the plotline, there is a plan to take over and destroy the nation – which voters in 2020 are seeing as the Anti-history anti-reality protesters.

The iZOMBiE virus is Covid-19 and the dead it creates are a small segment of the population whose numbers are blown out of proportion by simply reporting them in the pandemic context rather than the reality of the numbers and fatalities.

The way numbers are presented distorts the truth, as does the nature of the history and biology of the nations infected.

There is a reason Russia and Brazil were slow to be infected and why it took time for their cases to climb – neither nation is fully integrated into the global economy through commerce or tourism, but both are connected to fossil fuels. As the pandemic becomes established in those two nations, the growth of cases and fatalities will flag a key difference associated with heritage and blood type.

All blood is composed to double antigens from one of three types A, B, or the universal and original type-O. These are then referred to as A, B, AB, or O – factually, they are AO, AA, BO, BB, AB, or OO. What group you belong to is, as with the chromosomes that determine gender, is derived from your receiving one antigen from each of your parents. There is a third antigen which represents Rh; if you have it, you are Rh-positive; if not, Rh-negative.

In the United States, 35.7% of the population is A-positive and 37.4% are O-positive. Type-B is common in Northern India; Central Asians are also Type-B; in Denmark A-positive is common. That is the key to understanding the Covid-19 numbers.

It appears that Type-B blood is compatible with the virus and therefore effectively immune. On 15 May, Veronika Skvortsova, the chief of Russia's Federal Medical Biological Agency, stated most of the Russian patients were Type-A, and the fewest cases were Type-AB. Specifically, she said: "*An interesting fact that was noted by foreign specialists and has been verified by the Agency's centers. The overwhelming majority of those infected have blood type A. Next are types O and B. And, indeed, the rarest is type AB."*

In the case of Russia, a low death rate goes with them being composed of Eastern Europeans where we find the origin of blood Type-AB; Western Europeans were an origin point for Type-A blood. The percentage of Russians who are Type-B is more than twice that of Western European or Scandinavian nations. For Brazil, the blood types are the universal Type-O and European Type-A.

As medical science is discovering, Covid-19 is a virus intended to cull European Christians – conspiracy and apocalyptic freaks will soon realize that, like the Holocaust, this is as another way to claim the 144,000 righteous "Jews" for the rapture, and if it had killed undisputed criminals, a way to send the first batch of evil to their judgment.

Originally, Brazil (like Mexico) had proved a safe place for Jews escaping from the aftermath of the Spanish Inquisition – but the Inquisition followed them to the New World and soon those nations were transformed into "good pagan Catholic" countries. In Mexico, as the Inquisitors or Conquistadors arrived, Spanish Jews headed north to be absorbed into the Native American population.

In various books over the past decade, I've referenced a 1960s Hippy subway poster which declared: *"All of the people who ever lived are alive today."* Effectively, if one believes in reincarnation, it was saying all the souls who had previously lived had returned. In that context, all the souls are now here awaiting what Evangelicals would call Judgment Day.

LOL, think about that as the souls returned/resurrected for judgment being passed on Spain, France, and Italy as the source of Christian anti-Semitism. As we know, Democrats do not believe in such things – but enjoy a broad Jewish constituency.

This could bring us to the Tulsa, Oklahoma rally, on 20 June, where Trump told his audience, *"Testing is a double-edged sword. We've tested now 25 million people. It's probably 20 million people more than anybody else. Germany's done a lot. South Korea's done a lot."*

A Johns Hopkins University database released 24 June, tells us the U.S. reported 2,347,102 confirmed cases and 121,225 deaths from COVID-19. Combining Trump's numbers with theirs and only one-percent of those tested have the Wuhan virus; only five-percent of those died – yielding about 50 deaths per hundred thousand, where the normal death rate is 723; since the virus generally killed only the elderly and sickly, it can be considered a culling virus and serves an evolutionary purpose by creating a healthier population.

In the developed world, about 20 to 30 people out of every million die on any given day.   Over a typical year that is about 7.5 to 10.5 per thousand, with a different rate for younger compared to the elderly – Covid-19 focused on the elderly and others who are known to be approaching their natural expiration date.

On 18 June 2020, the Supreme Court [SCOTUS] ruled that acting Secretary of Homeland Security Elaine C. Duke had failed to properly justify what appeared to be an arbitrary termination of the rights granted to children illegally brought to the United States. It is critical to note that those rights were granted via an illegal Obama Executive Order that created the program known by the acronym "DACA."

The Obama action was illegal because a POTUS cannot in any way modify, rescind or negate any Statutory law through the use of an Executive Order – to do so is an illegal use of executive power.

When Obama issued the order, he knew it was "illegal" but, under "Executive Authority and Power" he could issue a temporary suspension of enforcement parameters – hence the Executive Order was entitled as being "Deferred Action" because it was deferred he had not 'changed" the law, but he did create the DACA status in a manner that inferred a "contract" that could not easily be broken by a subsequent POTUS.

Mainstream media [MSM] was thrilled by the ruling and so we had headlines like: *"U.S. Supreme Court blocks Trump bid to end 'Dreamers' immigrant program"* which told readers that the ruling had *"...dealt President Donald Trump a major setback on his hardline immigration policies,..."*

In fact, the court had only invoked the ancient biblical Rule of Solomon which, in modern law, is reflected in the idea that any action taken in good faith – and without knowledge that it is illegal or wrong – is to be excused. In this instance, the creation of an implied contract with those covered by DACA; the validity and nature of that contract is the real issue that must eventually reach the court or be resolved through the legislative action the House has, since the Obama order and up to the November 2020 election, not deemed anything but a political football.

Justice Clarence Thomas explained it in the minority opinion: "*DHS created DACA during the Obama administration without any statutory authorization and without going through the requisite rulemaking process. ... the program was unlawful from its inception. ... the Trump administration rescinded DACA the same way that the Obama administration created it: unilaterally, and through a mere memorandum.*"

However, Obama created what amounted to a legal contract with children under DACA and Secretary Duke had arbitrarily set a termination point without providing any legal justification or logical basis for her action. And, because it was a Presidential Order, DACA recipients had every right to believe they should remain covered by the program.

As we've discussed in earlier books, Congress is the source of the problem – they should have immediately passed a law to amend the relevant Immigration Act to grant legal status to those in the country in 2012 – when the Obama EO went into effect. That failure rests with the Republicans who controlled the House from 2011 to 2019 and therefore showed their inherent disrespect for children.

It is a disrespect because they were "forced" into the criminal act parents and did not become illegal immigrants via any personal decision or action; in biblical terms, the children are being punished for the sins of their parents – which creates a serious moral problem for the non-hypocrites among those Right-wing evangelicals. Of course, the general masses of hypocrites have no problem violating scripture at every opportunity.

Honest Americans would recognize the reality that, once the children were here, they have generally shown themselves to be superlative "citizens" with many of them achieving advanced degrees and joining the ranks of those we term respected professions.

Both sides in the SCOTUS decision recognized the law from different vantage points, but they all were supporting a Biblical Law – the Rule of Solomon – which holds that if you are ignorant of the law you're morally safe. But once told of your knowledge deficiency, you are henceforth liable for the consequence – those who vote for Biden will be running right into the wall of responsibility.

One thing the polls are telling us is constituency structure – who is supporting which presidential candidate. The Biden camp has support from Black women, 87%; Urban North Easterners 72%; Religiously Unaffiliated, 67%. So two-thirds of Biden's base is not into any organized religion and probably disregard scriptural things that are timeless and, when written, might actually have been ahead of their time.

Trump's base is White Evangelical, 78%; White non-college men, 62%; Rural Southerners, 60%. We can explain much of the impeachment related attacks and propaganda on the New York and California College crowd, though the base behind the protests seems harder to define – especially when they destroy statues of Jefferson and Washington, while also destroying black businesses.

It seems we're back to "1984" and George Orwell:

"Every record has been destroyed or falsified, every book rewritten, every picture has been repainted, <u>every statue and street building has been renamed</u>, every date has been altered. And the process is continuing day by day and minute by minute. <u>History has stopped. Nothing exists except an endless present in which the Party is always right.</u>"

Thus we see streets being painted with 'Black Lives Matter', and 'George Floyd Ave' street sign appearing to replace the Chicago Avenue sign at the intersection with 38th Street where Floyd was killed.

In New York City, it was reported on 24 June that Black Lives Matter would be painted on the street in front of Trump Tower and that introduces a new aspect to the 56, 57, 58 that has run through this book series.

Located on Fifth Avenue, between 56th and 57th Streets, in Midtown Manhattan, the Trump Tower is a 58-floor, 664-foot-tall mixed-use skyscraper whose address spans 721–725 Fifth Avenue, and serves as the headquarters for the Trump Organization.

The coincidence is cute. The address spans four numbers to define the presidential election quadrennia. The structure's height is quadrennia Trump won, while Obama's term is the streets. The only issue is his second term, and that is also in the building's height – 664 feet yields 6+6, which is the span from Bush's Great recession in 2008 to the Chinese Wuhan economic collapse in 2020; that leaves us with the second 4 needed to predict a second term.

Reagan, Bush, Clinton, Bush, Obama – the five who preceded Trump and created all the issues the nation has had to deal with in Trump's period in office. Or, we can look at Trump as the fifth POTUS since Reagan and the dawn of the Reaganomics concepts that created the non-pandemic related massive National Debt.

But that's playing with numbers and making them fit. Were we to just accept a symbolic prophecy, the four numbers related to the election quadrennia could infer Trump was both destined to be POTUS and also hold the office for only one term – it's "A prophecy of America's Destruction" that was in the title of my 2014 book, "Death Over Life." That figurative choice for national survival has become a very real choice in terms of the pandemic. And it is a choice that keys to the choice between Biden and Trump.

Wall Street experts are beginning to accept a Biden victory – again we have the recurrent number – they are polling 57-percent.

Meanwhile, on 25 June, Biden asserted: "People don't have a job, people don't know where to go, they don't know what to do. Now we have over 120 million dead from COVID."

Imagine, the man who would be POTUS doesn't grasp that the jobs are there and there's no place to go -- because of the pandemic. He did catch his error was: "..., *I mean, 120,000 dead from COVID. And you have so many—now we're past 2 million — I mean, and we're talking about it like it's over. I mean, it's over. My God.*"

Obviously, over a third of America's population hasn't died, but he doesn't grasp the economic ramifications of a lockdown. And the multiplying by a thousand, he also did that in the February debate with Sanders when he declared: "[NICS] *has caused carnage on our streets, 150 million people have been killed since 2007 when Bernie voted to exempt the gun manufacturers from liability, more than all the wars, including Vietnam from that point on.*"

Biden actually asserted, and might even believe, guns killed roughly half the population since the passage of "NICS" or National Instant Criminal Background Check System. He declared half the nation had died during a 13-year period overlapping the eight years when he was Vice President. And, apparently, nobody noticed.

CHAPTER Twelve – Reflecting

"Fear of the mob is a superstitious fear.

"It is based on the idea that there is some mysterious, fundamental difference between rich and poor, as though they were two different races, like Negroes and white men. But in reality, there is no such difference.

The mass of the rich and the poor are differentiated by their incomes and nothing else, and the average millionaire is only the average dishwasher dressed in a new suit.

"Change places, and handy dandy, which is the justice, which is the thief?

"Everyone who has mixed on equal terms with the poor knows this quite well. But the trouble is that intelligent, cultivated people, the very people who might be expected to have liberal opinions, never do mix with the poor.

"For what do the majority of educated people know about poverty?"

~ George Orwell, Down and Out in Paris and London

Stretch out the words of George Orwell and think about the events emerging in the latter part of 2020 that will define the nation for the balance of the century.

FINE – You don't get it.

Look back to the Vietnam War era, to Hippies and journey back 56-years to a time when the world abandoned the world they had seen and been raised with possible role models for couples life: "Leave it to Beaver", "Mr. Adams and Eve", "I Love Lucy", and "The Honeymooners."

That comic life of the Conservative wife-in-the-kitchen blue-collar world transitioned into the Hippy age of 'free love' where recreational drugs created anti-war protests, race protests, and produced Timothy Leary telling us to "Turn on, tune in, drop out."

It was 57-years-ago that Leary was forced to exit Harvard; it was 54-years-ago when his stoner philosophy became a recognized motto among the Hippies whose surviving members comprise the elderly segment of western culture. Nothing has changed.

American disruption of Vietnam dominated a period between 1 November 1955 and 30 April 1975 – do we see it as a bit more than 19-years, or a bit less than 20-years? And now that Boomers have finished the 49-year journey from grade school to Social Security retirement, again they are looking at the nation in a 19-going-on-20 year war combined with protests over racial inequality and other things that have never been properly addressed by those in power.

It was 57-years-ago November that the world witnessed the assassination of John F Kennedy. Back then, the United States was engaged in breaking its word to those who had been a wartime Allie against Japan – a promise that electoral free and democratic choice would end colonialism.

Kennedy's assassination, on 22 November 1963, was followed by the assassination of Martin Luther King on 4 April 1968; if we go with the mystic, and use Covid-19 as the death pattern there would be a new pandemic – sometime around 20 April 2024. If the focus is on the economy, then the crash of 24 February 2020 would see some similar event around 7 June 2024.

But, of course, that's nonsense. There is no mystical power, no pattern of events, no relationship between the past and future that goes beyond intentional decisions made by those living through the events that affect causality.

In the 1960s, the Boomers were raised in a period that knew only war. Their parents had survived the Second World War; the first of them was almost a decade old when the Korean conflict was placed on hold – only to be replaced by the Cold War and Nikita Khrushchev – whose son Sergei moved to America, became a citizen and died on 24 June 2020 – apparently a self-inflicted gunshot to the head – at the age of 84, in his Rhode Island home.

The Khrushchev-Kennedy Cold War involved was marked by "Brinkmanship" augmented by the "Mutually Assured Destruction" threat so many seem to want to return to constant attacks on Russia. It seems there is a section of the nation who would love a modern version of the 1962 "Cuban Missile Crisis" – 57-years-ago during the Week of 16-28 October 2019; 21 November making the anniversary of the end of the related blockade of Cuba.

It seems rather comical, 57-years-ago the media attention was consumed MAD, and now there are so many Americans focused on senility in the Presidential candidates and governmental MAD.

Done properly, there is no question the nation could achieve the promised Mutually Assured Destruction that helped contribute to the Hippy movement. But that was predicted as "*A Prophecy of America's Destruction*" which Americans have the power to change in the November election – though it is reasonable to say they would prefer to be ruled by the long-term Swamp Denizens.

Historic links are funny. In 1925, Adolf Hitler's story of his philosophical struggle, "*Mein Kampf*", was published and he became wealthy. That wealth survived the Great Depression; that, his book was an international bestseller is forgotten because 7-years later he sought and acquired elected office. His rise to power gave us the World War, American involvement in the June 1944 Allied invasion of Normandy – 57-years later New York was gifted with the 9/11 destruction of the World Trade Center.

In "*Mein Kampf*," Hitler spends a great deal of space warning of Russian intentions. But that message was lost amid the Christian anti-Semitic rhetoric that dated back to the Inquisitions and forced conversions which the spanned centuries – yet, because we ignore history, he is given all the credit for the anti-Semitic rhetoric that we could reasonably attribute to Shakespeare's "*Merchant of Venus*."

The Cold War was the world ignoring Hitler's warnings about Russian desires for dominance over former Pale of Settlement areas where their Jews had been segregated during the time of the Czars – the common birthplace of Hitler and Albert Einstein was on the fringe of or beyond the historic Pale.

But, as with everything else, that has little to do with what we can call an element of the "*Trump Existential*."

Here we are playing with imaginary cycles which, if they were real would mean we are at a very critical point both in the history of American and the world.

Is China supposed to finally take over?

Or will Islam have the proper Jihad promised in the Koran – the battle that the western culture refers to as the Apocalypse?

Is Joseph R Biden the right person to prepare the nation for a fantasy war that is integral to the growth of Western culture? Is he even the person who can handle the correcting of the economy and dealing with the next round of the pandemic?

Are we MAD? Or are we devoted to returning to the conflict that defined MAD? Which candidate has the appropriate mentality?

We had Vietnam, which covered 19.5 years between 1955 and 1975; we now have Bush's war to murder Saddam Hussein – which has been an ongoing disruption of Islamic nations since September 2001, and, in March 2021, will equal the duration of Vietnam – with the advantage of there being no draft to mobilize objection.

In '*The Art of War*', Sun Tzu tells us: "*There is no instance of a nation benefitting from prolonged warfare.*" Yet, as events of the past 75-years show, the United States persists wanting to engage in wars that are "boots-on-the-ground," constitutionally undeclared, military actions whose only purpose is to murder and destabilize.

Look at American behavior since the end of the Second World War – it's so proud of having a military budget that larger than the next ten nations combined. Yet, it lost in Korea, lost in Vietnam, has not succeeded in the "War on Terror." Terrorism is still there and with the BLM protests providing a platform for burning buildings, killing people, the huge military budget has done nothing beyond diverting money from domestic programs and enhancing domestic terrorism.

As of 2020, the American nation has shown itself a nation in love with committing mass murder, the destruction of landmarks and historic sites. Deprive citizens of the right to inflict harm and they will harm themselves. And, as we saw with Vietnam, America is a nation that opposes Democracy unless voters agree with their preconceived outcome. The answer to Hillary losing was for the two regions that wanted her – California and New York City, the source of the 7.5 million votes that yield a 3 million vote "popular victory" – to immediately initiate a search for anything that could be twisted into a Trump impeachment.

Comically, as has been declared throughout this book series, Trump will support anything that makes economic sense or offers a basis to gain praise. The economic stimulus invoked by pandemic created needs has shown the wisdom of a Universal Basic Income – and could be achieved if the elimination of welfare or other forms of basic public assistance is factored into the cost.

Again it is comical – Reagan and Conservatives have sung the "a rising tide lifts all boats" song without realizing, economically, it refers to the smaller boats which will rise first. Complaints about people not working are stupidity – unless you are referring to slaves – because, as Calvin Coolidge phrased it, "*... the chief business of the*

American people is business. They are profoundly concerned with producing, buying, selling, investing and prospering in the world."

In that, the critical aspect is "selling." It is not important that people work, it important they have the funds to buy the products produced by those who choose to work.

Those who do work will have true wealth. And people like to work. They also like to study and learn, volunteer their energy, and time to help others. Some do like to goof-off – when you force them to work they continue to do what they like and that only serves to reduce production or service efficiency. But those who like to be slave masters must find a way to create the slaves.

UBI does not make people "goof-off or sponge off the system. It does lower the need to be dishonest while expanding the ability to be creative, and reducing the economic liability associated with being unemployed or temporarily laid-off.

A UBI set at 150% of poverty, paid to every citizen over the age of 18, would stabilize the economy and eliminate welfare.

Naturally, Social Security would continue and be a reward to those who work as an added benefit when they retire. We would no longer have a silent reality that our elderly require welfare benefits to supplement retirement income.

In terms of wages. The minimum wage should also be set at 150% of poverty – meaning a minimum wage worker doubles their income by working. Those higher on the ladder would, of course, benefit.

Granted, there are always those who enjoy being criminals, and when dealing with them, the UBI can also serve a valid purpose. If someone is convicted of a crime, while they are incarcerated their UBI would be reassigned to cover the cost of that incarceration, and maybe even contribute to the cost of the prosecution.

If someone is on life support or requires extended intensive care, their UBI could be put towards helping pay that cost. When we hear about the cost of education, since UBI would start when a citizen turns 18, there is no reason it couldn't be used to fund their higher or advanced education – it is their money, and anything that serves a productive benefit provides a benefit to the nation.

Since UBI is intended to enhance the economy and provide a stable, reliable, financial foundation for the nation, the funds should be retained in the country. Accordingly, unless an individual is on government or corporate business which requires them to be foreign residents if they are living abroad, they are not entitled to receive the UBI payments. Congress might consider suspending the payment to those who have physically relocated outside the nation; if the individual fails to provide notification of their ex-pat status, all funds paid since the last provable date of domestic residence will be returned – a failure to do refund the money will be deemed a felony fraud, and their passport will be suspended with no right to renewal.

To cover social security needs – possibly universal Medicare as well – there would be no cap on income subject to payroll taxes. The current cap has those below the lower-middle-income bracket paying the full cost of Social Security, while the upper levels are exempted at some point within the first five months of every year.

What economic benefit would this produce?

First of all, the Welfare system would no longer be needed for citizens. It is important that the focus is on benefitting citizens, and that they not be convicted felons or those who utilize the UBI money to allow themselves the benefits afforded by moving to a "cheaper" economy in another nation. If they are going to goof-off, they will do so here; if they are retired and on earned Social Security, allow them the freedom to enjoy their senior years wherever they wish.

UBI is a foundation, it ensures everyone would have money to spend to support the national economy – under normal economic multiplier rules, this means every dollar provided by UBI generates 7-10 dollars to the local GDP, and then moves to the next economic region to enhance their GDP. If it is kept in the national economy, if American companies provide domestically manufactured goods, the GDP grows domestically. If outsourced to China or some other nation, the balance of trade must compensate for the loss of capital.

But, just in terms of the basic local multiplier, each dollar of UBI income will generate and yield at least $2.5 in tax revenues – UBI pays for itself. It can be argued otherwise. But to do so really means you are arguing an inherently unhealthy economic structure – a national economy that has no justification for surviving. In many ways, you are asserting the slave economy that doomed the South to failure and justified the ongoing strength of New England.

Now think in terms of the past four years of hate that, for the past four years, has targeted Trump, and the nation. It is a hate that haters have focused on themselves and their children – except they do not have children. To have children, even a single child, means to have a vested interest in the future.

Look at the world. To have a stable population, it is necessary to replace those who are alive at roughly the rate at which they die.

In Hebrew culture, the commandment to *"Go forth and multiply"* has been taken to mean couples should be parents of two children – on of each gender. In terms of fertility rates, this means an average of 2.1 children per fertile female.

We have reached that point in history where we talk in terms of "overpopulation." In pragmatic terms, the world has slipped into negative population growth and is approaching a fertility rate of one per couple or fertile female.

Remember the Hippy-era subway sign? *"Half the people who ever lived are alive today."* If souls come back, we might think that all there ever were are here today. Of course, the numeric depends on when you begin your count the meaning of "lived" – does a fetus that dies at birth have a life? Or does a life only belong to those who have contributed to society and its continuation?

"A Prophecy of America's Destruction" is only an observation of the behavior that manifested or revealed itself in the attacks of Donald John Trump – and Constitution, because the founders were wise enough to the Electoral College because the Constitution did its job and bestowed on the Presidential Election the same balance it did on the Legislature when it gave us a House of Representatives to represent the people and the Senate representing the States.

To enter the future, people must learn to think. The ignorant are devoted to the destruction of history and life of negativity.

A manifestation of negativity comes with the destruction of monuments – a manifestation of the idea *"History is written by the victors."* It is predicated on the idea *"The victor will always be the judge, and the vanquished the accused."*

Occasionally, as Orwell observed, an anti-establishment will emerge and attempt a rewriting of history in an attempt to become the *"Big Brother"* victor. There is a cultural phenomenon seemingly ingrained in every culture – segments of populations are anarchists, they hold that only force and violence are a means to affect change.

But, President Calvin Coolidge said: *"Don't expect to build up the weak by pulling down the strong."*

Throughout this book series, the governing concept has been to pay attention to the Willy Wonka hints Trump continues to toss about. And, since the death of George Floyd, the pandemic has been ignored by the anarchists and the media has become hypocritical in its dealing with social distancing and masks – anarchists are excused from social responsibility and encouraged to create media visuals.

When we see the things Trump is criticized for – the way he attacks in what has been termed a childish manner – we might think about something else attributed to Sun Tzu: "*If you know the enemy and know yourself, you need not fear the result of a hundred battles. If you know yourself but not the enemy, for every victory gained you will also suffer a defeat. If you know neither the enemy nor yourself, you will succumb in every battle.*"

How do you learn about your enemy?

Don't you seek out their vulnerabilities? Is childish taunting a non-threatening method to see if they are emotional and short-tempered? How do test what you believe you've observed?

If that is what you do, take another look at what Trump does.

Politicians and inept leaders tend to be short-tempered – we have seen this with Joe Biden and his calling a student a '*lying dog-faced pony soldier.*'

Biden is sensitive to challenge or anyone questioning his thinking – especially when he is wrong. Public opinion governs the politician but not the salesman. As pointed out in the first two books in this series, Trump is PT Barnum, and it is Barnum who is credited with: "*I don't give a damn what you say about me, just so you spell my name right.*"

We hear about lies. Biden lies about matters of substance – this is repeatedly being established by Fact-Check groups. Trump also "lies" through exaggeration or attributing to others the things his target demographic believes or wishes to hear. But, it would be nice if we addressed reality.

All warfare is based on deception

Covid-19 can spread asymptomatically. Initially, this was not recognized and over several months health officials minimized risks and pushed misleading messages despite mounting evidence.

Interviews with doctors and public health officials in more than a dozen countries show that a two-month delay was a product of faulty scientific assumptions and academic rivalries. There was also a reluctance to fully accept the drastic measures associated with virus containment.

Various models suggest that earlier, aggressive action might have saved tens of thousands of lives. A Munich based team, headed by Dr. Camilla Rothe, was among the first to warn of asymptomatic transmission, Germany's response seems to have kept the problem in check.

After reviewing the patterns related to the NYC epicenter, the CDC estimated that 35% of coronavirus cases are asymptomatic, and about 40% of all transmissions can be attributed to those who are asymptomatic – a CDC "best estimate" on asymptomatic fatality rates was set at 0.4%.

On 1 July, the fatality rate among the known cases was below 4.9% and the media was reporting expert estimates at ten times the established cases – all of whom being asymptomatic, and therefore indicating the actual fatality rate is below the CDC estimate, and that the nation is developing a widespread *herd immunity*. But CNN and other media persist in asserting their doom-and-gloom perspective.

The way numbers are presented distorts the truth, as does the genetics of each nation infected.

There is a reason Russia and Brazil were slow to be infected and why it took time for their cases to climb. In the case of Russia, a low death rate goes with them being the origin of blood Type-B and Eastern Europe being the origin of blood Type-AB; Western Europe gave the world Type-A blood.

As medical science is discovering, Covid-19 is a virus intended to cull Western Europeans – conspiracy and apocalyptic freaks will soon realize that, like the Holocaust, this is as another way to claim the 144,000 righteous "Jews" for the rapture, without flagging that prophecy is being fulfilled. But such "theory" only serves those who believe in such things – diverting attention from human biology.

In various books over the past decade, I've referenced a 1960s Hippy subway poster: *"All of the people who ever lived are alive today."* Phrased another way: all the souls that ever were are here.

LOL, think about that as the souls returned/resurrected for judgment and that judgment being passed on Spain, France, Italy. You know the Republican evangelicals are going to find a way to play with variations of that idea, while Democrats will yell "it's crazy."

Let's focus on reality.

At the 20 June, Tulsa, Oklahoma rally, Trump said, "*Testing is a double-edged sword. We've tested now 25 million people. It's probably 20 million people more than anybody else. Germany's done a lot. South Korea's done a lot.*"

Using Trump's numbers in conjunction with those released by Johns Hopkins University on the morning of 24 June, the U.S. had 2,347,102 confirmed COVID-19 cases and 121,225 deaths. That means only one percent of those tested had the "Kung-Flu"; only five percent of those have died from it. In terms of average deaths, that's about 50 deaths per hundred thousand Americans, where the normal death rate is 723. And the virus has generally killed only the elderly and those potentially fatally ill (hence, a culling virus).

There is a harsh reality, many of those who are dying would have died anyway; because of the lockdown, many who would have died in traffic accidents or other "outside activity" causes haven't. It is possible annual figures will show no significant change from the historic statistical models for the United States.

In the developed world, about 20 to 30 people out of every million die on any given day. Over a typical year, that is about 7.5 to 10.5 per thousand, with a different rate for younger compared to the elderly – Covid-19 focused on the elderly and those who are known to be approaching their natural expiration date.

Medical News & Perspectives June 29, 2020, Taking a Closer Look at COVID-19, Health Inequities, and Racism, Jennifer Abbasi: In the US, black people account for 13% of the population, but where race is known, they are 24% of COVID-19 deaths. Blacks, Latinos, Native Americans, and Asian Americans are all disproportionately represented in the case statistics. The United Kingdom, France, and other nations have also reported this racial disparity – indicating the issue is genetic and not social discrimination.

Finally, there is the Obama-Trump economic issue.

Here's the reality of the past twenty years.

When Bush entered office his agenda was an attack on social security. That was disrupted by 9/11. But it is important in understanding the Obama-Trump economic recovery and the Great Recession that necessitated it.

Bush attacked the Baby-Boomers -- the first of whom was born in 1945, and with the opportunity to retire at 62, was exiting the workforce in 2007. Bush's agenda ensured a crash based on the realities of demographic change in 2007/8.

When Obama took office, in 2010, the Boomer-generation was turning 65 and had three years related to the Great Recession to adjust their retirement thinking.

If you study the economic charts, you start to see that adjustment kick in, and by 2015, the boomers were turning 70 and you see the unemployment figures reflect them exiting, with a sharp change be giving as the reached maximum benefit age and jobs began to open, and new jobs serving the retired boomers being created.

When Trump came in, in 2017, the bulk of the boomers were retired or well-defined and the employment vacancies grew faster than the Baby-Bust could fill the shift. Suddenly there were opening for minorities and the statistics show the record low unemployment and record-high employment that treated women and minorities

Because women were delaying marriage and/or childbirth, they became an economic force into themselves. This was added to be widows feeling more comfortable consulting and working with other women.

Trump knows how to handle those demographics and has demonstrated he's preparing for the demographic reality that begins in 2025 and then culminates in 2035 when the last Boomer turns 70, and the vast majority of his generation has died.

If America is to survive, it must plan for the demographic reality that will define the latter half of the TRUMP or BIDEN DECADE that is defined by events between 2021 and 2025.

Look at the European Union. Isn't it obvious that Europe has decided to self-destruct?

Britain chose BREXIT as their 2016 to 2035 strategy -- with the 49-year K-Wave economic cycle crash due to impact in 2027.

[1929 provides the undisputed anchor point, with 1978/79 oil shock servicing to mask or mute the K-Wave for that year and, finally, we have 2027. Readers will recognize the K-Wave pattern follows the ancient Hebrew economic unit of measure – the Omer. Those familiar with market sell-offs or downturns know they tend to happen in the fall, so the end of October has significance.]

As of July 2020, America is poised for a record recovery, with the previous fiscal quarter showing a 17.7% recovery from the Wuhan-pandemic crash that Trump might call a Kung-Flu kick initiated crash. If the trend continues, the financial markets might return another 15% by the November election. That would bring the S&P 500 to an all-time record above 3,400 and the DJIA above 30,000 by the final quarter and going into the election.

The calls to defund police is just one of the anarchist tactics to institute economy damaging policies that would negatively impact the pandemic recovery.

In NYC, Mayor Bill De Blasio wants to cut police budgets by one-sixth, and duplicate those cuts in multiple areas that will cause major layoffs and undermine the NYC economy. If he can succeed there, he will do economically what pandemic mismanagement did to spreading the pandemic across the nation.

We can anticipate similar actions from local administrations that support (or fail to condemn) BLM related vandalism and have been associated with the four-year impeachment process which we can assume will continue if Trump is re-elected.

Among Swamp Denizens and anarchists, the national driving force is a goal of ensuring *"The Prophecy of America's Destruction"* comes to fruition.

Among the Republicans, there is opposition to the renewal of $600-per-week federal unemployment benefits scheduled to expire at the end of July; the Democrats went on break and are scheduled to return seven days before the expiration – meaning the swamp denizens are structuring their schedules to nullify renewal.

One of the fun things emerging as the nation approaches the Fourth of July is that the Far-Right and Idiotic-Left (who are not a wing of the Left) are competing for who can best screw the nation.

Hundreds of Bush-43 Republicans, calling themselves "Bush alumni for Biden," and "Lincoln Project" Republicans, are all betting heavily on Biden being the one. Indications are, he gets elected, has his third or fourth brain aneurysm, and his non-POTUS Cousin Vice President politely bows deeply to the Swamp Denizens and becomes POTUS in 2023.

CHAPTER 13 – Viral Time

"We are marshaling the full power of the federal government and the private sector to protect the American people." ~ Donald J. Trump, 27 January 2020

In Book-8 of this series, I wrote *"'Everything is up in the air': coronavirus fears upend US election campaigns."* But those fears, while they have meaning, also are relatively meaningless.

When we reached the middle or 15th of May 2020, the world had recorded the COVID-19 Dashboard reported 4.6 million cases and 310 thousand deaths. But, if we were to look at *Worldometer* – a webpage reporting population changes – we see that every day over 280 thousand children are born and more than 120 thousand died. So, every 36-hours we replace all those who reportedly died in the 5-months associated with the pandemic. Phrased another way, in the roughly 150 days of the "official" outbreak, only two deaths a day can be associated with the pandemic.

The CD reports an Infant Mortality rate of 5.79 deaths per 1,000 live births – about 22,000 infants die every year, in a nation that does not believe Healthcare should be free, does not support M4A and has a large segment of its population insisting that a fetus which will die or cause the death of its mother when it dies should go to term, rather than be aborted so the mother can have a healthy baby. Those same anti-abortion activists oppose Medicare for All – again, so they can ensure a sickly Citizen, one that would be the ideal target for the next COVID-19 pandemic, comes into existence.

The known timeline for the Wuhan COVID-19 virus reveals numerous things about who did what and when. One harsh reality is that actions aimed at blocking Trump's ability to take any action eventually came back when the virus appeared. One such action was inherent in Nancy Pelosi's proposed *"H.R.2214: National Origin-Based Antidiscrimination for Nonimmigrants Act or the NO BAN Act"*, introduced 10 April 2019. She intention was to impose change on presidential *"Authority to suspend or restrict the entry of a class of aliens."*

Had it been enacted, President Trump could not have issued Executive Orders restricting travel from virus-infected regions or the 22 April 60-day suspension of entry by Green Card applicants. That would have increased cases of Covid-19 in California.

In May 2019, Senator Mitch McConnell pointed out that the "[Democrats] *seemed to be hoping for a national crisis for the sake of their own politics.*" My the end of the month, rabble-rousers had their crisis in the 31 May death of George Perry Floyd Jr; thereafter, all who were not with them were Johnny Rebs whose existence was to be erased because someone in history dared to discover a western hemisphere continent, had the audacity to develop their portion of it into a Democratic nation and, nearly a century later, fight for the Constitution as it was written.

Subsequently, they failed with the impeachment effort that was begun with the 9 November 2016 announcement of the election results. Their failure was gifted with the COVID-19 global pandemic – this is the basic timeline for some of the events that accompanied the events defining the end of 2019 and then 2020.

The Covid-19 pandemic created an awareness of the need for border controls – which include travel bans – and the Trump administration came into power with a promise that a "Wall" would replace the "Fence" that was authorized by the 2006 Secure Fence Act. Trump has been attacked for wanting the improvements to the original structure.

Perspective is needed and can be derived from the fact that Hilary Clinton and Barack Obama spearheaded the 2006 Act. There is also the reality of the August 2008 Democratic Party Platform in which we find the border security no opposed by California Democrats was a critical element of the Obama Platform:

"We cannot continue to allow people to enter the United States undetected, undocumented, and unchecked. The American people are a welcoming and generous people, but those who enter our country's borders illegally, and those who employ them, disrespect the rule of the law. We need to secure our borders, and support additional personnel, infrastructure, and technology on the border and at our ports of entry. We need additional Customs and Border Protection agents equipped with better technology and real-time intelligence."

As we look at the Covid-19 timeline, we see that there is an apparent policy of ignoring contemporaneous reality whenever it allows opposition to either Trump or historic Democratic Platform positions. There is a commonality of approach based on the idea of being determined to *"cancel culture"* rather than make an effort to enhance or improve it.

Now, to bring this volume to an end, let's record the numbers as they appeared on 27 June, as we head into July and the fireworks at Mount Rushmore.

As promised, we are revisiting the April Fool's Day pandemic numbers, and doing so one week before the Fourth of July.

The Global fatality percentage baseline established by the previously selected nations has been augmented by three additional nations – Russia was late to the party and the prevalence of blood Type-B antigens has revealed its immunity (it would be amusing to hear conspiracy theorists argue Russia manufactured the virus and ensured their people were immune before they planted it in Wuhan, China); Portugal is adjacent to Spain, but its population is also a bit different in genetic structure; Brazil has entered as a news hotspot; finally Sweden – a nation that decided to ignore the pandemic and, in terms of fatality percentages, has faired better than Italy, Spain, United Kingdom, France, and Canada.

As we saw before, the United States appears to be consistent with – a good model for – the global population, where the overall fatality rate for both has remained approximately equal in the 5.3% area.

Globally, there were 9,871,711 confirmed cases with 495,781 dead (as of 3:15 PM EST), but that was on the 27th, and on the 28th the global number jumped to 10,070,339, with 500,306 fatalities – taking the percentage down to 4.97%.

Curious how, as virus numbers go up – and set records – they represent a more positive perspective on the pandemic. It is rather comic – the media desire to provide every new piece of data as if it were an increasing problem or evidence of a response failure; then to yell at Trump or Pence because they see things in a positive light.

Trump has a known, but ignored, history of reading various diverse works. He may well know Sun Tzu: *"Victorious warriors win first and then go to war, while defeated warriors go to war first and then seek to win."*

Even if he does not know the words, Trump has instinctively been able to apply the meaning behind the words. There is normal preparation for combat which contributes to victory. But, apart from the normal preparation, always carry a positive attitude. It tempers your armor and deflects the barrage of arrows while adding strength to your attack, it weakens the enemy.

Those working to pull down statues of the founding fathers or those of critical importance to the national existence are fighting against the reality of personal existence. Every African-American who takes it upon themself to denounce the history of slavery is, in fact, cursing the fact they are American – because, with the slavery, their ancestors would have remained in Africa and they would never have been born.

If not for Columbus and the Jews who sponsored him, there would be no America. Slavery was systemic in Europe – Columbus did not bring it, it was brought by the Spanish regime that was also slaughtering Jews – the Spanish Inquisitors were the Nazis of their era, Mexico and Brazil became a safe-haven for Spain's victims.

When the British came to New England they discovered the hackmatack tree – a tree whose surface root is at the proper angle to the trunk, with the proper strength, to right make it perfect to serve as an exceptionally strong once piece bow and keel. That tree made possible the New England shipbuilding industry which provided the Triangle Trade and made America the merchant transport rulers of the seas until the development of steel ships.

The Triangle Trade brought already people enslaved by their fellow Africans – or by Arabs – from Africa to the New World. Their descendants are, based on modern DNA studies, partially European. Therefore, without the mixing of the races, they would never have existed.

As readers know, over the past decade, my writing focus has been on areas that do not create "bestsellers" – the area of ancestry and genealogy. And that brings us to someone well known to those who support racial equality – Dr. Martin Luther King Jr.

Research into King's ancestry shows that like most African-Americans he is of mixed race. But he is also, like Barack Obama, a descendant of the 4-Sisters. And when they attack Thomas Jefferson they are attacking MLK's family along his European ancestral line.

After the death of his wife, Jefferson entered into a long-term relationship with his sister-in-law. Because of anti-miscegenation views and laws, he could not marry her because she was also the daughter of an Mulatto-slave who was a daughter of an Africa-slave and the sea captain on whose ship she was brought to America.

Jefferson gave us the constitution; they hate him for that. The idea he owned slaves – his children, who he properly educated – is their excuse. Jefferson believed in education and, beginning 25 January 1819, founded the University of Virginia. They hate him for that too.

But that goes to history and the reality behind those who have shaped and continue to shape the nation. For now, we have the problem of a pandemic and how America is fairing in the face of a culling virus.

As we did earlier in the book here are some of the numbers that will allow us to compare national responses to the coronavirus (fatality % - deaths v Cases):

14.46% - 34,716 / 240,136 Italy

11.39% - 28,341 / 248,766 Spain

13.99% - 43,598 / 311,727 United Kingdom

14.93% - 29,781 / 199,473 France

08.19% - 8,568 / 104,651 Canada

08.11% - 5,280 / 65,137 SWEDEN

05.48% - 4,641 / 84,726 China

05.04% - 125,340 / 2,488,037 ***United States***

Global Baseline 05.02%

04.71% - 10,364 / 220,180 Iran

04.61% - 8,968 / 194,458 Germany

04.39% - 55,961 / 1,274,974 Brazil

03.79% - 1,561 / 41,189 Portugal

01.43% - 8,958 / 626,779 Russia

The United States population is equivalent to 4.25% of the total world population and has a population diversity which does not significantly deviate from a random sample of the global community. It is therefore reasonable that America would evidence a pandemic fatality rate presented for the global community.

As seen above, initial presentations of the virus have followed the lines of commerce; therefore, the pandemic spread was through the industrialized or global commerce supply lines which we already know connect supplier with the consumer – the United States being the ultimate consumer. Thereafter, the spread went to the secondary suppliers, industrialized regions of the lesser developed nations, and remaining consumer minorities. Ultimately, the spread illustrates the importance of the various nationalities in the global community.

Within a nation, this can be phrased in terms of urban versus rural populations – 82.8 % of U.S. population is urban. And within the urban setting, the primary spread is among those who provide "essential services" or are the "invisible" blue-collar workers who the ones cleaning and doing the servicing or repairs while everyone else sleeps. These invisible workers are also those who serve the tourist industry – who are employed in hotels and restaurants. And they are those working in the shops and supermarkets that fill basic needs.

The Fourth of July weekend has seen many disruptive actions and the opening of the nation.

The media is cheering the spread of the virus and yelling about how the lack of social distancing and masks will help promote its spread.

There is a bit of a mental disconnect in their propaganda drive to find cause to denounce the President and cheer the crushing mob of protestors who are noted for the lack of social distancing and all too often a lack of masks – when worn, they are generally to conceal the identity of those looting, vandalizing, or simply desecrating the flag and other national symbols.

As I have repeatedly pointed out, America is at that point in its history where the critical choice of status is to be made by those who claim to be its citizens.

Historically, Spain, with its history of learning and commerce dating back to biblical times, should have been a great nation. But, in 1492, it decided to attack its founders. Even the benefits of the New World trade, it could only blow the opportunities in a sea of hate.

A thousand years after the writing of the Book of Revelation, capped by an invasion of Britain in 1066, France had risen to power and controlled Europe. The French Revolution ensured that would never be again – they made it a point to murder the descendants of the 4-Sisters.

Led by the Royal family that still serves a role today, Britain became master and then fell to its child – the United States.

Now the goal is to complete the prophecy and destroy America and with it return China to its ancient role as "Global Merchant".

Thus we see anarchy and the cellar campaign of the man who would be China's puppet. Let's recap the 2020 timeline:

<u>COVID-19 & GEORGE FLOYD TIMELINE</u>

17 November 2019 –

- The first known death of no precisely identified infection or incubation period was presented, but three weeks appeared to be the norm – the novel coronavirus can, therefore, be said to have originated prior to the last week in October 2019.

14 December 2019 –

- – France's First virus Case.

-

18 December 2019 –

- – Donald J. Trump impeached for Article I: Abuse of Power; Article II: Obstruction of Congress.

-

27 December 2019 –

- Based on a sample taken, but not tested until May, French authorities announce the first case of COVID-19 arrived between 14 & 22 December. Up until then, they had declared the first official cases of coronavirus in the country — three people who had all recently been in China — was 24 January, or four days after China confirmed the first human-to-human transmission.

-

31 December 2019 –

- The Wuhan, China government health authorities confirm the treatment of dozens of COVID-19 cases. They had been treating the cases as pneumonia of unknown cause. China informs The World Health Organization (WHO). The next day, on 1 January 2020, the concerned market in Wuhan was closed for environmental sanitation and disinfection.

- 01 January 2020 – New Year's Day, 1863, President Lincoln's 'The Emancipation Proclamation' – which technically violated the Constitution {if Southern States were still part of United States} – became official.

-

05 January 2020 –

- WHO published: "*On 31 December 2019, the WHO China Country Office was informed of cases of pneumonia of unknown etiology (unknown cause) detected in Wuhan City, Hubei Province of China. As of 3 January 2020, a total of 44 patients with pneumonia of unknown etiology have been reported to WHO by the national authorities in China.*"

- WHO's statement triggered limited elements of the Obama Pandemic Playbook. The first three dealing with mitigation are: "*1. Limiting spread of disease; 2. Mitigating the impact of illness, suffering, and death; and 3. Sustaining critical infrastructure and key resources in the United States.*" The third item would mean the economy itself, as well as medical resources – but those were outsourced to China, so, under the Obama guidelines, paramount importance must focus on the economy or ability to pay for Chinese medical resources. In terms of action and resources for State, Local, Tribal, and Territorial (SLTT) Governments: "*In the event of a suspected or emerging biological incident (Phase 1c), the Federal Government may conduct enhanced public health surveillance and increase coordination among Federal partners and SLTT authorities.*"

-

11 January 2020 –

- China reported its first death, a 61-year-old man who was a regular customer at the market in Wuhan.

- This is three years to-the-day after Dr. Anthony Fauci says there will be a "surprise outbreak" of a pandemic in the U.S. within a few years.

-

14 January 2020 –

- Dr. Fauci notes, beginning on 14 January, NIH "moved very quickly" on vaccine trials and development. At the time, it was noted that the 2003 SARS outbreak required about 20 months from the release of the viral genome to get a vaccine ready for human trials; the epidemic caused by the Zika virus in 2015 brought the timeline down to 6 months; it was hoped COVID-19 would take 3 months to Phase 1 – it took 62 days.

- In May, Fauci predicts that phases two and three of the trial will occur in the late spring and early summer, without any guarantee the vaccine will be effective – but Fauci offered a positive outlook on the vaccine progress: *"The NIH has been collaborating with a number of pharmaceutical companies at various stages of development."*

15 January 2020 –

- A 35-year-old man from Washington State returns from a trip to Wuhan, China (he later becomes first recognized death).

- *"Between the second half of January and the first half of February,"* [15 Jan to 15 Feb]:]there were likely enough infected people in Boston *"to generate local transmission,"* said Alessandro Vespignani, the principal investigator behind the Northeastern model.   Samuel Scarpino, a Northeastern mathematical epidemiologist (not a member of Vespignani's team) said: "*From my perspective, [the model] really fits with what we're seeing on the ground. The peak of cases in the Boston area happened much earlier than we would have expected given the reported cases. ... there was a much larger outbreak here than we realized earlier, and that really explains the peak timing, the early surge in deaths and cases. We were dealing with a few things in the US that made it very complicated. Because it was flu season, there were a lot of respiratory cases. It's much harder to notice a handful of unusual cases when there's just so many people that are ill. We knew by mid to late January that this disease was spreading rapidly through China. We should've been ready. We should've had things in place building into February, certainly by the beginning of March, to have really high testing capacity.*" (Trump's travel ban would be official on 31 January; the virus was on the west coast and was already on the east coast, as was confirmed by a test the next day.)

- House Speaker Nancy Pelosi holds a vote to send articles of impeachment to the Senate – it passes along partisan lines; Pelosi gives away commemorative pens used in the signing.

-

16 January 2020 –

- Tulsi Gabbard told her campaign stop audience, "*Politicians who say there isn't enough money to pay for health care or education or infrastructure have been lying to us about 'progress' in the war in Afghanistan when they knew/know it* *is unwinnable—lying to justify spending $4 billion a month for 18 years and counting."*

- Congresswoman Nancy Pelosi joined community leaders on a tour of Chinatown to support local small businesses facing losses due to fear associated with the pandemic. Pelosi spoke of precautions taken by the city, noting Chinatown is safe and hoped many would join her in visiting Chinatown – the exact opposite of what she and her cronies assert should have been done because Trump should have ordered a lockdown.

-

17 January 2020 –

- Trump warns airlines of his plan to halt China travel.

-

20 January 2020 –

- first confirmed United States case of COVID-19 in the state of Washington.

-

21 January 2020 –

- Responding to the first U.S. case of coronavirus, the secretary of the Department of Health and Human Services appeared on Fox News to report the latest on the disease as it ravaged China.

- The Trump administration informs airlines servicing Asia of plans to institute a travel ban.

- A man believed to be the first to enter the United States from China carrying the coronavirus, arrives from Wuhan.

22 January 2020 –

- The United States and other countries confirmed cases, the first of which was in Japan, South Korea, and Thailand.

-

23 January 2020 –

- Chinese authorities lockdown Wuhan – a city of more than 11 million – canceling planes and trains leaving the city. Spread of disease to Taiwan, Japan, Thailand, South Korea, and the United States had claimed 17 lives with more than 570 others infected.

- Singapore, an island nation of 5.8 million people relies on 1 million foreign workers to build and maintain its gleaming infrastructure, reports its first case – by the end of April, it will have 13,625 cases (80 percent migrant workers) and 12 deaths.

- House impeachment managers make opening statements.

-

27 January 2020 –

- Joe Biden asserts *"the Trump administration's shortsighted policies have left us unprepared"*; a few days later, he would later call Trump's echoing of the Chinese travel ban response "xenophobic" and "racist".

- The "Experts" miss COVID-19's silent spread and assume that only active cases could spread the disease; in June, the error will be formally acknowledged and Trump's policies are the correct approach – thought NYC Mayor Bill De Blasio ignored and therefore caused the pandemic spread across the nation...as would be acknowledged when the various Universities studying the spread attribute 65% of contagion to the NYC policies.

- German laboratories begin using commercially made Covid-19 tests, modifying tests used as they are validated.

-

29 January 2020 –

- – Trump launches Coronavirus Task Force.

- The NAVARRO MEMO details cost and concerns related to the COVID-19; while Trump was upset by the content, he had already begun to institute a Travel Ban which became official on 31 January. Joe Biden reacted declaring Trump to be a xenophobic racist and declaring the ban was not warranted.

- Twenty-six days later, Navarro said: *"increasing probability of a full-blown COVID-19 pandemic that could infect as many as 100 million Americans, with a loss of life of as many as 1-2 million souls."* By that time, Trump had already taken action, and the very next day Pelosi advocated mass gatherings at the San Francisco Chinatown businesses.

30 January 2020 –

- WHO: *"Director-General of the World Health Organization, following the advice of the Emergency Committee convened under the International Health Regulations, declared the current outbreak of COVID-19 a public health emergency of international concern,"* and Temporary Recommendations are then issued which include a statement that there is no need to restrict travel.

- Senators begin asking two days of questions of both sides in the impeachment trial of President Trump.

31 January 2020 –

- – Secretary of Health and Human Services declared a public health emergency under the Public Health Service Act (42 U.S.C. 247d, section 319).

- The Senate votes vote on whether to allow further witnesses and documents in the impeachment trial.

- – Presidential Proclamation 9983, *"Improving Enhanced Vetting Capability and Processes for Detecting Attempted Entry Into the United States by Terrorists or Other Public-Safety Threats,"* is amended to include restrictions or a ban on China-related travel. The legality of this type of ban was upheld by the U.S. Supreme Court in 2018 and cleared the way for updates adding or removing countries from the list.

- Epidemiologist Dr. Michael Osterholm, in NYTimes article, classifies the China travel ban as *"more of an emotional or political reaction,"* rather than one justified by any medical necessity.

- A day after the WHO declared COVID-19 a global health emergency, Azar declared it a public health emergency. That same day, during the first Coronavirus Task Force briefing, Azar told the public: *"I want to stress: The risk of infection for Americans remains low."*

- At this point, 213 people had died and nearly 9,800 had been infected worldwide.

-

01 February 2020 –

- Joe Biden reacts to the Travel band with Tweet: *"We are in the midst of a crisis with the coronavirus. We need to lead the way with science – not Donald Trump's record of hysteria, xenophobia, and fear-mongering. He is the worst possible person to lead our country through a global health emergency."*

- On 1 February, a student at the University of Massachusetts Boston who had recently traveled from Wuhan, China, tested positive.
- In February a sample isolated from a patient examined via an electron microscope image from the US National Institutes of Health shows the virus that causes COVID-19.
-

02 February 2020 –

- The federal government begins restricting travel from China.
- The first coronavirus death was reported outside China is a 44-year-old man in the Philippines.
- An ACLU statement declares that *"travel bans & quarantines don't work."*
- The Phillippines has it's first reported Covid-19 death.
-

03 February 2020 –

- The Lancet Respiratory Medicine {updated 1 March} *"On Dec 31, 2019, China alerted WHO to several cases of pneumonia associated with an unknown virus."* In May, Trump would mistake the stated opening "December" date as the original publication date, and be rebuked by Lancet publishers. It is worth noting the Dec 2019, Volume 7, Number 12, p993-1084, e37-e40 included articles on "Personalised mechanical ventilation in acute respiratory distress syndrome" which is the final stage of COVID-19. On 2 June, it would be revealed that, based on a flawed article that appeared in both the Lancet and the New England Journal of Medicine, both WHO and government Covid-19 policies had been altered.
- House impeachment managers call the President a threat to national security as they begin closing arguments without a statutory base crime or "High Crime" being alleged.
-

04 February 2020 –

- – Trump's State of the Union makes fighting COVID-19 the national priority by saying: *"Protecting Americans' health also means fighting infectious diseases. We are coordinating with the Chinese government and working closely together on the coronavirus outbreak in China. My administration will take all necessary steps to safeguard our citizens from this threat."* In response, Speaker Pelosi declares the SOTU address a lie and rips up her House copy of the document.

- – Trump Issues Emergency use authorization for diagnostic tests

- Echoing Pelosi, Chuck Schumer Tweets: *"President Trump's speech tonight was much more like a Trump rally than a speech a true leader would give. It was demagogic, undignified, highly partisan, and in too many places, untruthful."* No *"untruthful"* specifics are ever provided, but both Pelosi and Schumer appear to be calling Coronavirus a lie – Schumer's NYC will become the epicenter of the spread; Pelosi encourages crowds in San Francisco's Chinatown.

-

05 February 2020 –

- A cruise ship in Japan quarantined thousands.

- The Senate, voting along partisan lines, acquits the President on both articles of impeachment, 52-48 and 53-47.

-

06 February 2020 –

- 57-year-old Patricia Dowd, an auditor at a Silicon Valley semiconductor manufacturer, developed flu-like symptoms and abruptly died in her San Jose kitchen, triggering a search for what had killed her. Her Flu tests were negative, but, as noted, it wouldn't be until 22 April that China reports false negatives in 30% of tests. Dowd had traveled to Beijing in November; her death indicated the virus entered California in December.

-

07 February 2020 –

- Secretary of Health and Human Services Alex Michael Azar II repeats a message: *"The immediate risk to the American public is low at this time."*

- Dr. Li Wenliang, a Chinese doctor, who first tried to raise the alarm about COVID-19 died of the virus.

-

09 February 2020 – Trump Task Force Briefs Governors

-

10 February 2020 –

- Vice President Pence said a group of major health insurance companies have agreed not to charge patients co-pays when they get tested for coronavirus. But reliance on those private firms reveals a basic problem with the current medical health system – in an emerging crisis people avoid being tested due to the cost, and that endangers the whole nation.

11 February 2020 –

- – Trump Expedites Development of Vaccine

- World Health Organization proposed an official name for the disease the virus coronavirus causes: Covid-19.

- The Chinese death toll is 1,113; confirmed cases 44,653; 24 other countries report a total of 393 additional cases.

-

12 February 2020 –

- The Dow Jones Industrial Average [DJIA] reaches 29,551 to set an all-time record that marks an end to the longest bull market in history – the decline continues until 23 March and closes at 18,592.

-

14 February 2020 –

- Azar continued to say *"the immediate risk"* to Americans was low and travel restrictions had worked: *"So I think so far, our measures have been quite effective."*

- France announces the first coronavirus death in Europe, an 80-year-old Chinese tourist had died in a Paris hospital.

-

19 February 2020 –

- After a two-week quarantine, 443 passengers began leaving the Diamond Princess cruise ship; at least 621 people aboard the ship were infected.

- Democrats debate in Las Vegas. Sanders opens by saying, *"In order to beat Donald Trump, we're going to need the largest voter turnout in the history of the United States."* He adds, *", …we should join the rest of the industrialized world, guarantee health care to all people as a human right, raise that minimum* *wage to a living wage of $15 bucks an hour, and have the guts to take on the fossil fuel industry,…"*

- Part of Sanders' concluding remarks: *"…the bottom line is, all of us are united in defeating the most dangerous president in the modern history of this country. That we agree on. But where we don't agree, I think, is why we are today the only major country on Earth not to guarantee health care to all people, …, when 500,000 people sleep out on the street, why hundreds of thousands of bright young kids can't afford to go to college, and 45 million remain in student debt. …Bottom line here: Real change never takes place from the top on down, never takes place from an oligarchy… We need to mobilize millions of people to stand up for justice. That's our campaign."*

-

20 February 2020 –

- Codogno Hospital intensive care unit (ICU) Lodi, Lombardy, Italy, admits a patient in his 30s admitted who tests positive for Covid-19. The patient's medical history revealed atypical pneumonia that was not responding to treatment. The next day an emergency task force was formed by the Government of Lombardy and local health authorities to lead the response to the outbreak. On 8 March, Lombardy was quarantined and strict self-isolation measures were instituted.

-

21 February 2020 –

- – Presidential Proclamation 9983 Travel Ban goes into effect.
- Iran announced two coronavirus cases in the country, then said both patients had died, and 2-days later, Iran announced two additional deaths.
- The coronavirus-driven global recession and an oil-price war triggers the biggest decline in Stock markets, in both Europe and the United States, since 2008.
- Italy reports its first Covid-19 death with 19 cases.

-

22 February 2020 –

- First official Covid-19 death is reported in Italy.

-

23 February 2020 –

- Italy reports major surge in cases; Lombardy region, officials locked down ten towns after a cluster of cases suddenly emerged in Codogno, southeast of Milan. Schools closed and sporting and cultural events were canceled.

- Sen. Bernie Sanders predicts: "*We are going to win across the country because the American people are sick and tired of a president who lies all of the time.*"

-

24 February 2020 –

- – Trump administration asks Congress for $2.5 billion, and authorization to transfer of $535 million appropriated for the Ebola virus, for coronavirus response; $8.5 Billion to combat spread is offered.

- – Pelosi goes on TV to invite people from across the nation to gather in San Francisco Chinatown.

- Iran emerges as a second focus point when it reports 61 cases and 12 deaths.   Cases in Iraq, Afghanistan, Bahrain, Kuwait, Oman, Lebanon, the United Arab Emirates, and Canada, have been traced back to Iran.

-

25 February 2020 –

- On Fox News, Azar says: "*But thanks to President Trump's historically aggressive containment efforts, we've actually contained the spread of this virus here in the United States at this point. I think part of the message to the American people is we all need to take a bit of deep breath here.*"

- Dr. Nancy Messonnier warning includes "Social Distancing"

-

26 February 2020 – Ash Wednesday – Lent begins

- Latin America reports its first case, a 61-year-old São Paulo, Brazil man, who had returned from a business trip to Italy, tested positive for the coronavirus.

- On February 26 & 27, the biotech company Biogen held a conference where 100 of the 175 attendees were infected with the novel coronavirus – initiating a Massachusetts outbreak that contributed to the coronavirus spread in North Carolina, Tennessee, Indiana and Florida.

•

27 February 2020 –

- During February, 2 million travelers arrived in the U.S. from Italy and other European countries.

- The Province of Hubei, China has experienced sustained local transmission and has reported by far the largest number of confirmed cases since the beginning of the outbreak, lately, the situation in China showed a significant decrease in cases.

- WHO continues to advise against the application of any trade restrictions or travel bans involving countries experiencing COVID-19 outbreaks. Anti-Trump individuals want Trump to "listen to the experts" – so oppose travel bans.

- WHO receives reports from 38 countries of additional health measures that significantly interfere with international traffic concerning travel to or from China or other countries, ranging from denial of entry of passengers, visa restrictions, and quarantine for returning travelers.

•

28 February 2020 –

- Infections in Europe spike with Northern Ireland and Wales cases traced back to Italy; nearly 60 cases Germany and 57 were reported in France.

- Nigeria, Africa's most populous nation, reports the first case in Sub-Saharan Africa.

- At a rally in South Carolina, Trump discusses 'Democratic Hoaxes': "*They tried the impeachment hoax. That was on a perfect conversation. … And this is their new hoax. We have 15 people in this massive country and because of the fact that we went early. We went early, we could have had a lot more than that. … So a statistic that we want to talk about, go ahead. … So a number that nobody heard of, that I heard of recently and I was shocked to hear it, 35,000 people on average die each year from the flu. Did anyone know that? … They say usually a minimum of 27[,000], goes up to 100,000 people a year die. And so far we have lost nobody to coronavirus in the United States. Nobody. And it doesn't mean we won't and we are totally prepared. It doesn't mean we won't, but think of it. You hear 35 and 40,000 people and we've lost nobody and you wonder the press is in hysteria mode.*" On 17 April, Bill Maher restates Trump's *"the press is in hysteria mode"* phrase as media *"panic porn"* – while the media uses the 'hoax' reference to falsely claim Trump called the COVID-19 a hoax and continues to deflect from their pattern of perpetuating hoaxes.

- Trump also states: *"I also created a White House virus task force. It's a big thing, a virus task force. I requested 2.5 billion dollars to ensure we have the resources we need. The Democrats said, 'That's terrible. He's doing the wrong thing. He needs eight and a half billion, not two and a half.' ... I'll take it. I never had that before. ... These people are crazy. We must understand that border security is also health security. "* He enumerates the things he claims to have achieved, and say: *"While the extreme left has been wasting America's time with these vile hoaxes,"* and then enumerates things achieved with the longest economic expansion in the nation's history.

-

29 February 2020 –

- – Trump Issues Level 4 Travel Advisory for South Korea and Italy – a *"do not travel"* warning. All travel to Iran is banned and entry barred to any foreign citizen who had visited Iran in the previous 14 days.

- The United States reports its known coronavirus death, but it would later be discovered to be the third death.

- Federal regulations on testings are lifted to allow private labs to develop tests and treatments for COVID-19

-

?? February 2020 –

- On 01 July it is revealed that, at some point in February, Adam Schiff, in his role as chairman of the House Permanent Select Committee on Intelligence, was briefed about Russia offering the Taliban bounties in Afghanistan, but he took no action in response to the briefing [arguably an act of treason]; he has also acknowledged President Trump was never briefed on bounty intelligence.

-

01 March 2020 –

- President Trump declares United States COVID-19 outbreak constituted a national emergency began 1 March – the formal Proclamation 9994 was issued 13 March 2020.

- New York State records its first confirmed Covid-19 death.

- A Speculative study by Columbia University released 21 May, indicated 54,000 fewer would have died if a lockdown had begun on 1 March rather than 19 March. When the study was released, 93,000 had died, a third of them in the New York metropolitan area which an earlier analysis blamed for 65% of COVID-19 deaths.

- WHO reports excluding China, there are were 6,009 Covid-19 cases spread over 53 countries.

-

02 March 2020 –

- On 14 April, a NYTimes article, *"The Huge Cost of Waiting to Contain the Pandemic"* makes a hindsight assertion that the *"Social Distancing policies, including closing schools and avoiding groups of more than 10,"* imposed on 16 March should have been imposed on 2 March, when only 11 deaths were recorded in the country.

- However, the article acknowledges Dr. Fauci said, *"Obviously, you could logically say that if you had a process that was ongoing and you started mitigation earlier, you could have saved lives... there was a lot of pushback about shutting things...,"* which means there was objection from all quarters. Also acknowledged was the fact an early mitigation argument was also leveled against Obama in 2002 and 2009.

-

03 March 2020 –

- SUPER TUESDAY – Joe Biden's wife body-blocks protester. Biden later jokes: *"I'm probably the only candidate running for president whose wife is my Secret Service. Whoa, you don't screw around with a Philly girl, I'll tell you what."*

- Italy reported 2,200 COVID cases; an American returning after spending several months in Milan arrives at New York's JFK Airport and is only asked if she had been to China or Iran.

- Coronavirus arrived and was established in Massachusetts at the end of February, but its prevalence is denied.

-

04 March 2020 –

- California declares emergency over coronavirus as death toll of 10 in Washington is added to by one in California and new cases emerged around New York City and Los Angeles; over $3 billion – of the $8.3 appropriated by Congress – is to go to research and development of coronavirus vaccines, test kits, and therapeutics.

- Trump signs the Coronavirus Funding Bill.

- Citing "Presidential Proclamation 9983, issued on January 31, 2020", Pelosi once again promotes passage of H.R. 2214 <u>to end the travel ban</u> imposed to prevent COVID-19 exposed individuals from entering the country.

- After meeting with front-line medical workers, Governor Baker and other Massachusetts state officials reiterated that the risks posed by Covid-19 were low – the spreading Biogen cluster was downplayed or ignored.

-

05 March 2020 –

- British Chief medical officer Prof. Chris Whitty tells MPs coronavirus plan is at 'mainly delay' stage, and older people may in the future be told to avoid crowded places.

- Utah considers decriminalizing polygamy.

- In Europe it's estimated airlines will lose $113 Billion due to COVID-19 – Airline share prices fall 25%.

- Based on testing conducted 27 & 28 February and 2 March, Hong Kong officials report finding COVID-19 virus in pets.

- Based on 26 February ruling by 2nd Circuit Court of Appeals in Manhattan, administration moves forward on withholding Federal funds from *"Sanctuary Cities."*

- Based on his Super Tuesday victories, Biden asserts: "*Look, I think the one thing the president doesn't want to do from the very beginning is face me because I will beat him. Period.*" Apparently, Biden has not noticed an emerging issue related to COVID-19, because he makes no mention of it.

- The Department of Commerce study reports a study finding that a staggering 97 percent of all antibiotics in the United States came from China. They also report that 80 percent of the ingredients used to make various drugs within the United States are also from China or outsourced from other nations. It is pointed out that Trump has sought repatriating various industries and the Chinese could weaponize our dependence on them, while the media uses repatriation opposition as a tool to score political points against the president; the Right-wing media paints Biden as pro-China.

- Senator Mitt Romney (R-Utah) tells reporters: "*There's no question but that the appearance of looking into Burisma and Hunter Biden appears political, and I think people are tired of these kind of political investigations.*" The Senate Homeland Security and Governmental Affairs Committee is engaged in obtaining relevant subpoenas.

- New York City mayor Bill de Blasio rides the crowded subway to demonstrate Covid-19 is not an excuse to disrupt normal routines. While riding the subway on a day when there were already four confirmed cases, he tells reports: "*I'm here on the subway to say to people nothing to fear, go about your lives and we will tell you if you have to change your habits but that's not now. We have the best public health professionals protecting us. All over the city, there are doctors, nurses, and disease detectives trying to keep everyone safe and so far we have had really good results. Right now, New Yorkers need to keep the warning, which is wash your hands, use an alcohol-based hand sanitizer, cover your mouth when you cough — the basics.*"

- Massachusetts' Berkshire Medical Center has three cases of Covid-19 that trace to a basketball game.

-

06 March 2020 –

- Bernie Sanders, when was asked in his first Town Hall (Fox News) about Trump's Travel Ban: "*If you had to, would you close down the borders?*" He responded: "*No...What you don't want to do, right now you have a President who has propagated xenophobic anti-immigrate sentiment from before he was elected...*" Sanders then invoked the scientists and confined his view to the community level then deflected to make the issue one of immigrants and not the normal business traveler who might be infected. It should be noted the question was "*If you had to...*" and Sander's response was spin a compulsory national health action into an immigrant issue elevated to a political one.

- Former Massachusetts Governor Deval Patrick and former Maryland congressman John Delaney, endorse Biden against Sanders. Digging deep into Biden's 40-year record versus his own record, Bernie Sanders says: *"I was there on the right side of history, and my friend Joe Biden was not."*

- Italian government planning to lock down Lombardy region due to coronavirus outbreak.

- MSM promotes the 'Trump botched the response" scenario that will become the trump Derangement Syndrome talking-point.

- When the Boston Public Health Commission broke the news of the city's second, third, and fourth coronavirus infections on March 6, the department took a cautiously reassuring tone: *"There is currently no evidence of community transmission in Boston ... risk remains low, but this situation is evolving rapidly and changes day-to-day."*

- Dr. Howard Zucker NYS Department of Health Commissioner Statement: *"Yesterday, we convened a meeting with county health officials from across the state to hear from them firsthand and get their input before we promulgated state regulations concerning Coronavirus. The Governor has also been discussing the situation with County Executives in affected areas this week. Having received the input of our stakeholders, we are issuing regulations, and thank them all for their input."*

- Governor Charlie Baker and Boston Mayor Marty Walsh go before news cameras to tell the people of Massachusetts not to worry. The Health and Human Services secretary denied there was a risk of community spread, and that they had the necessary testing kits and personal protective equipment on hand. When asked if the St. Patrick's Day Parade would be canceled, Walsh rejected the idea, saying: *"No. We're not there yet. ... Massachusetts is home to world-renowned hospitals and leading health care experts that are planning and preparing our communities. The general public in Massachusetts remains at low risk."*

- After the news conference ended, the governor and his family headed to the airport to begin a scheduled six-day vacation in Park City, Utah.

-

08 March 2020 –

- Biden mentioned the circular firing squad, one form of which is Democrats attacking Democrats rather than both focusing on why they would be the best nominee to take on Trump. We have Sanders' comments on the problems in Biden's record. Yet, in an 8 March interview, Senator Sanders stated: *"I believe Joe can beat Trump, and if Joe is the candidate I'll do everything I can to make sure that he does."* One might wonder if Bernie didn't effectively endorse Joe and concede the nomination.

- Donald Trump Jr. Says: *"You know what will be great, I'll let you host it. You moderate a debate between Hunter Biden and myself."* Basically, Don Jr. threw down a gauntlet that is never picked up, because of the reality the Bidens are trying to dodge: *"Hunter Biden, his father becomes VP. All of a sudden he goes over to Ukraine and he's making 83 grand a month."*

- On NBC, Dr. Anthony Fauci says there should be 400,000 more kits available tomorrow, and 4 million within five days; he warns of the need for greater "social distancing." The U.S. has 500 cases and 22 deaths.

- It's observed that Senator Warren has "broken character" and that "inconsistency" will cost her the nomination. It is also observed that Biden and Sanders remain true to character – their gestures, quirks, flaws, and strengths, are all familiar to their base demographic which recognizes their basic brands.

- Civil rights activist Jesse Jackson endorses Sanders.

- Iran records almost 6,000 Covid-19 infections with 145 dead; Italian deaths exceed 230; WHO reports 105,500 cases with nearly 3,600 deaths; Saudi Arabia places the governorate of Qatif in the oil-producing Eastern Province into lockdown.

-

09 March 2020 –

- Joe Biden and Bernie Sanders issued a joint statement saying they were consulting public health experts about coronavirus risks so they could plan changes to their campaign strategy in response to election officials in primary states considering early voting.

- In a 1:27 PM tweet, Bernie Sanders says: *"Joe Biden thinks we should 'return to normal.' / Normal means 87 million uninsured or under-insured. / Normal means fossil fuel companies destroying the planet. / Normal means the rich getting richer while the poor get poorer. / We cannot return to normal. We need real change."*

- World Health Organization (WHO) Director-General Tedros Adhanom Ghebreyesus concedes the threat of a coronavirus pandemic *'very real'*, but it is also *'first pandemic in history that could be controlled.'*

- As oil prices dropped and Covid-19 concerns increased, the Financial Markets slid downward raising concerns among the generation of older Americans who rely on those markets for their pensions. TDS groups translate this into a concern for money over life and attack Trump's policies because they are aimed at a quick economic recovery.

- Massachusetts Governor Baker returns early from Utah, as Mayor Walsh announces he is reversing his earlier decision and was canceling the St. Patrick's Day Parade.

-

10 March 2020 –

- Joe Biden becomes the presumptive Democratic nominee. And warns, "*our very democracy is at stake in this election.*"

- Biden retreats to recreation room-turned-broadcast center, where he stays until May 26, when he emerged to attend a Memorial Day service, his lead over Trump increased by not being visible – though cringe-worthy gaffes continued. Only two people a day actually have contact with Biden (former Virginia Gov. Terry McAuliffe would assert in June).

-

11 March 2020 –

- Trump Restricts Travel From Europe saying: The EU "*failed to take the same precautions [as the U.S.] and restrict travel from China and other hotspots. As a result, a large number of new clusters in the United States were seeded by travelers from Europe."*

- The national security asserts China 'covered up' coronavirus, and Secretary of State Mike Pompeo tells CNBC China had put the U.S. "behind the curve" in responding to the virus.

- China declared its virus peak had passed and new cases in Hubei fell to single digits for the first time. National Health Commission spokesman Mi Feng states: *"Broadly speaking, the peak of the epidemic has passed for China. The increase of new cases is falling."* The Chinese senior medical adviser, Zhong Nanshan, says: *"My advice is calling for all countries to follow WHO instructions and intervene on a national scale. If all countries could get mobilized, **it could be over by June.**"*

- Sen. Lamar Alexander (R-Tenn.) blocked quick passage of a Senate Democrat legislation intended to require employers to provide 14 days paid sick leave in a public health emergency.

- The World Health Organization declared the coronavirus a pandemic and urged aggressive action from all countries to fight and the DJIA falls 1,464 points of 4,000 over a two day period. And WHO identifies Iran and Italy as the focus.

- Seattle Officials announced public schools are closed; large gatherings were banned in San Francisco and Washington state, the hardest-hit U.S. state, with 29 deaths.

- A Twitter post identifies interesting timeline facts: Donald Trump has been in government for 3 years; Joe Biden has been in government for 44 years; Nancy Pelosi has 33 years; Bernie Sanders has 29 years, yet they blame Trump because the pandemic infrastructure they built isn't strong enough.

- Massachusetts has 95 confirmed cases of the virus – 77 were tied to the Biogen conference.

-

12 March 2020 –

- Biden acknowledges need for action but says: *"neither should we panic or fall back on xenophobia, labeling COVID-19 a foreign virus does not displace accountability for the misjudgments that have been taken thus far by the Trump administration."* However, he fails to specify just what those *"misjudgments"* were.

- In another release, Biden declares his approach would be to rely more heavily on global alliances and listening more closely to the recommendations of scientists, saying from the shelter of his basement: *"This administration has left us woefully unprepared for the exact crisis we now face."*

- (Friday the Thirteenth in Asia) Asian stocks go into freefall and markets punch through downward-limit circuit breakers. The Chief Asia Market Strategist for J.P. Morgan, Tai Hui, states: *"Government bureaucracy simply has not kept pace with the nature of the outbreak and market expectations. We need to see the number of new infections stabilize ... we also need to see fiscal and monetary policy support implementation. Hence, we are not looking at a specific time or valuation to advise investors to add back equities."*

- Mitch McConnell describes the House approach to COVID-19: *"One is reminded of the famous comment from President Obama's first chief of staff: 'You never want a serious crisis to go to waste'."*

- Trump Executive Order designed to end a reliance on foreign supply chains. Issues: 1. 90 percent of all U.S. antibiotics were manufactured in China. 2: China has prevented the export of surgical face masks, severely limiting supplies in the U.S. and countries around the world. 3: Navarro tells the NYTimes: *"China has managed to dominate all aspects of the supply chain using the same unfair trade practices that it has used to dominate other sectors – cheap sweatshop labor, lax environmental regulations, and massive government subsidies. As President Trump has said, what we need to do is bring those jobs home so that we can protect the public health and the economic and national security of the country."*

- Media details the claim that *"Joe Biden Plagiarizes President Trump's Coronavirus Plan."* Politico and other fact-checking groups had previously documented Biden plagiarized paper in law school and was almost expelled for unethical behavior. He also has a record of claiming to be on the size of a winning position when the historic record establishes he opposed it.

-

13 March 2020 –

- – Trump declares National Emergency mentioned above.

- Chinese government data obtained/reported by Hong Kong's South China Morning Post states the first case of someone in China suffering from the novel coronavirus, Covid-19, can be traced back to 17 November 2019.

- Statistical models to projecting extent of COVID-19 casualties suggest more than a million Americans could die if the nation does not take mitigation action to halt its spread as quickly as possible. It is projected that, over a one-year period, between 160 million and 210 million Americans could be infected with between 200,000 and 1.7 million fatalities.

- Globally, projections indicated between 20 percent and 60 percent of the global population could be infected.

- Letter objecting to records investigation of the Bidens is sent by Records Representative to President Obama, Anita Decker Breckenridge. (Note, Biden claimed Obama had approved the Ukraine extortion when he bragged about it in C-SPAN.)

- Rep. Tulsi Gabbard, introduced a resolution to provide an income of $1,000 per month *"until COVID-19 no longer presents a public health emergency."*

- Candidate Joe Biden uses video manipulation to distort and misrepresent Trump's COVID-19 statements. In defending the misrepresentation, Biden's campaign spokesman, Andrew Bates, says: *"Donald Trump is the most dishonest president in American history and one of the least credible human beings in the world. We don't trust his next-day cleanup attempt, and he has made many comments in that same vein. And the claim that the American Dream was 'dead' in the final year of the Obama administration – during the longest streak of job growth in American history – is categorically untrue and another reminder of Donald Trump's deep cynicism."*

-

14 March 2020 –

- House passes bill to prop up the economy from coronavirus in a 363-40 vote. At a late-night Friday press conference in the Capitol, Nancy Pelosi states: *"We could have passed our bill yesterday. But we thought it was important to assure the American people that we are willing and able to work together to get a job done for them."*

- The current population of Spain is 46,754,778 as of Saturday, March 14, 2020. This is the equivalent to 0.6% of the world population; it is 30 on the list of countries by population; the population density is 94 per Km2 (243 people per mi2); total land area is 498,800 Km2 (192,588 sq. miles); 80.3 % of the population is urban (37,543,537 people in 2020); the median age in Spain is 44.9 years; Spain 6,391 cases 196 deaths Spain 2020-03-14. By July, it is recognized the Latin and African populations are at higher risk – with the possible implication of a genetic or blood type correlation.

-

15 March 2020 –

- The CDC recommends no gatherings of 50 or more people in the U.S. for the next eight weeks (until after 10 May). But Trump adds additional caution and advised citizens to avoid groups of more than 10 (a Hebrew minyan).

- Treasury Secretary Steven Mnuchin: "*What I'd focus on is what do we need to do right now because it's clear we need to get economic relief to the economy right now. If the medical professionals are correct and we're doing all the things, I expect we'll have a big rebound later in the year.*"

- Oil prices go below $30 a barrel, sparking additional fears the government disease lockdowns for disease mitigation would trigger a global recession.

- Governor Baker joined other governors in announcing that all schools would be closed for three weeks, and limits visitor access to assisted living facilities and hospitals; he also bans elective surgeries. Responding to photos showing throngs of rowdy patrons outside Boston pubs in advance of St. Patrick's Day, Baker orders the state's restaurants and bars shutdown for everything except takeout, starting 17 March.

-

16 March 2020 –

- – Trump Issues National Guidelines to slow the spread

- Latin America feels the effects of the virus. A nationwide quarantine is announced in Venezuela for March 17. Ecuador and Peru implement countrywide lockdowns; Colombia and Costa Rica closed their borders.

- Brazil's president, Jair Bolsonaro, encourages supporters to engage in mass demonstrations against his opponents in Congress.

- French government orders a lockdown on 16 March – their first "official case had been 24 January. In May a delayed test revealed a *"patient infected with Covid-19 one month before the first reported cases in our country"* whose *"lack of recent travel suggests that the disease was already spreading among the French population at the end of December 2019."* This infers the disease might have reached New York.

- Canada shuts borders to foreign nationals who are not either permanent residents or U.S. citizens.

- Social distancing triggers human sensitivity to changes in the social norms; some find the suddenly change confusing and find it difficult to accept the open-endedness of sudden the change in routine imposed by lockdowns. For some, there is selfish altruism which invokes positive feelings in response to acts of generosity.

- The increased use of Amazon triggers the hiring of 100,000 new employees with a pay raise from $15 to $17/hour. Their operations VP, Dave Clark, said: *"We are seeing a significant increase in demand, which means our labor needs are unprecedented for this time of year."*

- Doctors in Australia report there are 'unacceptable' shortages of protective equipment.

- Globally, 174,100 cases and 6,700 deaths are attributed to the Covid-19; in the U.S. 71 had died, with over 4,100 infected. Italy's financial capital Milan recorded 1,218 deaths.

- Nationally, responses and guidance related to Covid-19 vary chaotically; the mayor of Philadelphia, Jim Kenney, is saying: *"I would recommend you wash your hands, you stay out from within three feet of people, and go out and have dinner – and tip your waitstaff because they're struggling right now."* The recommended social distancing norm is six feet, and in the midst of conflicting messages, Trump sees the opportunity for harmony and tweets: *"Everybody is so well unified and working so hard. It is a beautiful thing to see. They love our great Country. We will end up being stronger than ever before!"*

- An observation is reported: *'The coronavirus highlights the awful paradox that makes global warming heating feel so inevitable.'* {Jeff Sparrow, Guardian Australia columnist}

-

17 March 2020 – 21st day of Lent

- France imposes a nationwide lockdown.

- The EU bars most travelers from outside the bloc for 30 days.

- MUFG Union Bank Chief financial economist, Chris Rupkey, warns: *"If the public stops spending, then the economy will go into a recession, and frankly, the market's steep losses are saying that day isn't just coming, it is now."* Economic analysts concur and advise: *"Italy will be Europe's canary in the coal-mine for the post-Covid economy."*

- Senate Majority Leader Mitch McConnell rejects the idea of remote voting that, on 13 May, would be proposed as House Resolution 965. Republican minority leaders: *"Democrats are jamming through a rules change that would upend 200 years of precedent and have serious constitutional and institutional repercussions."*

- Article I, Section 5 of the Constitution requires a quorum be present – traditionally this has been taken to mean 218 out of 435 members must be physically present and only their votes count. Speaker Nancy Pelosi is, therefore, subverting the Constitution via a "rule change" when it must be done via a Constitutional Amendment.

- A Coronavirus stimulus package is being proposed.

- As one component in the trillion dollars stimulus program, President Trump asked Congress to speed emergency checks to Americans. Secretary Mnuchin states: *"We're looking at sending checks to Americans immediately... Americans need cash now and the President wants to get cash now, and I mean now, in the next two weeks."*

-

18 March 2020 –

- – Trump Invokes the Defense Production Act

- – Trump signs the Families First Response Act

- Michigan state Rep. Karen Whitsett test positive for COVID-19 (see 31 March) [and her husband is believed the source].

- Bonds plunge as currency markets collapse – only the Dollar and Euro hold their own and gain. The problem is attributed to the impact on demand and the disruption of global supply chain.

- Objection to Trump calling Covid-19 – which everyone knows originated in Wuhan China – a Chinese virus reveals the emergence of a counter-racist racism in which racism is used to attack accurate terminology. A few months later, a further example emerges with BLM when Vice President Pence uses the term "ALL Lives Matter" – and it is deemed racist because it dose not diminish the importance of Europeans, Asians, or Native Americans, while exalting the importance of those with an African heritage. Effectively, an era of "Black Privilege" is emerging in which being Black provides advanced placement and benefits. The Orwellian principle of reversal of meaning manifests itself in yet another form.

-

19 March 2020 –

- Vaccine Trials Start

- For the first time, China reports zero local infections.

- California lockdown begins when Governor Gavin Newsom, issues statewide 'stay at home' order over based on modeling that projects 56 percent of California residents could contract COVID-19 over an eight week period ending around the 15th of May. Two weeks earlier, House Speaker Nancy Pelosi was ignoring the pandemic to promote San Francisco tourism and social gatherings. Had she been successful, it could have caused a major epicenter to appear in California.

- 1/ Hydroxychloroquine is referenced at a White House briefing; Trump says: "*Now, a drug called chloroquine, and some people would add to it, hydroxychloroquine, so chloroquine or hydroxychloroquine ... [has] shown very encouraging, very, very encouraging early results. ... we're going to be able to make that drug available almost immediately.*"

- 2/ Thereafter the media attacks him for "playing doctor" and for several months, failed usage of Malaria drug is touted as evidence he was wrong. However, around 1 July the media reports "*Researchers at the Henry Ford Health System in Southeast Michigan have found that early administration of the drug hydroxychloroquine makes hospitalized patients substantially less likely to die."*

- 3/ The same "failures" the media harped on – underlying conditions that are already deemed potentially fatal – are the cited criteria for excluding patients from the treatment, or altering related treatments.

- 4/ Upon the release of the peer-reviewed findings, the White House says: *"Fortunately, the Trump Administration secured a massive supply of hydroxychloroquine for the national stockpile months ago."*

- 5/ *"Yet this is the same drug that the media and the Biden campaign spent weeks trying to discredit and spread fear and doubt around because President Trump dared to mention it as a potential treatment for coronavirus. The new study from the Henry Ford Health System should be a clear message to the media and the Democrats: stop the bizarre attempts to discredit hydroxychloroquine to satisfy your own anti-Trump agenda. It may be costing lives."*

-

20 March 2020 – Vernal Equinox – the Persian New Year

- Two months after President Trump orders China Travel Ban, 19 days after the first confirmed NY case, New York Governor Andrew Cuomo issues a statewide lockdown order; on 5 May, experts say the delay was responsible for 60-65% of the virus cases in the USA.

- New York Mayor Bill de Blasio unveils a special pandemic response team to coordinate relief efforts and finally labels coronavirus *"an unprecedented threat"* requiring a wartime mentality.

-

21 March 2020 – Persia Nauryz 'new day'

- Hawaii orders a first of its kind mandatory 14-day quarantine of arriving visitors and residents.

- Canada and the U.S. agreed to keep the border between the two countries closed to all but essential travel, on 20 May the restrictions are extended until June 21.

-

22 March 2020 –

- – Trump Funds National Guard Deployments for States that ask for assistance (which is consistent with Obama Pandemic Playbook).
- Prime Minister Boris Johnson orders lockdown that closed all nonessential shops, barred meetings of more than two people, and required all people to stay in their homes except for trips for food or medicine locks Britain down.
- Massachusetts has its first confirmed Covid-19 death – a man in his 80s.
-

24 March 2020 –

- The CDC instructs medical staff to report deaths as COVID-19 deaths even when no test has confirmed the presence of the disease. This requirement {*"COVID-19 should be reported on the death certificate for all decedents where the disease caused or is assumed to have caused or contributed to death."*} effectively increases the COVID-19 mortality rate, while decreasing 'normal' causality related to other deaths during the winter months.
- The Tokyo Olympics delayed until 2021. Previously, the 1916 Summer Olympics were canceled by World War I; 1940 and 1944 saw cancellation of the Summer and Winter Games due to World War II.
- India announces a 21-day lockdown affecting country's 1.3 billion; all domestic flights are halted – 500 reported cases in India.
- Massachusetts state order shuttering nonessential businesses
- State advisory for people to stay home was still weeks away.
-

25 March 2020 –

- British researchers begin gathering genetic data to determine if there is a genetic commonality among Covid-19 victims. In a research paper pre-published on 22 April, states: *"Here we report that 50% of the variance of 'predicted covid-19' phenotype is due to genetic factors. The current prevalence of 'predicted covid-19' is 2.9% of the population."* {Available online as: 2020.04.22.20072124v2.full.pdf with subsequent posting, of report on 26 May, by AAAS magazine SCIENCE}

-

26 March 2020 –

- – On Fox News' "Hannity", Trump mentions: "*I had Biden calling me xenophobic. He called me a racist, because of the fact that he felt it was a racist thing to stop people from China coming in.*"

- The United States leads the world in confirmed coronavirus cases – at least 81,321 confirmed infections and more than 1,000 deaths.

-

27 March 2020 –

- – USNS MERCY arrives in California

- – Trump signs $2.2 Trillion Economic Relief

- Prime Minister Boris announces he's infected with the virus.

- NY Governor Cuomo criticized those objecting to the urging people not to travel upstate from NY City after NYS Health Commissioner Howard Zucker, said a 14-day quarantine or travel ban on metropolitan area residents was medically unnecessary. (By May, NYC will be blamed for about 65% of the national coronavirus cases.)

-

28 March 2020 –

- Trump sends USNS COMFORT to New York

- Virginia, Maryland, and Washington, D.C., joined those who issued orders requiring their residents to stay home – 265 million Americans were being urged to stay home.

-

31 March 2020 –

- Karen Whitsett begins taking hydroxychloroquine her doctor prescribed. (See 6 April)

01 April 2020 –

- Kellyanne Conway notes that Biden is hiding "*in his bunker*" in Wilmington, Delaware.

-

02 April 2020 –

- Global cases top one million, and millions lose their jobs.

- Governor Baker spoke inside a Logan Airport hangar after the New England Patriots jet brought in a massive shipment of masks from China.

-

05 April 2020 – Holy Week begins – Palm Sunday

- In April, French Microbiologist Didier Raoult published the paper that led Trump to recommend hydroxychloroquine, an antimalarial drug (used in conjunction with azithromycin, a common antibiotic); early detection applications the two well known and approved drugs are 91.7% effective. It was also noted that there was a level of virus concentration where the treatment was ineffective.

- Prior to the Raoult paper publication, Trump states the drug is *"being tested now"* and that *"there are some very strong, powerful signs"* it works. He adds *"But what do I know? I'm not a doctor,"* adding, *"If it does work, it would be a shame we did not do it early."* He then added that 29 million pills had been purchased and stockpiled, and *"We are sending them to various labs, our military, we're sending them to the hospitals."*

- Trump's *"being tested now"* reference seems to have been to Dr. Raoult's study conducted between 3 March and 9 April, and an abstract of the results for the 1061 test subjects was published online: *"A good clinical outcome and virological cure was obtained in 973 patients within 10 days (91.7%)."* It was noted that: *"Poor clinical outcome was significantly associated to older age (OR 1.11), initial higher severity (OR 10.05) and low hydroxychloroquine serum concentration. In addition, both poor clinical and virological outcomes were associated to the use of selective beta-blocking agents and angiotensin II receptor blockers (P<0.05)."* Indicating age and blood pressure medication affects the treatment.

- The media immediately attacked Trump and denounced the hydroxychloroquine treatment as having detrimental effects – on 30 April, Dr. Raoult rebuked their irrationality, pointing out the assertion a drug that has been safely used for 80-years was suddenly declared dangerous. Citing America: *"L'hydroxychloroquine est le traitement de référence pour les pneumopathies {nfections du système respiratoire}, se permet-il de rappeler. Un Américain sur huit en prend une fois par an !"* [TRANSLATION: *"Hydroxychloroquine is the standard treatment for pneumonitis {respiratory system infections}. One in eight Americans takes it once a year!"*]

•

06 April 2020 –

•   Austrian economics news and opinion service, Mises Institute *Mises Wire*, published an article by Ryan McMaken which compared historic death rates with those during the COVID-19 period, in which they quoted, UK National Health Service pathologist John Lee: *"The simplest way to judge whether we have an exceptionally lethal disease is to look at the death rates. Are more people dying than we would expect to die anyway in a given week or month?"*

•   The story mentioned findings for several countries and stated that, in the United States, *"for March, the increase in total deaths is about equal to what we already saw as a pre-COVID increase from March 2018 to March 2019."*

•   Lee also noted the way COVID-19 was being reported was such that it could distort the figures: *"Making Covid-19 notifiable might give the appearance of it causing increasing numbers of deaths, whether this is true or not. It might appear far more of a killer than flu, simply because of the way deaths are recorded."*

•   A related analytical article, *"This Is Strange: Total US Deaths in March 2020 are Actually Down 15% from Average of Prior Four Years"*, looked at the CDC's National Center for Health Statistics Mortality Surveillance System website data, which revealed the total U.S. deaths for the first three weeks of March were DOWN 10% from the average of the prior four years for the same three week period.

•   Prime Minister Boris Johnson moved into intensive care.

•   Karen Whitsett credits hydroxychloroquine and Trump for "curing" her coronavirus infection and saving. According to Whitsett, "It was less than two hours" for relief from sinus infection, shortness of breath, and swollen lymph nodes to set in.

•

08 April 2020 – Passover begins in the evening

- Companies plan and start vaccine trials.

- Passover marks the "shelter-in-place" which Moses ordered be done by the Egyptian Hebrews to avoid a disease that was 'passing over' and claiming the firstborn sons. In coincidental analogous thought, the Covid-19 claimed mostly elderly males (logically earliest or firstborn of a family) and then the Omar comes into play in a manner that invokes what Congress called a "Stimulus Package." {Historians have connected the Passover legend to the Nile turning red and the custom of the eldest sone being given clams for the Egyptian holiday that fits the time frame. We would know it as the Red Tide bio-organism that periodically contaminates clam beds.}

-

09 April 2020 – PASSOVER

- The Omer Count began on Thursday Night, 9 April 2020 – It was counted every evening after nightfall, from the second night of Passover till the night before Shavuot {day 50}.

- The Omar ritual of the calendar count is derived from Torah, Leviticus 23:15: *"You shall count for yourselves from the day following the day of rest, from the day on which you bring the Omer as a wave-offering; [the counting] shall be for seven full weeks. Until the day following the seventh week shall you count fifty days."* {Lockdown to reopen period.}

- Leviticus 23:22: *"When you reap the harvest of your land, do not reap to the very edges of your field or gather the gleanings of your harvest. Leave them for the poor and for the foreigner residing among you."* {Stimulus Package}

-

10 April 2020 – 01 Days in the Omer – Good Friday

- Coronavirus cases surge in Russia. Two-thirds of country's 12,000 reported cases are in Moscow

- Global deaths surpass 101,000.

-

12 April 2020 – 03 Days in the Omer – Easter Sunday

- Boris Johnson is released from the hospital.

-

13 April 2020 – 04 Days in the Omer

- Some European nations begin easing restrictions.

-

14 April 2020 – 05 Days in the Omer

- The International Monetary Fund warned that the global economy was headed for its worst downturn since the Great Depression.

-

15 April 2020 – 06 Days in the Omer

- Citing a disagreement over lockdown measures, Brazilian President Jair Bolsonaro fired his health minister. Brazil is the largest country in Latin or South America.

- Kim Jong Un fails to appear at the birthday celebration of his late grandfather, state founder Kim Il Sung – North Korea's most important holiday – raising concerns about his health, since he hadn't been seen for four days; there was speculation he died after heart surgery.

-

16 April 2020 – 07 Days in the Omer

- President Trump encourages protests against some state restrictions.

-

17 April 2020 – 08 Days of Omer

- At a White House press briefing on Coronavirus Task Force, President Trump is asked about $3.7 million in funding to Wuhan laboratory by Obama under direction of Dr. Fauci for experimentation into what is now the Covid-19. This transfer of funds was to circumvent a 2014 moratorium on such testing in the United States.

- Reports included the 11 January 2017 statement by Fauci that the administration would experience a *"surprise outbreak"* – In a speech at Georgetown University, Fauci said that *"There is no question that there will be a challenge to the coming administration in the arena of infectious diseases. The thing we're extraordinarily confident about is that we're going to see this in the next few years."*

-

18 April 2020 – 09 Days in the Omer

- There are 42 states with "stay-at-home" orders; on 27 May, a research paper establishes the orders resulted in significant reductions in cases against the projected rates as confirmed by states that did not issue the orders.

-

19 April 2020 – 10 Days in the Omer

- Chile issues 'immunity cards' to people who have recovered from the virus.

-

20 April 2020 – 11 Days in the Omer

- Trump administration responds to an 18 April a letter from Rep. Grace Meng which said, *"Family members of nursing home residents have a right to know this information,"* it was determined that family members of nursing residents should be swiftly notified of any COVID-19 cases.

- President Trump announces a suspension of immigration.

-

21 April 2020 – 12 Days in the Omer

- Officials discover earlier known U.S. coronavirus deaths in Santa Clara County, California – two residents who died on 6 and 17 February.

- Trump announces he will direct USNS Comfort Hospital Ship to leave New York and return Norfolk, Virginia – it departs around 27 April.

-

22 April 2020 – 13 Days in the Omer

- Trump Executive Order: 60-day temporary suspension of United States immigration for new Green Card applicants.

- Over 47,000 Americans have died with 830,000 infected.

- It is reported that a February survey by Chinese doctors had examined samples from 213 patients and suggested the tests returned or had a false-negative rate of 30%.

-

23 April 2020 – 14 Days in the Omer

- – Pelosi requires an in-person vote on a rule change enabling proxy voting during the pandemic – the vote on proxy voting to be done when they assemble in person to vote on the new relief bill. Her senior aide stated: *"Bottom line here is that the speaker wants a bipartisan solution."* But the real effect was to create a means of delaying – as Daniel Schuman, policy director of Demand Progress, put it: *"Speaker Pelosi should have figured this out months ago. Pushing forward on a select committee that cannot meet and a task force that will require the House to reconvene to implement its recommendations is a recipe for continued delays in getting the House, and its committees, back to work."*

- U.N. Secretary-General Antonio Guterres warned that the COVID-19 outbreak risks becoming a human rights crisis in some countries might use it as an excuse to adopt repressive measures unrelated to the pandemic. He stated that: *"We see the disproportionate effects on certain communities, the rise of hate speech, the targeting of vulnerable groups, and the risks of heavy-handed security responses undermining the health response. Against the background of rising ethno-nationalism, populism, authoritarianism, and a pushback against human rights in some countries, the crisis can provide a pretext to adopt repressive measures for purposes unrelated to the pandemic. ... In all we do, let's never forget: The threat is the virus, not people."*

- In response to comments made by Dr. Bryan, Trump mused about a Covid-19 [medical] "disinfectant" that could be used ion or inside the body

- Pelosi creates controversy when she misrepresents Trump's statement and claims he said to inject Lysol.

-

24 April 2020 – 15 Days in the Omer

- The Guardian, a British newspaper, reports on a leaked *2019 National Security Risk Assessment* which details the threat of *"an influenza-type disease pandemic, predicts waves of a novel flu virus striking several months apart."* And warns *"Sustained human-to-human transmission in emerging airborne diseases is possible, which is why infection control procedures are critical to the mitigation of this risk."* When the document is reported, the United Kingdom has 149,569 cases and 20,381 deaths. There is no way to determine how many less there would have been if the warning were headed.

- House Speaker Nancy Pelosi falsely claimed that President Donald Trump told people to *"inject Lysol into your lungs"* social media followed-up with assertions Trump had said Lysol and Clorox should be injected or taken internally. She can justify her falsehood because Trump said disinfectant – meaning to remove an infection – when medical experts were seeking money to find research to find a treatment that could kill any virus as soon as it enters the body (a medically sound virus disinfectant), in contrast to a vaccine that would stop a specific virus.

- After Northeastern University researchers determine that NY had, prior to 1 March, over 10,000 virus cases with origins in Europe (probably Italy), Governor Andrew Cuomo blames Trump for not imposing European Travel Ban earlier – at a news briefing, Cuomo said: *"We closed the front door with the China travel ban, which was right. But we left the back door open because the virus had left China by the time we did the China travel ban."*

-

26 April 2020 – 17 Days in the Omer

- Tom Inglesby, director of Johns Hopkins Center for Health Security, says the U.S. was at the *"end of the beginning"* of the pandemic but it was overly optimistic to predict an end-stage by Memorial Day. His reference was a Pence statement on 23 April: *"by Memorial Day Weekend we will largely have this coronavirus epidemic behind us."*

- USA TODAY reports that, prior to COVID-19, a third of all death certificates cited the wrong cause of death: *"Inaccurate death reporting is a longstanding problem noted by numerous researchers in study after study."* Bob Anderson, chief of the mortality statistics branch at the National Center for Health Statistics stated: *"For example, cardiac arrest is not an acceptable cause of death, because everybody dies of cardiac arrest. That just means your heart stopped."*

-

27 April 2020 – 18 Days in the Omer

- In an interview on CNNSOTU, Nancy Pelosi says Americans and Green Card holds should not have been allowed to return from China after the 31 January travel ban.

- An interview with Dr. Deborah Birx follows Pelosi and Brix points out the seriousness of America's dependence on China and other nations for basic and critical health care supplies. Asked about Trumps's UV light or injection, she pointed out it was not as a treatment, but rather as a dialogue with the doctors. She chastised host Jake Tapper for not focusing on meaningful data and discussions related to differences in demographics between the US and Europe – such as the fact an average American is 8-years younger than their European counterparts.

- In the United Kingdom (UK), researchers rely on a study of twins to affirm that genetic factors explain 50% of differences between people's Covid-19 symptoms. One of the scientists, Prof Tim Spector, explained: *"The idea was to basically look at the similarities in symptoms or non-symptoms between the identical twins, who share 100% of their genes, and the non-identical twins, who only share half of their genes. If there is a genetic factor in expressing the symptoms then we'd see a greater similarity in the identical [twins] than the non-identical [twins] and that is basically what we showed."*

- The NYS Board of Electors cancels the primary election.

- CNN "AC360" Host Anderson Cooper [a homosexual] has a son via a surrogate; he is noted for routine attacks on Trump.

-

28 April 2020 – 19 Days in the Omer

- Coronavirus: Globally 3 million with 214,000 dead; America 1 million with 57,270 dead. One-third of cases with a quarter of the deaths. The cause of the discrepancy could be due to several possibilities: synchronization lag time; more testing, or better medical care, or healthier population in the U.S.A.; the true global numbers are misreported.

- American Dead attributed to COVID-19 now exceed Vietnam War-related deaths. But it's not "official" in terms of the CDC reported tally of 1 May.

- Hillary Clinton endorses Joe Biden, claiming that *"this is a moment where we need a leader, a president, like Joe Biden."* Trump's campaign manager responded that *"There is no greater concentration of Democrat establishment than Joe*

Biden and Hillary Clinton together. President Trump beat her once and now he'll beat her chosen candidate."

- New York Board of Elections cancels Democratic presidential primary. Elections officials said it cost more than $300,000 for a medium-sized county to hold a primary, plus the cost of sending pre-stamped absentee ballot applications to voters. [The NY Republican primary was called off in February when no other candidates besides Trump qualified for the ballot.]

- In a 28 April tweet, Rudy Giuliani commented on Hillary encoding joe: *"I'm sure Hillary "Women's Rights" Clinton was not concerned about the corroborated sexual assault allegation from a woman against Joe Biden. "For her, it must have brought back fond memories of her covering for Bubba. It's good Biden recognized her."*

-

29 April 2020 – 20 Days in the Omer

- Coronavirus gender gap observation and investigation is first reported – fewer women than men die; it is believed estrogen hampers the progression of the disease.

-

30 April 2020 – 21 Days in the Omer

- CNN's "New Day," Pelosi said she was 'satisfied' with how Biden has responded to sexual assault allegation brought by Tara Reade and then asserted the politically correct:

  "I have great sympathy for any women who bring forth an allegation. I'm a big strong supporter of the 'Me Too' movement. I think it's been a great contribution to our country. And I do support Joe Biden. I'm satisfied with how he has responded. I know him. I was proud to endorse him on Monday. He's the personification of hope and optimism for our country, and I was proud to endorse him. America needs a person like Joe Biden with his integrity and his vision for the future."

- Maryland Governor Larry Hogan says the state's National Guard was watching the 500,000 COVID-19 test kits his state bought from South Korea – to ensure Federal authorities did not take them. He told a HuffPost reporter, *"This was an extraordinarily valuable payload. It was like Fort Knox to us, because it's gonna save the lives of thousands of our citizens."*

- Reopening of economy is scheduled to begin in May. Report on economic activity for April will show retail sales fell 16.4% on top of the 8.3% drop for March – the largest two-month decline on record; J. Crew, Neiman Marcus, and J.C. Penney file for bankruptcy.

-

01 May 2020 – 22 Days in the Omer

- Planned Parenthood's president released a statement: *"we believe survivors – and saying we believe survivors doesn't mean only when it's politically convenient."* Effectively they came out against Biden and for Tara Reade.

- Business Insider reports: *"The campaign of Democratic presidential nominee Joe Biden has repeatedly insisted that journalists "rigorously vet" the claims of former Biden staffer Tara Reade, who says she was sexually harassed while working in Biden's Senate office and sexually assaulted by Biden himself in 1993. But Biden is refusing to allow public access to his senatorial archives, even though it may contain records that could shed light on Reade's accusations — and even as his own campaign operatives have themselves accessed the papers in the past year."*

- Biden's campaign managers are struggling with ways to get the 77-year-old candidate safely out of his basement and back on the campaign trail. At the same time, Trump was telling reporters he was less concerned with the campaign and more concerned with *"protecting the health and well being of the American people."*

- Biden's people seemed to take a shot at their own candidate, saying: *"People aren't just sitting in their basements. They're grocery shopping, they're going to get coffee, they're taking walks around the block. ... There are optics that could be done better."*

- House Speaker Pelosi claimed state and local governments are seeking up to $1 trillion for coronavirus costs – money for "heroes" is needed to prevent layoffs as governors or mayors stare down red ink in their budgets.

- Texas reopens, relaxing social distancing guidelines amid the coronavirus pandemic.

- 5.4-magnitude earthquake near the southern Puerto Rico city of Ponce, where it briefly knocked out power and resulted in structural damage.

- CDC official tally of deaths: 37,308 COVID-19; 719,438 dead from all causes; 97 expected deaths; 64,382 pneumonia dead; 16,564 pneumonia+COVID-19; 5,846 influenza dead; 90,165 deaths from pneumonia, influenza or COVID-19. As bad as the COVID-19 might be made to seem, pneumonia is worse.

-

02 May 2020 – 23 Days in the Omer

- NY Governor Andrew Cuomo labels demands to reopen state premature.

-

04 May 2020 – 25 Days in the Omer

- Despite effects of the coronavirus pandemic, Most American 51 percent of voters approve of President Trump's handling of the U.S. economy; 46 percent of those polled disapproved.

- European Traders responded to U.S. criticism of China, by scrambling to sell European stocks, so market opened down.

- The DJIA bounced around a bit but closed flat, and U.S. crude dropped 6% to $18.60 per barrel, and Brent crude dropped 1% to $26.19.

- U.S. held preliminary discussions to punish China for its role in the virus outbreak and the possibility of the U.S. canceling its debt obligations with China was raised, even while saying the full faith and credit of US debt obligations is 'sacrosanct' – inferring China would be sued for damages and its debt is a way any penalty would be "paid" or reimbursement made.

- Media reports: "Scientists have identified an antibody in a lab that they say can prevent the novel coronavirus from infecting cells." The research was published in the journal *Nature Communications*; the antibody is named 47D11.

- Medical researchers begin to search for the earliest victims of COVID-19 – earliest known death from Covid-19 in the U.S. occurred 6 February in Santa Clara County, California. It had been believed the earliest was on 26 February in Seattle.

- Coronavirus-related factory shutdowns in China, India, and other nations that had benefitted from outsourcing threaten a ripple effect on the availability of various important items – supply chain issues, result in empty store shelves and out-of-stock items on major retailers' websites. Items included are Laptops, iPhones, LCD Televisions, Computer Monitors, Video Game Consoles, Medical Supplies, Pharmaceuticals, Thermometers, Disinfectants, Hand Sanitizer, Toilet Paper, Toys, and even foods like Garlic or Freezers to store food in. The COVID-19 has exposed the realities of outsourcing and the dependence of a global economy in which various third world or developing nations became critical for survival.

●

05 May 2020 – 26 Days in the Omer

● Texas records the highest single day COVID-19 death rate while governor stated Texas has maximized testing capacity to conduct 15,000 to 20,000 tests a day, of the stated near-term goal of 30,000 per day.

● New York and New Jersey account for 446,725 of the known cases; Texas accounts for 32,810.

● Consistent with their ongoing anti-trump propaganda cover for Biden, CNN presents a timeline for the virus that ignored key facts and connections but properly utilized the delights of lawyer's lies. One such action is to detail TRUMP actions then interject that Hollywood Star Tom Hanks and his wife contracted Coronavirus in that period.

● What forms the "lawyer's lie" is the inferred link to Trump's COVID-19 actions, when the facts they conceal include Hanks and his wife being on location in Australia when they contracted the virus; nothing Trump's administration was doing was relevant to the Hanks' contracting the disease or recovering from it while guaranteed in Australia.

● A hospital near Paris reports performing test of sample from a pneumonia patient (taken 27 December) tests positive and shows the virus spread farther, faster than previously known. The 43-year-old man, who recovered, resides on the outskirts of Paris, had not traveled – but his wife worked in business servicing airline passengers from China.

● Judge orders Sanders, others to be reinstated on New York primary ballot which effectively reinstates canceled primary and allows him to amass additional convention delegates.

- NYTimes reports that the scattered outbreaks around the nation had their roots in New York City. Kristian Andersen – microbiology & immunology professor at Scripps Research – admits: "*It means that we missed the boat early on, and the vast majority in this country is coming from domestic spread. I keep hearing that it's somebody else's fault. That's not true. It's not somebody else's fault, it's our own fault.*" To which Nathan Grubaugh of Yale School of Public Health added, "*We now have enough data to feel pretty confident that New York was the primary gateway for the rest of the country,*" adding that 60 to 65 percent of the cases across the country could be traced back to New York and that earlier action there could have prevented the virus from spreading.

- .

07 May 2020 – 28 Days in the Omer

- 57 transcript interviews from 2017-2018, revealing what was said when lawmakers sought to determine whether members of the Trump campaign and Russia coordinated to tip the scales of the election are released after being concealed by Adam Schiff. Upon releasing them, Schiff said: "*Despite the many barriers put in our way by the then-Republican Majority, and attempts by some key witnesses to lie to us and obstruct our investigation, the transcripts that we are releasing today show precisely what Special Counsel Robert Mueller also revealed: That the Trump campaign, and Donald Trump himself, invited illicit Russian help, made full use of that help, and then lied and obstructed the investigations in order to cover up this misconduct.*"

- Biden sexual abuse accuser Tara Reade told Megyn Kelly she belied Biden Should Withdraw From Presidential Race and he "*should not be running on character.*" When asked if she would take a polygraph test to verify the veracity of her accusations, she said: "*I will take one if Joe Biden takes one. But I'm not a criminal.*"

- California Gov. Gavin Newsom reveals that "*This whole thing started in the state of California, the first community spread, in a nail salon. I'm very worried about that.*"

- As California entered a phased reopening it had reported 2,685 COVID-19 deaths.

- After an FBI plot to frame former national security adviser Michael Flynn is revealed, Attorney Barr drops all charges, Nancy Pelosi objects base on a coerced confession: "*Michael Flynn pleaded guilty to lying to federal investigators in the face of overwhelming evidence - but now, Attorney General Barr's Justice Department is dropping the case to continue to cover up for the President.*"

- Eleven Secret Service agents test positive for COVID-19, with another 23 Secret Service members recovered from the virus, and another 60 employees self-quarantining.

- New York Governor Andrew Cuomo issues Executive Order 202 to be in effect until 21 June 2020 limiting gatherings to 10 people or less.

-

08 May 2020 – 29 Days in the Omer

- Neiman Marcus department store, founded in 1907, declares bankruptcy; JC Penny announces it will also file bankruptcy within a few weeks.

- Charges against Michael Flynn are dropped and Judge might prevent it – covering-up for the FBI frame-job against Flynn.

- A 14.7% unemployment rate is announced, taking it to the worst level since the Great Depression. Reportedly, there are 20.5 million people who abruptly lost jobs due to COVID-19. Two months ago, the nation had the lowest unemployment rate in 50 years; now it's the highest in 80 years.

- College budgets were ravaged by COVID-19 – 25 institutions in New England were in danger of closing by 2027; because of the financial impact of the virus, a total of 345 institutions were in peril.

- Republican senators request meetings of State Department personnel in Burisma investigation and documents produced by 14 May.

- Pelosi wants to hold the 17-20 August Democratic National Convention in a large stadium.

- A new study suggests hydroxychloroquine largely ineffective for treating coronavirus with analysis revealing there was no "substantial difference" in hydroxychloroquine results.

- A leaked Barack Obama phone call reveals him making some unpresidential comments on the decision to drop the Mike Flynn case and the manner in which Trump handled COVID-19. Obama said of the pandemic handling: *"It has been an absolute chaotic disaster when that mindset of what's in it for me and to heck with everybody else, when that mindset is operationalized in our government."* He then says, *"… the response to this global crisis has been so anemic and spotty. It would have been bad, even with the best of governments,"* and concludes, *"So that's why I, by the way, am going to be spending as much time as necessary and campaigning as hard as I can for Joe Biden."*

-

09 May 2020 – 30 Days in the Omer

- The United States lost 20 million jobs with the threat that a wrong response could make the losses permanent, and place thousands of companies into positions where bankruptcy is the only course of action.

-

11 May 2020 – 32 Days in the Omer

- Barack Obama tweeted *"While we continue to wait for a coherent national plan to navigate this pandemic, states like Massachusetts are beginning to adopt their own public health plans to combat this virus – before it's too late."* – Senate Majority Leader Mitch McConnell: *"I think President Obama should have kept his mouth shut. You know, we know he doesn't like much this administration is doing. That's understandable. But I think it's a little bit classless frankly to critique an administration that comes after you."*

-

12 May 2020 – 33 Days in the Omer

- Covid-19 causes Price to fall by 0.8% on a seasonally adjusted basis in April, and the largest drop since December 2008. The cause is attributed to falling gasoline and energy prices. Economists are concerned that deflation might force business failures and remove jobs temporarily lost due to lockdowns.

- Dr. Anthony Fauci warned of *"really serious"* consequences if states reopen too soon, saying: *"Even under the best of circumstances, when you pull back on mitigation, you will see some cases appear. It's the ability and the capability of responding to those cases with good identification, isolation, and contact tracing will determine whether you can continue to go forward, as you try to reopen America."*

- Obamagate emerges from the Flynn prosecution.

-

13 May 2020 – 34 Days in the Omer

- The top Republican on the House Intelligence Committee Rep. Devin Nunes vowed pursuit of multiple new criminal referrals following revelations in the Justice Department's handling of the Russia probe conducted by Robert Mueller. Nunes stated: *"We're looking at doing criminal referrals on the Mueller team, the Mueller dossier team, the Mueller witch hunt, whatever you want to call it. That's where we are now in our investigation."*

- FBI goof reveals the name of Saudi involved in the 9/11 WTC destruction – a Saudi Embassy official in Los Angeles.

- In March, the New York state's last coal-burning plant, the Kintigh Generating Station in Somerset, closed; in 2020, the United States is on track to produce more electricity from renewable power than from coal for the first time on record – making Trump the Green Energy President, despite claims that the Paris Climate Agreement withdrawal would have the exact opposite effect. On 1 May, Texas wind power supplied nearly three times as much electricity as coal did nationally. Wind and solar are now the cheapest energy options, with natural gas providing 38% or the nation's electrical needs. According to Nat Kreamer, Advanced Energy Economy CEO: *"In some parts of the country, we're now seeing renewable penetration hit 60 or 70 percent on some days, and no one's screaming that they can't do that."*

-

14 May 2020 – 35 Days in the Omer

- COVID-19 Antibody test to determine whether someone has had Covid-19 is approved by Public Health England: *"such a highly specific antibody test is a very reliable marker of past infection and may indicate some immunity to future infection."*

- A National Review article By LARRY KUDLOW *"Trump the Disrupter"* is brought to my attention in a QUORA discussion and summarizes one element in the Trump Card series, the fact that Trump's 'Drain the Swamp' is about disrupting an establishment that has devoted itself to destroying America: *"Trump is not going to give up his economic populism or his America-first foreign policy. He has represented himself as the voice for the ailing American middle class. He is a disrupter. He will always be the outsider."*

- In accordance with Obama's Pandemic Playbook, the Trump administration announces the military will be mobilization to distribute potential coronavirus vaccine: *"You know, it's a massive job to give this vaccine. Our military is now being mobilized so at the end of the year we're going to be able to give it to a lot of people very, very rapidly."*

- The possibility of 100,000 deaths is asserted when the 14 May status was 85,886. By 8 July, there were 132,195 deaths.

-

15 May 2020 – 36 Days in the Omer

- Republican voters are accepting the relationship between climate change and human activity. Carbon-reduction has begun to emerge as a Conservative-led policy change position on Capitol Hill. It has been recognized that clean energy is a proven high-growth sector capable of adding well-paying jobs across America while also improving reduced pollution that benefits public health while reducing emission of greenhouse gases. Energy security has replaced Reaganite disdain for the use of solar energy and is emerging as a conservative value.

- The House votes to change rules, for the first time in its 231-year history, the Representatives will convene without being physically together – the lawmakers will vote remotely using proxies.

-

16 May 2020 – 37 Days in the Omer

- Dr. Deborah Birx expresses frustration over how the CDC is handling the COVID-19 data – they are generating inaccurate and delayed numbers on both virus cases and deaths. The CDC website says: *"Provisional death counts may not match counts from other sources, such as media reports or numbers from county health departments. Our counts often track 1–2 weeks behind other data."*

- U.S. Secret Service investigators reveal perpetrators of the infamous Nigerian scams – a well-organized Nigerian fraud ring – have begun filing bogus unemployment stimulus claims that could result in *"potential losses in the hundreds of millions of dollars."* The fraud came to light when still-employed people began to question receipt of confirmation paperwork in the mail. Scam operators had already been online asserting the letters a waste of federal funds.

- Obama delivered a virtual commencement address in which he claimed America's leaders had fumbled the response to coronavirus pandemic: *"More than anything, this pandemic has fully, finally torn back the curtain on the idea that so many of the folks in charge know what they're doing. A lot of them aren't even pretending to be in charge."* He also told his predominantly black audience the pandemic *"spotlights the underlying inequalities and extra burdens that black communities have historically had to deal with in this country."* He reminded them: *"Whether you realize it or not, you've got more road maps, more role models, and more resources than the Civil Rights generation did. You've got more tools, technology, and talents than my generation did. No generation has been better positioned to be warriors for justice and remake the world."*

- Trump Tweets: *"I'm not running against Sleepy Joe Biden. He is not even a factor. Never was, remember 1% Joe? I'm running against the Radical Left, Do Nothing Democrats & their partner, the real opposition party, the Lamestream Fake News Media! They are vicious & crazy, but we will WIN!"*

-

18 May 2020 – 39 Days in the Omer

- President Trump announces he's taking the malaria drug he had recommended and has been taking hydroxychloroquine and a zinc supplement daily *"for about a week and a half."* It requires medical supervision – the White House physician meets the advised standard. The White House has mandated face coverings for those in the West Wing, with daily testing for the president, vice president, and those they come in close contact with.

- House Democrats again move to impeach Trump. This time the want secret Mueller grand jury materials – a related letter from the House Committee letter said: "*If this material reveals new evidence supporting the conclusion that President Trump committed impeachable offenses. The Committee will proceed accordingly – including, if necessary, by considering whether to recommend new articles of impeachment.*" Arguing against any delays while the SCOTUS reviews the matter, the letter made it clear: "*This substantial delay will seriously endanger the Committee's ability to complete its impeachment investigation during the current Congress.*" The ultimate goal would, as with the original 2016/17 effort, be to install Mike Pence as POTUS; it also indicates that the House Democrats have no faith in Joe Biden winning the election.

- In what is the first relief fund of its kind, California initiated a program that allows undocumented immigrants to begin applying for financial support assistance during the COVID-19 pandemic. A $125 million coronavirus disaster relief fund is designated to support undocumented immigrants whose status renders them ineligible for federal stimulus checks and unemployment benefits – this amounts to making payments to roughly 10% of California's workforce. It also reveals the degree to which California has directly profited from illegal immigration that is supported and promoted by Nancy Pelosi and the rest of those who objected to a traditional Citizenship Question on the 2020 Census; it also shows the degree to which illegals are used to gerrymander or distort body-counts that serve top determine Representatives in both Federal and State legislatures.

- NYC employees undocumented or low-wage workers to scrub subways for coronavirus. This began with the 6 May, closure of the subways from 1 a.m. to 5 a.m. and the hiring of outside cleaners who set up around-the-clock shops in 14 end-of-line stations where they quickly mop and wipe down the interiors of trains before they're returned to service. Cleaners are not subject to health safety rules and a crew of twelve is allotted only five minutes to clean ten subway cars.

- Tiffany Trump (26-year-old) graduates Georgetown Law, her father tweets: "*Just what I need is a lawyer in the family. Proud of you Tiff!*" [Tiffany's aunt, President Trump's older sister, Maryanne Trump Barry is a retired federal appellate judge. So the tweet serves as inside humor.]

-

19 May 2020 – 40 Days in Omer – 19th Amendment in HOUSE

- A new documentary filmed in 2017 reveals Norma McCorvey, a.k.a. Jane Roe, [of *Roe v Wade*] switched sides on abortion in the '90s because she was paid [or bribed] to do so.

- Trump firing his Inspector General [IG] spawns left-wing anger resulting in the WH Press secretary stating: "*'No one seemed to care' when Obama fired holdover Igs. ... 'no one seemed to care' when former President Obama fired holdover inspectors general from the preceding administration, amid an uproar over a string of dismissals by President Trump.*" This was in-spite-of the fact several IGs had issued a letter asserting: "*'President Obama, you're inhibiting our investigations,' no one seemed to care then.*"

- Trump address issues related to over 40,000 National Guard members deployed to help in coronavirus relief – scheduled to end 24 June, or one day short of the 90-day qualification for federal benefits under the Post-9/11 GI bill. Many would gain reduced tuition at public universities if tour extended.

- Senate Majority Leader Mitch McConnell Confirms they will be *'Taking Steps'* to Issue Subpoenas to 'Variety of Obama Officials' connected to the illegal surveillance of Americans: "*It is unacceptable for any federal warrant application to include seven different inaccuracies and omissions. It was a FISA warrant to snoop on a presidential campaign. Here it is in black and white. Sadly, this was no isolated incident. The Mueller investigation showed those allegations collapsed. Senate Republicans are taking steps to issue new subpoenas to a wide variety of Obama administration officials.*"

- Speaking from his basement, Biden claims President Trump hasn't enacted the exact food program which was activated a week earlier as the Farmers to Families Food Box program.

- Biden blasts Trump for taking hydroxychloroquine, claiming: "*Look at the studies that have been done. It does much more harm than good. This is totally irresponsible.*" If taken in high doses or sustained long-term use, it can cause retinal damage. However, HCQ was synthesized in the mid-1940s for use against malaria, and in 1955 it was shown effective for both systemic lupus and rheumatoid arthritis. Clearly, Biden feels that eye damage outweighs the numerous established benefits and lives saved. As he said: *"Truth over facts."* The facts support the safety of HCQ, while the truth argues Biden believes all existing approvals of the drug should be reversed. Ignoring the facts and over 70-years of HCQ use, Biden says: *"There's no serious medical person out there saying to use that drug. It's counterproductive. It's not going to help, but the president, he decided that's an answer."*

- Serious medical people, like frontline National Health Service (NHS) health workers in the U.K. will be given HCQ. There is an issue of medical professionals saying, *"Chloroquine and hydroxychloroquine have been used for treating malaria for more than 60 years and are generally regarded as very safe drugs. Until recently 300m chloroquine treatments were given for malaria every year."*

- GOP Rep. Roger Marshall, an obstetrician, supports taking HCQ "prophylactically" and says he and his family are taking it – adding: *"I would encourage any person over the age of 65 or with an underlying medical condition to talk to their own physician about taking hydroxychloroquine and I'm relieved President Trump is taking it."* Thus, while the anti-Trump, non-medically trained, House Speaker and former Vice President denounce HCQ, a certified physician is both using it and approves of the President's usage of HCQ.

- In their roles as 'medical experts', Biden suggested, *"It's like saying 'Maybe if you inject Clorox into your blood, it may cure you.'"*; Pelosi enhanced her medical expertise to include obesity: *"I would rather he not be taking something that has not been approved by the scientists, especially in his age group and in his, shall we say, weight group, morbidly obese, they say."* As noted, HCQ has been in use since the mid 1940s; it has approved for prescription use since 1956 and that means it is, with customary safeguards or warnings, approved – it just lacks specific guidelines relative to the new COVID-19.

- A Ukrainian lawmaker releases phone conversations between Joe Biden and Ukraine President Poroshenko discussing the extortion details and establishing an achieved quid pro quo – it appears VP Biden received $900,000 in lobbying fees.

- The Ukrainian lawmaker, Andriy Derkach, claimed he has proof showing Hunter Biden's employer, Burisma Holdings, paid Biden the $900,000 in lobbying fees.

- Trump displays how governments use quid pro quo in his dealings with WHO, where mandatory payments to maintain its membership are paid in addition to voluntary donations – the United States provides about 15 percent of the agency's budget. On 14 April, Trump temporarily suspended the U.S. payments for 60 days; a letter threatening a permanent halt of funding stated, *"It is clear the repeated missteps by you and your organization in responding to the pandemic have been extremely costly for the world. ... It is clear the repeated missteps by you and your organization in responding to the pandemic have been extremely costly for the world. ... The only way forward for the World Health Organization is if it can actually demonstrate independence from China."*

- A leaked Pentagon memo revealed that top Department of Defense (DOD) officials were planning for the possibility that a "globally-persistent" coronavirus pandemic could affect the military operations well into 2021.

- A century ago, President Woodrow Wilson called Congress into special session on 19 May 1919 – three 19s yield 57 – and two days later they voted 304 to 89 for the 19th Amendment that granted women the right to vote.

-

20 May 2020 – 41 Days in the Omer

- Senate Republicans issue the first subpoena for wide-ranging investigations into Obama administration abuse of authority and the Biden-Burisma Ukraine extortion.

- China resumed attempts to 'downgrade' Taiwan status – the Island nation was first to war of COVID-19 pandemic.

- Since the coronavirus broke out, the Trump administration has deported over 900 Children under the Pandemic Border Policy – in some cases, without notifying their families.

- SCOTUS rules the Mueller Investigation documents qualify as Grand Jury testimony and are therefore not available for House of Representatives investigation.

- Canadian Prime Minister Justin Trudeau says of extending the border crossing limits, *"This is an important decision that will keep people in both of our countries safe.*" The U.S. Canadian will remain closed to all but essential travel until June 21.

- Commenting on last Susan Rice email written on 20 January linking Obama to Michael Flynn, Press Secretary Kayleigh McEnany: "*As Shakespeare said, 'Thou doth protest too much, Susan Rice.' He didn't add the 'Susan Rice' part.*"

-

21 May 2020 – 42 Days in the Omer

- British Analysts assert the possibility that a No-deal Brexit '*would overwhelm local emergency teams*'. In "Death over Life" {2014}, 2016 was pegged as a potential problem point; as if events were scripted, UK voters approved BREXIT while the United States election of Donald John Trump triggered dramatic, possibly psychotic, actions apparently intended to elevate Mike Pence to POTUS via impeachment. As with the US, the UK is dependent on China for PPE needed to address the Wuhan virus. The British government made it clear that it would not seek an extension of the Brexit transition period on 31 December – the COVID-19 pandemic, combined with a shortage of EU medical personnel, threatens to complicate British mitigation and treatment abilities. A leaked report indicated: "*The NHS are understandably a priority, but other key agencies, particularly those attending deaths in the community (police, fire, medics, funeral directors) have had difficulties in accessing PPE. It's not just PPE, there has been a critical shortage of body bags, with suppliers providing them at 10 times the normal price.*"

- A PEW Research poll shows 60% of Americans believe social-distancing slows the spread of COVID-19. It also appeared that faith in medical-science had increased – more among the Democrats than Republicans.

- A Reuters analysis of the pandemic showed the death rates in Democratic counties were triple those in Republican ones. In terms of the 2016 election, those counties voting for Hillary Clinton had 39 coronavirus deaths per 100,000 residents; in those voting for Donald Trump, the rate was 13 per 100,000. Democrats are densely urban, while Republicans rural, and that difference defines disease transmission.

- Senate adjourns without further legislative action to address the ongoing coronavirus pandemic. Senate Majority Whip John Thune expressed the need to evaluate the effect of the current stimulus: *"It's illogical to say we've spent $3 trillion and we wouldn't want to take a look whether it's being efficient before we rush headlong and push another $3 trillion out the door."*

- Trump visits Ford ventilator manufacturing facility and faced criticism for not wearing masks during media photo-op – it is later shown, via candid photos, that he was wearing his mask while touring the facility.

- Trump made the comment: *"In our lifetimes, the company founded by a man named Henry Ford – good bloodlines, good bloodlines – if you believe in that stuff."* The latter was taken to reference Ford's anti-Semitic rhetoric and beliefs that inferred race superiority. Trump then said to Ford CEO William Clay Ford you have *"good bloodlines."* The media seemed to ignore the reality of centuries of history and that era in American history, by making connections to Nazi Germany bestowing on Henry Ford in 1938; of course, it is a matter of history that IBM produced the system to track the tattooed numbers on the arms of Holocaust victims. Media focus on Trump's "amazing DNA" comments places them at odds with the historic reality of *Jonathon's POTUS Cousins* and all Presidents being descended from the 4-Sisters.

- Trump says U.S. won't close if there is a 2nd COVID-19 wave: *"People say that's a very distinct possibility. It's standard. And we're going to put out the fires. We're not going to close the country. We're going to put out the fires. Whether it's an ember or a flame, we're going to put it out. But we're not closing our country."*

- Dr. Anthony Fauci told the Senate: *"I hope that if we do have the threat of a second wave we will be able to deal with it very effectively to prevent it from becoming an outbreak not only worse than now but much, much less."* He also warned that *"reopening states too quickly would cost lives."* The President placed that in context by adding: *"A permanent lockdown is not a strategy for a healthy state or a healthy country. Our country wasn't meant to be shut down. We did the right thing but now it's time to open it up. A never-ending lockdown would invite a public health calamity. To protect the health of our people we must have a functioning economy."*

- The Guatemalan President Alejandro Giammattei scolded U.S. for deporting migrants with coronavirus – 119 have tested positive for the virus, and are 5% of the country's 2,512 cases – *"We understand that the United States wants to deport people, but what we do not understand is why they send us flights full of infection."*

-

22 May 2020 – 43 Days in the Omer

- Media persists in denouncing HCQ based on hospital patient results. When used on intensive care patients (as opposed to outpatient care), HCQ produces a 34% increased mortality; a 137% increased risk of arrhythmia; HCQ with an antibiotic 45% increased risk of death, and a 411% increase in heart arrhythmia. The key fact – the observed patients are already at death's door. HCQ remains a drug that has been proven by 65 years of real-world use.

- Minnesota farmers are being impacted by COVID-19.

- President Trump declares places of worship to be "essential services."

-

23 May 2020 – 44 Days in the Omer

- With the Bank of England base rate at 0.1% (one-tenth of a percent) they indicated they were paving the way for negative interest rates. Because of the language drafted into the fine print of many mortgage agreements, their rates will fall to a possible low of one-tenth of one percent.

- As he hides in his cellar, Biden ad slams Trump: *"'The death toll is still rising.' 'The president is playing golf.'"* Of course, viewers of videos see the President exhibiting extreme social distancing while getting out, exercising, in healthy fresh air. This was the same day Dr. Birx announced hospitalizations were declining. Biden's campaign offers no solutions or any suggestions that might prevent those who already contracted COVID-19, in addition to immune deficiency or severe illness they already had, from dying. Nor has Biden presented anything that would suggest he could prevent any further need to hospitalize those with existing medical conditions who contract coronavirus. The COVID-19 is a culling virus – it remains asymptomatic in the healthy, but kills those who already require medical supervision.

- President Donald Trump issues travel restriction order for Brazil as it accrues the second-highest number of COVID-19 cases in the world. Exemptions include permanent residents, spouses of permanent residents, siblings and children of U.S. citizens, and parents of U.S. citizens under 21. At the time of the order, Brazil had one-quarter the number of U.S. cases.

-

24 May 2020 – 45 Days in the Omer

- Charlemagne tha God warns: "*On top of possible Russian interference and voter suppression, [Democrats] have to worry about voter depression. That's people staying home on Election Day because they just aren't enthused by the candidate.*" Speaking to the possibility of Klobuchar as Vice President, he said that Biden choice would serve to further damaged voter turnout and "*You know, they got to make some real policy commitments to black people*"

-

25 May 2020 – MEMORIAL DAY 46 Days in the Omer

- The OUT FROM UNDER blog announces: "*The #NOJOE Democratic movement has officially begun and we invite any like kindred Republicans and Independents to join in.*" Their objective: "*#NOJOE is the battle cry for all who want a good government.*" A good government is defined as one that has honest, rational, and sane leadership – Joe Biden is seen to qualify to a far lesser degree than Trump, and Trump is widely seen as inferior.

- Massachusetts Open for Business – shops and retailers all across the state welcomed customers back for the first time since the coronavirus pandemic forced them to close more than two months ago. But it was not quite business as usual. As shops opened, the recorded deaths had reached 6,416 with 44 reported on Memorial Day, and the total people who have tested positive for COVID-19 rose to 93,271, with 596 newly reported cases.

- California allows places of worship to reopen, and resumes in-store retail shopping.

- Dr. Michael Ryan, WHO's emergencies chief, affirms there was no indication of any hydroxychloroquine safety problems within the WHO trial to date. WHO director-general Tedros Adhanom Ghebreyesus stated: "This concern relates to the use of hydroxychloroquine and chloroquine in COVID-19," then added that the drugs are approved treatments for people with malaria or autoimmune diseases – underscoring that the claims of HCQ dangers are unjustified.

- For the first time in ten weeks, Joe Biden exits his basement to lay a wreath at a local veterans memorial. The media focus was on the full lower face masks he and his wife Jill wore. In contrast, President Trump performed the traditional wreath-laying without a mask.

- While being arrested and pinned to the ground by an officer who has his knee pressing on the upper spine/neck of George Floyd, Floyd has a heart attack and dies. The event is labeled a murder and the four officers involved are fired; the officer whose knee was on Floyd's neck is charged with third-degree murder and manslaughter. An independent autopsy report on 1 June refutes the official one and claimed asphyxiation as the cause of death.

- The fact Floyd was a Black man, had served to trigger pent up emotions related to a Covid-19 recession and resulted in a series of violent protests across America that spread to parts of Europe – echoing "Black Lives Matter" associated protests that began in Minnesota, where the death occurred.

-

26 May 2020 – 47 Days in the Omer

- The genetic testing begun in March discovered a mutation that increases the risk of dementia – the nation saw Ronald Reagan leave office and then be confirmed to have Alzheimer disease. For the ten weeks ending with Memorial disease, the world saw Biden hiding in his basement, forgetting the real details about his grandchildren, not remembering, confusing Covid-19 victim and unemployment statistics – and generally making the gaffes he's so famous for with ever-increasing regularity...even when the words are fully scripted. The same genes that cause dementia of the type Biden evidences have been found to dominate in COVID-19 victims.

- The researchers found 9,022 of almost 383,000 Biobank participants of European ancestry studied had two copies of the e4 variant, while more than 223,000 had two copies of a variant called "e3" – which also presented as a dementia risk that was fourteen times higher. Within the study, 37 people who tested positive for Covid-19 had two copies of the e4 variant of ApoE, while 401 had two copies of the e3 variant. In ethnicity terms: *"American Indians, Asians, and Mexican Americans have the highest frequency of E3 (over 84%); Africans and African Americans have the highest frequency of E4 (20.1% and 31% respectively)."*

- The APOE gene makes the protein apolipoprotein E (ApoE) that is associated with a production, delivery, and utilization of cholesterol in the body. The E4 variant makes a protein characterized by faster cholesterol metabolism resulting in a higher blood cholesterol level – it is recommended that they follow a high-carb, low-fat diet. Since testing is needed to determine individual genetic profiles, a health provider must be involved, increasing the need for M4A and routine annual check-ups.

- David Melzer, a Professor of epidemiology and public health at Exeter University, presented his comments in the *Journal of Gerontology: Medical Sciences*: *"It is pretty bulletproof – whatever associated disease we remove, the association is still there. So it looks as if it is the gene variant that is doing it ... This association is not driven by people who actually have dementia."*

- Prof Tara Spires-Jones, a neurodegeneration expert with the University of Edinburgh, stated: *"It is possible that the role of ApoE in the immune system is important in the disease and future research may be able to harness this to develop effective treatments."* It would appear there is a golden lining to the COVID-19 experience, one which could yield treatments for mental deterioration that was never a problem in the days when half the population born in any given year was dead before the reached the POTUS age of eligibility.

- YouTube has a bot deleting comments that contain certain Chinese-language phrases "communist bandit" and "50-cent party." Amazon has a bot screening eBooks that identified a 2014 book on the relevance of Biblical prophecy to the 2016 election as containing inaccurate data on Covid-19, which is a disease that evolved six-years after the book, "Death over Life", was published. On Twitter, "fact-checking" was being employed as a cover for an openly anti-Trump employee to fill the function of silencing the Presidential tweets. Trump asserted: *"Twitter is completely stifling FREE SPEECH, and I, as President, will not allow it to happen!"*

- Twitter flagged a comment about mail-in voter fraud with a <u>blue</u> [Left-wing color] exclamation mark and the statement *"get the facts about mail-in ballots."* Comically, there was also a 2004 video of House Prosecutor Jerrold Lewis Nadler telling his colleagues of the factual evidence he had of ballot fraud of the type could easily occur through the call for general and widespread voting by mail.

-

27 May 2020 – 48 Days in the Omer

- Dr. Fauci reveals how the United States can mitigate a second wave Covid-19 outbreak – there are 686,000 cases recorded in New York, New Jersey, Pennsylvania, and Massachusetts representing roughly 41% of all cases in the nation; NY alone has 22% of the national total while having only 5.8% of the national population. In that context, Fauci said: *"New York was a very special situation because it really got hurt very badly. God forbid, I hope we never get anywhere near seeing anything near like New York again."* Fauci stated: *"I use the words 'second wave' with some reservations. It doesn't necessarily have to be a true second wave in the sense of a major outbreak. And whether that happens or not depends on how we're prepared to respond."*

-

28 May 2020 – 49 Days in the Omer.

- Globally, Covid-19 cases surpass ten-million; deaths surpass half-million; fatality rate is 4.87%. The United States fatality rate is slightly lower, at 4.83%, and while the case numbers grow, the herd immunity increases, and fatality rates fall. The experts remind people this is just the beginning – the media is suppressing that it is the beginning of *Herd Immunity*, and act as if that immunity is bad. They place a negative spin of the projection there are ten infections for every known one – that is, the *Herd Immunity* is extensive and 26-million people might now be immune (meaning the real fatality rate is less than one-half-of-one-percent).

•

29 May 2020 – Shavuot {Day 50}

• The Supreme Court rejects challenges from California church to public gathering restrictions. Roberts joined the liberal justices to form a 5-4 majority.

• The Commerce Department reports that Americans' personal incomes in April managed rose $1.97 trillion (10.5 percent). Tens of millions of people lose their jobs, wages and salaries fell significantly – federal benefits more than made up for it. The personal savings rate increased to 33 percent. Consumer spending fell by 13.6 percent.

•

30 May 2020 –

• Minnesota Governor Walz fully mobilized National Guard for the first time in the state's 164-year history. Walz estimated that about 80% of rioters were not from Minnesota, only around 20% of rioters are from Minneapolis, St. Paul area; an 8 p.m. curfew is imposed.

•

31 May 2020 –

• Five days after George Floyd's death, police decided to take a different tactic and many are setting down their batons and joining the protestors in peaceful protest demonstrations. It is clear that they accepted Trump's statement of opposition to violence and solidarity with those seeking an end to racism, and to honor George Floyd rather than destroy communities.

• Genesee County Sheriff Chris Swanson told Flint, Michigan protestors *"We want to be with y'all, for real. I took my helmet off, laid the batons down. I want to make this a parade, not a protest."*

[01 June 2020 – 31 May to 1 June 1921, Tulsa race massacre – Biden thought this was what Juneteenth referenced – also known as the destruction of "Black Wall Street," the wealthiest black community in the United States.]

- Biden uses the convergence of Covid-19 and Floyd's death as a means to shift the dialogue away from his being locked away in his Wilmington basement. Biden went outside to meet demonstrators near his home and presented a different optic. The issue is the propriety of that optic. Do you arrest those destroying stores and looting? Does the president interfere in the misconduct of local law enforcement? Trump said, "*We need law and order in our country. If we don't have law and order, we don't have a country.*"

- But, when it came to real actions, Biden was "quiet", he was playing optics of meeting someone on the street against actually expressing anything – instead, others were left to interpret. The optics showed no attempt to lead, though one Biden statement did express vague ideas: "*We are a nation in pain, but we must not allow this pain to destroy us. We are a nation enraged, but we cannot allow our rage to consume us. We are a nation exhausted, but we will not allow our exhaustion to defeat us. … The only way to bear this pain is to turn all that anguish to purpose,*" *Biden added. And as President, I will help lead this conversation — and more importantly, I will listen, just as I did today visiting the site of last night's protests in Wilmington.*" But what in that idealistic abstraction stops the breaking of store windows, stops the setting of fires, stops the looting?

- New York City imposes its first curfew since World War Two – 700 people are arrested for violating it.

- Floyd Protestors start toppling or defacing various Civil War-era monuments – including the defacement of a monument to the all-volunteer 54th Regiment which stands across from the Massachusetts State House. The all-black regiment was led by a white Colonel named Robert Gould Shaw who, at 25, died in combat leading his volunteer all-black Regiment into combat. The destruction of monuments to those who either fought for freedom or uphold the Constitution would, over the following weeks, became one of the global movement's more defining actions. Another emerging movement was "Defund the Police." {Shaw was a 4-Sisters descendant and a POTUS Cousin. His parents were friends of the abolitionist-author Harriet Beecher Stowe and he shared her anti-slavery views. The Black Lives Matter [BLM] activists attacking Civil War monuments clearly display a cognitive dysfunction that influences other policies, like "Defund the Police."}

- Defend the Police, remove them from their role as enforcers of the laws, they are the "enemy' so echo the words of George Orwell: "*When I see an actual flesh-and-blood worker in conflict with his natural enemy, the policeman, I do not have to ask myself which side I am on.*" These words were, as Orwell stated, written about his experience in the Spanish Civil War (936 to 1939) and "*against totalitarianism and for Democratic Socialism, as I understand it.*" Thus consistent with the first two quadrennial election cycles of the new age in American history – as defined by Senator Bernie Sanders – a self-proclaimed democratic socialist.

-

02 June 2020 –

- Governor Cuomo accuses New York City Mayor De Blasio of underestimating the scope of the protester problem, while De Blasio calls on community leaders to step in to help quell the violence: "*Do not let outsiders attack your community, do not let a violent few attack your community, do not let criminals attack your community, stand up.*"

- Multi-state primary: To clinch the nomination, Biden requires an 89% win across the primary states. Both Trump & Biden must win Indiana; Idaho, Iowa, Maryland, Montana, New Mexico, Pennsylvania, Rhode Island, and South Dakota.

- McConnell blocks Senate Democrat condemnation resolution over Trump's response to protesters in the Nation's Capitol.

- Research reveals the most dangerous Covid-19 transmission source are the asymptomatic – 80 percent of the cases are asymptomatic.

- Motivated by Twitter "Fact-Checking" presidential tweets – while ignoring those of Iran and others who promote violence as national policy – Leaders of three civil rights groups, Color of Change, The Leadership Conference on Civil and Human Rights and the NAACP Legal Defense and Educational Fund, unify to attack Facebook CEO Mark Zuckerberg's refusal to censor the posts made by the President of the United States.

-

03 June 2020 –

- Affirming other data, the British news journal, The Guardian, reported: *"Solar, wind and other renewable sources have toppled coal in energy generation in the United States for the first time in over 130 years, with the coronavirus pandemic accelerating a decline in coal that has profound implications for the climate crisis."*

- 2019 total US energy consumption by source: Renewables 11%; Petroleum 37%; gas 32%; coal 10%; nuclear 8%; other.

- Yielding to the ACLU, who said, *"While AB 2261 purports to protect privacy, it does the opposite. The bill invites tech companies and law enforcement to self-regulate their use of face recognition, and places no meaningful restrictions on their ability to deploy this invasive technology against the people of California,"* California lawmakers block expanded the use of facial recognition technology by law enforcement.

04 June 2020 – Senate votes on 19th Amendment

- A century ago, Southern Democrats filibustered against the right of women to vote, they then abandoned the effort.

- The Senate votes on right to vote, 76% of Republican Senators voted in favor, 60% of Democrat Senators voted against; the final vote is 37 Republican Senators and 19 Democrats favor granting of women the right to vote. Final ratification of the 19th Amendment is achieved 18 August 1920 and the voting right woman enjoyed prior to the drafting of the Constitution was restored.

-

05 June 2020 –

- As data related to OBAMAGATE/BIDENGATE unfolds, The Hill tweeted: Sen.@tedcruz: *"All of them thought Hillary was going to win. Nobody would know that they had abused law enforcement and intelligence to target their political enemies."*

- In relation to the Floyd Protests, Caleb Hull (@CalebJHull) tweeted: *"Absolutely perfect that the press is whining about not social distancing at the WH after they've spent the last week encouraging mass protests in the streets."*

- A lengthy NYTimes article entitled, *"The Fullest Look Yet at the Racial Inequity of Coronavirus"* reveals that the virus is more deadly among Black and Latin segments of American society. This report is fully consistent with global population observations. The article states the data shows, *"Black and Latino people have been nearly twice as likely to die from the virus as white people."*

•

06 June 2020 – Normandy landings D-DAY celebration

• The White House tweets: *"On June 6, 1944, our Greatest Generation bravely stormed the beaches of Normandy. 'Those who fought here won a future for our nation. They won the survival of our civilization. And they showed us the way to love, cherish, and defend our way of life for many centuries to come.'"*

• The New York Times reports that neither Former President George W. Bush nor Senator Mitt Romney would support the re-election of President Trump. It was also reported that Biden planned to release his "Republicans for Biden" coalition at a later date. However, on 8 June, Bush Spokesman Freddy Ford said the Times story was bogus, *"...completely made up. He is retired from presidential politics and has not indicated how he will vote."* However, neither George W. nor his wife Laura voted for any candidate in 2016, so the indication that they would be voting could infer, if he wins, they will claim to have supported Trump.

•

07 June 2020 –

• Tesla Chinese division announces: *"'One million mile' electric car battery is now 'ready to produce.'"* Contemporary Amperex Technology Co Ltd (CATL), claims it can produce a battery pack that can last for about 16 years, powering an electric vehicle for 1.24 million miles. In addition to Tesla, BMW, and Toyota will be using the battery.

• Former Republican Secretary of State, General Colin Powell, claimed Congress does nothing about Trump's "lies" and that the American people must "vote him out." {Powell is another POTUS Cousin and 4-Sisters descendant.}

• On CNN's "State of the Union," Powell unequivocally stated: *"I certainly cannot in any way support President Trump this year."* And, with regard to Biden, Powell said, *"He is now the candidate, and I'll be voting for him."* However, based on his reasoning and history, it appears Powell is a swamp denizen whose family was caught in the swamp draining process.

- In response to Collin Powell's endorsement of Biden, Trump tweeted: *"Colin Powell, a real stiff who was very responsible for getting us into the disastrous Middle East Wars, just announced he will be voting for another stiff, Sleepy Joe Biden. Didn't Powell say that Iraq had 'weapons of mass destruction?' They didn't, but off we went to WAR!"*

- Benjamin S. Carson M.D., Secretary of Housing and Urban Development warns: *"A house divided against itself cannot stand. We the American people are not each others' enemies. We must be smart enough to recognize that and not allow ourselves to be manipulated into thinking that we hate each other and destroying ourselves."* He also addressed Powell's comments about President Trump: *"I admire Gen. Powell and he certainly is entitled to his opinion and the way that he wants to conduct himself, but I generally don't find it particularly useful to demonize other people."*

- 1) Brazil stops releasing Covid-19 death toll and cleans data from its official site. In a related issue

- 2a) Using NASA satellite survalence technology, researchers determine a likelihood that the Wuhan Virus began during the summer of 2019; Tom Diamond, president of RS Metrics said, *"At all the larger hospitals in Wuhan, we measured the highest traffic we've seen in over two years during the September through December 2019 time frame."*

- 2b) Dr. John Brownstein, of Harvard Medical, the research team behind the study analyzed commercial satellite imagery *"observed a dramatic increase in hospital traffic outside five major Wuhan hospitals beginning late summer and early fall 2019."* The data was timed: *"It has to be right at noon, because you basically want direct sunlight. You don't want shadows to prevent our ability to count the cars."*

- 2c) On focus was the Wuhan's Tianyou Hospital, one of the city's largest the parking lots, on 10 October 2018, there were 171 cars; a year later, 285 cars were seen – an increase of 67%.

- 2d) Recalling, Taiwan notified WHO of an undefined novel virus in November 2019, if the satellite analysis is correct, the Chinese covered up the virus for at least four months and have only reported the deaths during remission period; this explains how a large concentrated population that is roughly equivalent to the New York City metropolitan area reported fatalities that were on 15% of NYC. One must conclude that China lied and eventually it will be revealed that European infections began in the last three months of 2019; this infers infections reached NYC before Christmas.

- 2e) Consider Trump's view on American reliance on China's supply chain and technological transparency; then consider what a State Department spokesperson told ABC News: *"The Chinese government's cover-up of initial reporting on the virus is just one more example of the challenges presented by the Chinese Communist Party's hostility toward transparency. The Chinese government has a responsibility to share information on the virus and support countries as the world responds to COVID-19."* Having thought about it, it is important to note that the Biden family is closely linked to "Chinese Transparency" regarding financial connections.

- BLM demonstrators in Britain topple a statue of Bristol slave trader Edward Colston.

- BLM co-founder Alicia Garza said on NBC's "Meet the Press," *"When we talk about defunding the police, what we're saying is 'invest in the resources that our communities need'. Why can't we start to look at how it is that we reorganize our priorities so people don't have to be in the streets protesting … in a global pandemic? Are we willing to live in fear that our lives will be taken by police officers who are literally using their power in the wrong way? Or are we willing to adopt and absorb the fear of what it might mean to change our practices, which will ultimately lead to a better quality of life for everyone."* Clearly, creating *"a better quality of life"* involves the destruction and refutation of slavery's contributed to history – something which dates to ancient Greece and Rome, but was repudiated by the Bible whose doctrines are antithetical to the BLM movement.

- Britain's BLM Floyd Protesters turn destructive attention to the Oxford University statue of Cecil Rhodes claiming: *"Oriel College abhors racism and discrimination in all its forms. The Governing Body are deeply committed to equality within our community at Oriel, the University of Oxford, and the wider world. ... As a college, we continue to debate and discuss the issues raised by the presence on our site of examples of contested heritage relating to Cecil Rhodes."*

- 3a) A record drop in unemployment after a record increase is something to cheer. But being negative is the way to win in America, as Joe Biden revealed in a video statement tweeted by The Hill (@thehill) on Sun, Jun 07, 2020: "*Donald Trump still doesn't get it. He's out there spiking the ball completely oblivious to the tens of millions who are facing the greatest struggle of their lives.*"

- 3b) True, due to government lock-downs used to mitigate the pandemic, tens of millions are still out of work. The numbers are positive and indicate pre-pandemic economic strength is re-emerging.

- 3c) Trump's "*spike the ball*" reversal declares the beginning of a new record-setting era that will become part of the legacy of whoever is sworn in on 20 January 2021. The pandemic recession, which began in February, reflects the traditional 11-year cycle keyed to the end of the Bush Great Recession. The average recession lasts eleven-months – in an election year, the length of a recession would be determined by the election outcome. In keeping with the average, the Wuhan-recession should end by February 2021, with the formal declaration of that end in June 2021.

- 3d) Biden's negative reaction to Trump's positive view of the jobs recovery infers that, as President, he would prove to be incapable of capitalizing on the end of the pandemic to form a basis to exercise a historic opportunity for economic and social reforms that would form a solid economic foundation in preparation for the next pandemic or epidemic to emerge as a result of the dynamics of climate change. The pandemic triggered the eleven-year cycle, but there is a larger K-Wave cycle due to impact Europe around 2027 – it is already visible in the UK and EU restructuring that is being complicated by migrants from Africa and the Middle East.

- 3e) For the United States to survive the next 56-quadrennial cycles, it will be necessary to dramatically restructure society during the next two cycles. The Obama-Trump transitional period will probably be one of the greatest eras of change in history. Biden has signaled a willingness to reinstate those

19th-century practices that finally failed in the 20ᵗʰ-century and yielded the Bush-43 war and economic collapse debacle.

- 3f) Biden will point to transient Wuhan-pandemic negatives made permanent by his failings, then blame that permanence on Trump; he will allow China to usurp American economic power and independence; complete the Reagan-Conservative outsourcing agenda intended to bring the nation to its knees; then facilitate the global apocalypse so deeply desired by the far-Right evangelicals that is apparently timed for 2033.

-

08 June 2020 –

- To demonstrate that the state is open again while wearing a mask, Governor Cuomo uses the New York subway system.

-

09 June 2020 –

- HuffPost article points to the 13 May arrest of a 22-year-old mother, a black woman, in Brooklyn, New York, for refusing to wear a mask, while police officers are not wearing them. The pattern shows 2/3rds of those arrested are black. Angela Cooke-Jackson, a California State University public health researcher, observed: *"What the police are showing me is that they're not protecting anybody, let alone Black and brown people. How simple would it be to do that?"*

- Tuesday, Eric Trump tweets: *"The DOW went from 19,173.98 on March 20th to 27,250.00+ today (35% in 90 days)! The United States has come roaring back to life and there is no doubt the best is still ahead!"* Thursday, fears of a resurgence of the virus – triggered by the BLM protests – sent the DJIA down 1,861.82 to close at 25,128.17.

- HBO Max removes 1939 classic, "Gone With the Wind," from its movie list. The film represents the first African-America (a woman, Hattie McDaniel) to receive an Academy Award (for best supporting actress) – a milestone of equality and the attack on systemic discrimination. This was a breakthrough movie that engaged both Black and white audiences to the extent that Box Office receipts were one hundred times the production cost. In many ways, the stereotypes became the touchstone for measuring social change.

-

10 June 2020 –

- The United States registers two million Covid-19 cases, and 113,500 fatalities – Harvard doctor projects 200,000 deaths by September. [By July, U.S. deaths surpassed 134,000]

-

12 June 2020 – Anne Frank {born 1929} wrote in her diary: "*How wonderful it is that nobody need wait a single moment before starting to improve the world*"

- History is being erased. Statues destroyed and the names of military bases and streets change; George Orwell has proven prophetic: "..., *every statue and street building has been renamed,... History has stopped. Nothing exists except an endless present in which the Party is always right.*"

- Activists seek to remove statue of Abraham Lincoln depicting him standing at podium, a slave whose chains are falling off as Lincoln announces Emancipation proclamation, claiming the Park Square (Boston) depiction a kneeling slave gaining freedom as the 16th president towers over him is disturbing. The replica of the Freedman's or Emancipation Memorial in Washington, D.C. was a gift given to Boston on 30 May 1879. It was pointed out that black men "taking a knee," has the symbolic effect of them returning to the posture in the statue where Lincoln's hand magical waves over the slave, breaking shackles imposed by the Constitution.

-

13 June 2020 –

- Atlanta, Georgia Wendy's is scene of a black man, 27-year-old Rayshard Brooks, who fell asleep in his car at the drive-thru, being wakened and harassed by police and then shot. Then BLM protesters burn down the Wendy's; the police offer who shot Brooks is fired.

-

14 June 2020 – Donald John Trump {born 1946}

-

15 June 2020 –

- A CNN poll shows 60% of Biden support is based exclusively on voting against Trump, while 70% of Trump's support is for him to continue. Former Obama White House spokesman Eric

Schultz pointed out that the networks consider Trump good for business and provide him with far more free election coverage than they do gaffe-prone Biden. It could be argued that the MSM wants Biden to be POTUS so they can rip him apart when takes office; so they conceal flaws they can reveal later.

•

18 June 2020 –

• In a 5-4 decision, SCOTUS rules the Trump administration cannot cancel the Obama administration Deferred Action for Childhood Arrivals {DACA} program. The majority opinion ignored the legality of Obama's action, citing: "*We do not decide whether DACA or its rescission are sound policies. We address only whether the agency complied with the procedural requirement that it provide a reasoned explanation for its action.*" In the underlying case, acting Secretary of Homeland Security Elaine C. "Duke 'failed to supply the requisite reasoned analysis.'" Basically, there was no logic provided for the underlying action; that opened the door to further action to rescind the Obama Executive Order.

•

19 June 2020 – Juneteenth, dating to 1865, is the oldest nationally celebrated commemoration of the ending of slavery in the United States, specifically, when the Emancipation Proclamation was read to Texas slaves; in 1980 it became an official Texas holiday. To BLM, the statue of Lincoln and Alexander commemorating it was worthy of destruction (an action you'd expect from KKK).

• Portland wakes up to enjoy an overnight gift from Antifa: The statue of George Washington had been was toppled from its century-old perch and covered in graffiti – "White fragility," "Damn white men," "you're on native land," "BLM" & other messages are written on the moment. Nearby, was scrawled "Defund white men" – inferring a racist action perpetrated by Blacks or Native Americans.

• Zogby International POLL asked likely voters if Biden 'Early Stages Of Dementia' the breakdown of those say its likely: medium-size cities 61%; suburbs 52%; large cities 55%. By gender: Suburban women 49%; urban men 62%. National election choice polling had Biden 43% and Trump 48%.

- Protestors in Washington, D.C. toppled and burned a statue of Confederate Gen. Albert Pike

- South Carolina Republican Congressman Jeff Duncan called on Speaker Nancy Pelosi (D-Calif.) to reverse her Orwellian erasure of history order for removal of portraits of previous House Speakers who served in the Confederacy.

-

20 June 2020 – SUMMER SOLSTICE longest day of the year;

-

21 June 2020 –

- The statue of Theodore Roosevelt outside the New York City Museum of Natural History, depicting him on horseback and flanked by two walking men, one Native American, the other African, scheduled for removal – because it is deemed racist to have his companions walking rather than on horseback.

-

22 June 2020 –

- Trump expands immigration ban to include work visas – the intent is to allow domestic workers to get the jobs before they go to foreign ones; it threatens a shortage of workers.

-

27 June 2020 –

- In France, Covid-19 exposed the fact that race does matter. A senior researcher focusing on immigration and discrimination at France's National Institute for Demographic Studies (INED), Patrick Simon, indicated that being color blind hurts when fighting disease. Medical researchers have a need to know the ethnic representation of Covid-19 cases and deaths. *"Not to see minorities as a means of protecting them doesn't hold. 'It's necessary to bolster the information we have to protect people."*

- The response to the killing of George Floyd, which ignited the Black Lives Matter protests that extended to Europe, has given rise to create an officially color-blind society. Covid-19 is revealing that, in such a color-blind society, being of a given race or ethnic heritage could result in a deadly form of natural racial discrimination far worse than "racism."

- In Louisville, a 27-year-old photographer is shot, protesters fir back at alleged shooter, wounding him.

- In St. Louis, an armed couple greets protesters who were headed to the house of Democratic Mayor Lyda Krewson.

- Observing the preponderance of guns, Edward Davis, former commissioner of the Boston Police Department, notes how hard it is to tell the *"good guys from the bad guys.* [because] ... *Nobody knows who's a right-wing extremist, who's a left-wing extremist, who might have pulled the trigger."* In effect, he noted that the swamp denizens on both sides are no emerging.

-

28 June 2020 –

- Citing the racist thinking and policies of the 28th President, Princeton University announced the removal of "Woodrow Wilson" from its public policy school; henceforth to be known as the Princeton School of Public and International Affairs – ending a 72-year identity.

- Four white men attack an 18-year-old biracial Jewish woman; first throwing lighter fluid on her, then igniting it, with the result that she suffered 3rd-degree burns – making Madison, Wisconsin the site of an anti-Semitic racist attack. When the news broke, the victim, Althea Bernstein, received a phone call from Duchess of Sussex Meghan Markle, who, aside from being a descendant of the four-sisters, is also biracial Jewish.

- It was reported: "Democratic senators are feeling increasingly optimistic about their chances of winning back the Senate majority in November."

- 1/ A European survey report reveals European citizens have been "traumatized" by the pandemic, and based on the media attacks on Trump: *"Europeans' trust in the US is gone. Many have been appalled by the [America's] chaotic response to Covid-19; the lack of solidarity it showed with Europeans in the 12 March closure of its border to members of the Schengen area; and its lack of leadership in tackling the coronavirus crisis at the global level – or even engagement with the issue (beyond a war of words with the World Health Organization)."*

- 2/ Two days after the survey, the European Union announced it will reopen its external borders to 15 countries, but that the

United States will not be among them. The denial of access to U.S. tourists means the EU is voluntarily removing billions of dollars from its economy while providing motivation for the American summer tourist trade to be domestic and enhance a reboot of the economy.

•

29 June 2020 –

- 1/ AOC sends a letter about a lack of economic priority that has caused defunding portions of The City University of New York [CUNY] budget expressing concern over the laying off of *"potentially thousands of adjunct faculty by June 30 and cut course offerings for the fall by as much as 35 percent."* As she pointed out, *"The CARES Act allocated more than $100 million to CUNY for institutional support during the crisis, with an explicit provision about keeping employees on payroll."*

- CUNY School of Professional Studies [CUNY SPS], which has been leading online education in New York, enrollment is up 30% over the past four years – during which time Trump has promoted repatriation of highly skilled graduates and has said he'd also prefer to see them in the area of work visas.

- On 4 May 2015, de Blasio announced a two year, $80 million, cash infusion in the CUNY, and an additional $70 million to provide all New Yorkers with broadband access by 2025. For 2021, the Mayor cut about $110 million from education funds. United Federation of Teachers President Michael Mulgrew: *"Now is not the time to cut direct services to students and school communities when they are going through so much."*

- Responding to anti-Russia rumors about bounties for killing American troops, Pentagon spokesman Jonathan Hoffman stated: *"The Department of Defense continues to evaluate intelligence that Russian GRU operatives were engaged in malign activity against United States and coalition forces in Afghanistan. To date, DOD has no corroborating evidence to validate the recent allegations found in open-source reports."* Trump tweets: *"Possibly another fabricated Russia Hoax, maybe by the Fake News @nytimesbooks, wanting to make Republicans look bad!!!"*

- In Italy, aftereffects of Covid-19 have accentuated observed pre-pandemic economic issues. There are indications of an economic cascade effect that could bring down the nation – something the is to happen with this 112th Pope.

- After all the talk about Nazis, China has implemented what passes as a eugenics policy to curb its Muslim population by imposing mandatary birth control and sterilization. Joanne Smith Finley, of Newcastle University, stated: *"It's genocide, full stop. It's not immediate, shocking, mass-killing on the spot type genocide, but it's slow, painful, creeping genocide. These are direct means of genetically reducing the Uighur population."*

- The Democrat Party tweeted an attack on Mount Rushmore, negatively portraying an upcoming Trump 4th of July event at the historic monument as further evidence, *"Trump has disrespected Native communities time and again. He's attempted to limit their voting rights and blocked critical pandemic relief. Now he's holding a rally glorifying white supremacy at Mount Rushmore–a region once sacred to tribal communities."*

- In a related story in a British newspaper The Guardian, Oglala Lakota tribe member Nick Tilsen is quoted saying of the site that depicts the faces of four presidents: *"Mount Rushmore is a symbol of white supremacy, of structural racism that's still alive and well in society today."* In now appears that the Presidents, George Washington, Thomas Jefferson, Theodore Roosevelt, and Abraham Lincoln, are to be equated with neo-Nazis and KKK members in a manner consistent with that described by George Orwell.

-

30 June 2020 –

- Former congressman Carlos Curbelo observes: *"It is different now, and people are waking up to the reality of having this kind of president."*

- Since the 2016 passage of BREXIT, when the UK initiated its downward course, and the pandemic affirmed the damage to NHS, the British economy has been in recession; there are now claims of a pending V-shaped recovery. The Obama-Trump longest expansion in history ended only because of the pandemic and, thanks to the Covid-19 stimulus, we now see the validation and economic wisdom of UBI – meaning the U.S.

could quickly return to record levels and global economic power before the 2024 elections.

- The 2nd quarter finishes with record financial market growth and what could be interpreted as confirmation of the Trump recovery forecast. A chief market strategist at TD Ameritrade, JJ Kinahan, stated: *"What everybody sees is if we can get something that puts an end to the spread or the spread becomes less, there is literally so much money out there that the Fed has put out there that when we turn, it is going to be a rocket ship the other way."*

- While the S&P 500 indicates economic positives appearing at a time when there is available cash combined, the EU is reported to be functioning under a delusion 'TRUMP FAILED US' and, effective 1 July, has excluded Americans from its "safe list" of countries allowed non-essential travel – a tourist travel exclusion imposed by EU means that money gets spent domestically. (Much to the chagrin of those who would like the economy to take on reported European characteristics.) Interestingly, several of the 15 nations on the "safe list" have a significantly higher Covid-19 fatality rate than the U.S. but lack the persistent negative media attention targeting Trump.

- With California, Texas, and Arizona vying to become the new epicenter for the pandemic, Dr. Anthony Fauci noted 47,000 new cases were recorded over the previous 24-hours and said: *"Clearly we are not in total control right now. I am very concerned because it could get very bad."* However, that is new test documented cases and not deaths or critical care unit growth. During the same period, the fatality rate dropped.

- Walmart decides the phrase "All Lives Matter" is racist and discontinues third party sales of merchandise with that expression on its website. However, "Black Lives Matter" does not seem to be race-specific and is continued to be sold.

- Biden informs donors: *"I'm going to get rid of the bulk of Trump's $2 trillion tax cut, and a lot of you may not like that, but I'm going to close loopholes like capital gains and stepped-up basis."* This will raise the taxes of 82% of middle-class voters but has no effect on the elite 1%. And to achieve this objective, he would need both the House and Senate to be under Democratic control.

- After Biden's tax restoration statement, it was announced that former George W. Bush administration Republicans formed a super PAC, "43 Alumni For Biden." This emphasizes the party evolution and degree of defection by swamp denizens to be seen since Trump declared he would "*drain the swamp*." Along with the "Lincoln Project," the "43 Alumni For Biden" are creating the strongest, most organized, economic support base for the Biden nomination and campaign – comprised of elite Conservative Republicans from the one-percent.

- Before going on their Spring Break, House democrats unveil their vision of 'solving the climate crisis' by 2050. This comes a week after reports of that the Arctic has its warmest period in history – on 22 May, Khatanga, Siberia, which is well above the Arctic Circle, recorded a temperature of 78 degrees, about 46 degrees above normal. On 20 June, another Siberian town record 100.4 degrees. These temperatures are being echoed to a lesser degree in the antarctic, and are resulting in warmer seawater which will accelerate ice melting. In short, by 2050, the geography of America's coastlines will be changed to such a degree that no act of the House will have meaning. As the pandemic has shown, decreased human activity will have a greater effect – and that activity will drop significantly when the Baby-Boomers die and the Baby-Bust, with low energy electronic, defines the environment around 2035.

-

01 July 2020 – USMCA goes into effect

- On 1 Jul 2020, ABC News tweeted: "*A 22-foot-tall statue of Christopher Columbus was removed from outside the Columbus, Ohio, city hall after the city's mayor called for it to come down.*" Of course, if Columbus were honest, and not just giving in to bigoted mob rule, they would also change the name of their city.

- In compliance with the minimum wage included in USMCA, Japanese auto companies triple Mexican pay – the pay raise was based on the requirement that 40% or more of parts for each passenger vehicle be manufactured by workers who are paid at least $16 per hour to qualify as tariff free in the region. Trump used this feature to both boost U.S. production and provided a higher hourly rate than Mexico. This infers he would happily sign a Minimum Wage increase to $16 or $20.

- Covid-19 news continues to get interesting. Coronavirus autopsies of 38 brains, 87 lungs, and 42 hearts revealed some surprising results – the damage is consistent with a mosquito-borne disease that occurs in tropical and subtropical areas of the world, Dengue fever.

- A peer-reviewed Henry Ford Health System Study revealed that Treatment with Hydroxychloroquine significantly cut the death rate among Covid-19 patients. This was a large-scale retrospective analysis of 2,541 patients hospitalized between 10 March and 2 May 2020 – around the time the media was attacking Trump for touting the potential benefits of the well-known malaria drug. The study showed Hydroxychloroquine reduced the probability of death by 50%. Where it was not effective, involved patients with serious underlying diseases.

-

02 July 2020 –

- The City of Boston removes the Freedman Emancipation Statute of Abraham Lincoln and Archer Alexander – depicting a slave rising to freedom is hated by those claiming to represent the idea of Black Lives Matter. The fact is, they want the slaves on their knees and therefore promote taking a knee. The story of the freedman, Archer Alexander (1812-1880), was told by William Greenleaf Eliot, the grandfather of the Poet T.S. Eliot. The 1880 census, shows that Alexander was residing with the Eliots, and is recorded as a Mulatto.

- A tweeted video of a White House Press Secretary briefing at 9:01 AM – Question: *"Why is [Trump] digging in on race in this way?"* Kayleigh McEnany: *"If you're saying that the fact that he does not to rename our bases, if you're considering that racist, then apparently 56% of America is as well."*

- The 2nd quarter employment numbers reveal the recovery rebound has begun: Record jobs gain of 4.8 million in June smashes expectations; unemployment rate falls to 11.1%. As per the pandemic history, the "Expert Economists" surveyed by Dow Jones had expected only a 2.9 million increase and a jobless rate of 12.4%.

- Responding to record 55,274 virus cases recorded over a 24-hour-period, Trump stated: *"There is a rise in Coronavirus cases because our testing is so massive and so good, far bigger, and better than any other country.   There is a rise in Coronavirus cases because our testing is so massive and so good, far bigger and better than any other country. This is great news, but even better news is that death, and the death rate, is down.*" When the goal is herd immunity, the ideal is an increase in cases without fatalities.

- Sen. Mitch McConnell states: "*While we have far-left mobs attacking statues of our Founding Fathers from coast to coast, we have far-left politicians attacking the institutions those founders left us.*"

- Sen. Josh Hawley states: "*The cancel culture that is tearing down statues of George Washington, and Ulysses S. Grant, Abraham Lincoln, Theodore Roosevelt for heaven's sakes -- this cancel movement seeks to divide us, not unite.*"

-

03 July 2020 –

- With the global BLM movement, with its attacks on historic monuments, it seems Copenhagen's Little Mermaid is racist and vandals added graffiti saying 'racist fish' and seem to hold the works of Hans Christian Andersen to be racist. Possibly the protestors object to a 19-year-old African-American, Halle Bailey, in the Disney movie role of "The Little Mermaid"

- Trump prepares for the Mount Rushmore fireworks, while the media attacks him for a lack of social distancing and the danger of forest fires the current Arizona climate conditions might foster. The media fears of Covid-19 spread due to the gathering, have caused Mexico to close its Arizona border – in effect, it has Mexico building a virtual or effective wall.

- On CNN they misrepresent the testing related increases in cases. They reference America's curve rising while in the EU the new cases are decreasing. As previously mentioned, those countries have a fraction of the population and therefore the same number of tests will return different numbers. Sweden has a population equal top New York City and its bedroom communities – naturally, their curve will flatten. Look at the curves for Italy, France, Spain, or Britain – they are flattening but the fatality rates are double that emerging for the U.S.A.. It is not the positive tests, it is the number of people with the virus who die – CNN and other anti-Trump fake news media make it a point to misrepresent the realities if doing so will allow an attack on Trump.

- As the nation prepared for the Fourth of July, CNN and others were actively promoting fireworks everywhere but where the President was. They were also avoiding the fact that Biden is having his cognitive abilities tested on a regular basis – indicating fears that he might develop a new brain aneurysm or that damage done from previous ones might be worsening. As we close this book, a prediction already posted online in June 2020: If elected, Biden will not be able to complete his term; he would be replaced by his Vice President in, or before, 2023.

- Speaking at Mount Rushmore, Trump states said the nation's history was '*under siege from far-left fascism.*' In keeping with our 57-year-cycle, it should be noted:

- 1/ the Vietnam era defined by the year 1963 and marked the beginning of the anti-war protest reaction to Kennedy's use of 'military advisors' to guide the emerging combat involvement.

- 2/ that year included 28 August 1963, when Potus Cousin and descendant of the 4-Sisters, Rev. Dr. Martin Luther King Jr led the first 'March on Washington' where he delivered his famous '*I Have a Dream*' speech.

- 3/ 1963 was a year of racially related actions in the search for the 'equality' systemically denied African-Americans.

- 4/ This was also the period that gave rise to counter-culture or fascist groups – "Weather Underground" and "Black Panthers" – and saw culturally disruptive behavior of the type presented by BLM and the anti-police CHOP districts.

- At Mount Rushmore, President Trump effectively threw down the gauntlet, pointing to the landmark sculpture and saying: "*This monument will never be desecrated. These heroes will never be disgraced. Their legacy will never, ever be destroyed. Their achievements will never be forgotten. And Mount Rushmore will stand forever as an eternal tribute to our forefathers and our freedom.*"

- Historically Mount Rushmore was known by the tribal name as "The Six Grandfather" – but that was before "grandfathers" of American history were carved into its face. Cheyenne River Sioux Tribe Chairman Harold Frazier said: "*Nothing stands as a greater reminder to the Great Sioux Nation of a country that cannot keep a promise or treaty than the faces carved into our sacred land on what the United States calls Mount Rushmore."* Again, Frazier's statement reflects the cyclical behavior pointed out concerning the American pattern of 'breach of contract' defining a post-World War Two National character.

•

04 July 2020 – FOURTH OF JULY

- An amazing day in the history of the world – one that many have wanted to denounce by destroying statues to its creators.

- Strange Holiday – celebrated with a Chinese invention called gunpowder, the driving force behind the evolution of warfare, invented and used as Fireworks. But the driving force behind the evolution of war.

- Nashville, Tennessee creates a replacement for dangerous fireworks – a DRONE LIGHT SHOW. America is seeking to truly enter the third decade of the 21st Century in style. And it is more evidence that the Old Silk and Spice Road is a thing of the past. Do we really need to continue the dependence on China to add spice to our life?

- In a Fourth of July proclamation, City manager David Lynch, declared Newton Falls, Ohio to be a "Statuary Sanctuary City" and invited any community that wanted to remove its historic monuments to send them to Newton Falls. His proclamation recognizes: "*The great leaders of our country and Western civilization, though flawed in many ways, have risen to great achievement such as the founding of our nation, the ending of slavery, establishment, and protection of our national parks, the establishment of antitrust laws to protect our citizens from over aggressive monopolization of industry, and the discovery of the New World itself.*" There now exists a "general amnesty" for the statues of George Washington, Abraham Lincoln, Thomas Jefferson, Ulysses S. Grant, Patrick Henry, Francis Scott Key, Theodore Roosevelt, and Christopher Columbus.

•

05 July 2020 –

- 1/ The Frederick Douglass statue vandalized on anniversary of his famous Fourth of July Rochester speech – delivered on 5 July 1852 – when he asked: "*What to the Slave is the Fourth of July?*" Concluding then as we could now, "*There is not a nation on the earth guilty of practices more shocking and bloody than are the people of the United States, at this very hour."*

- 2/ We gave up slavery only after a war because we needed the blood rather than the simple Constitutional Amendment of 1870.

- 3/ Thereafter, we replaced slavery with military adventurism and war; today America has the largest military budget of any nation (or ten nations combined) and seems to want to utilize it to the fullest – has Trump expanded military adventurism or is he disengaging from those operations? Has the nation shown more support for those who expand the killing than they do toward Trump who wants to end it?

- 4/ Is BLM a movement of peace or violence, vandalism, and social disruption that has destroyed monuments to Frederick Douglas – a former slave – and to Abraham Lincoln, the man who freed slaves, accompanied in a statue by the freed slave Archer Alexander depicted as rising to his feet in freedom?

- 1/ Senator Tammy Duckworth said Trump "priorities are all wrong" and that "He should be talking about what we're gonna do to overcome this pandemic. What are we going to do to push Russia back?" She then complained that in denouncing the attacks of Mount Rushmore and the Statues of those depicted there, "He spent all his time talking about dead traitors."

- /2 So to Duckworth, the first President, and the author of the Constitution who became the third President, are traitors because they owned slaves when the Constitution said they could. She made it quite clear that, in the modern viewpoint, obedience to the Constitution makes one a traitor.

-

06 July 2020 –

- POLITICO "White House defiant as Covid-19 deaths approach 130,000" on same day the MSM is touting an increase in the Covid-19 cases by 47,158 while ignoring the fact the mortality rate had dropped to 4.2%. The media continues to emphasize that which can be interpreted as negative. But the pattern of the numbers has been toward herd immunity and an end to the pandemic.

- CNN continues to attack Trump for "President's unfounded claim that 99% of coronavirus cases are 'totally harmless'" –

they are therefore arguing math similar to that put forward by Joe Biden's 25 June statement about 120 million Americans having died from the COVID-19 coronavirus disease. In the case of the 99% harmless, CNN must be arguing against the pre-existing conditions being a factor in mortality numbers; it is known that asymptomatic cases are generally unnoticed and, therefore, cause no harm to the carrier. It is also worth noting that, in January, the expert projections called for a 1% mortality. As of July, U.S. mortality had fallen to 4.4%, even as the number of hospitalized cases increases throughout the southern states.

• Israel begins a lockdown: Synagogues are to be allowed only 19 worshipers at a time; restaurants will be allowed 20 diners inside and 30 outside.

• Comic observation. If one wanted to see a satirical or comic form of 2020 events, they could watch a 2005 movie starring Zooey Deschanel, "Hitchhiker's Guide to the Galaxy" where the current mainstream media is represented by "Marvin, the Paranoid Android" whose persistent depression manifests as extreme negativity.

•

[As readers might suspect, both Zooey {TV series "New Girl'} and her sister Emily {TV series "Bones"} are descendants of the 4-Sisters and POTUS Cousins.]

07 July 2020 –

• After six months of denial, WHO acknowledges that Covid-19 presents "evidence emerging" of the airborne spread. Their published statement still infers their basic denial of the reality that the novel coronavirus can be transmitted by circulation or linger in the air withing confined or closed spaces.

• Per the one-year notice requirement, Trump gives United Nations formal notice that the United States is withdrawing from its World Health Organization membership effective 6 July 2021.

• With documented infections exceeding 3 million, the media makes ignores the 13 March projection that between 160 and 210 million could be infected and yield 1.7 million fatalities. As the number of cases grows, the number of fatalities has fallen –

indicating the annualized expert projections and the President's 'one-percent' statement appear to be accurate.

- Confirmed cases: 3,035,231; deaths: 132,041; the fatality rate posted as 4.3%. Sunbelt ICU facilities are being taxed to their limits.

- Brazilian President Jair Bolsonaro is infected with Covid-19 and states he will be treated with hydroxychloroquine. Based on late stage outcomes, WHO has rejected any and all use of the hydroxychloroquine regime; based on peer-reviewed early usage outcomes, the treatment is being used.

-

08 July 2020 –

- Congress began to discuss a fifth Covid-19 relief bill

- Joe Biden adopts the Progressive platform points, indicating a willingness to compromise with Republicans, something the Progressives are warning him against. As stated by Nomiki Konst, a progressive activist, *"Biden is transparently taking a bet to win over a group of anti-Trump Republicans but at the expense of what? Potentially losing some of the largest movements in history? ... His excitement is extremely low and that should always be alarming for candidates. It's the Hillary Clinton strategy all over again."*

- Mexican border towns close the border to American tourists. At the Arizona border, Sonoyta's mayor, José Ramos Arzate stated, *"We invite US tourists not to visit Mexico. We agreed on this to safeguard the health of our community in the face of an accelerated rate of Covid-19 contagion in the neighboring state of Arizona."*

- A link between Covid-19 and brain damage has emerged and patients in the study did not experience respiratory symptoms at all, instead "the first and main" symptom of COVID-19.was the neurological disorder. Canadian Neuroscientist Adrian Owen was reported saying: *"if in a year's time we have 10 million recovered people, and those people have cognitive deficits ... then that's going to affect their ability to work and their ability to go about activities of daily living."*

- Rudy W. Giuliani tweeted: *"Dr. Anthony 'Doomsday' Fauci just said: 'it's a false narrative to take comfort in a lower rate of death.' Would he be happier with a higher rate?"*

- On a podcast, Dr. Anthony Fauci said: "*What we're seeing is exponential growth, it went from an average of about 20,000 to 40,000 and 50,000. That's doubling. If you continue doubling, two times 50 is 100.*"

- In Bridgeport, Connecticut, the city council decides to remove the statue of Christopher Columbus from Seaside Park, and in so doing states it was "*out of an abundance of caution for preservation of the historic artifact, the need to respond to modern-day sensitivities, as well as public safety at large.*"

- A tell-all book by President Trump's niece, Mary Trump, will be released on 14 July. The publisher, Simon & Schuster, has printed 75,000 copies of the work which describes the Trump family as dysfunctional, and the timing of her book, "*Too Much and Never Enough: How My Family Created the World's Most Dangerous Man,*" promises to add some spice to the pre-convention campaign season.

-

09 July 2020 –

- Joe Biden asserted the police were over militarized, and have therefore "*become the enemy*". Stating in a USA Today op-ed: "*I've long been a firm believer in the power of community policing — getting cops out of their cruisers and building relationships with the people and the communities they are there to serve and protect. That's why I'm proposing an additional $300 million to reinvigorate community policing in our country. Every single police department should have the money it needs to institute real reforms like adopting a national use of force standard, buying body cameras, and recruiting more diverse police officers.*"

- In a 7-to-2 decision, the Supreme Court ruled that New York can seek Trump's financial records. While apparently favorable to the New York City prosecutor, the 74-page decision with dissenting opinions also enumerated the valid objections and arguments that the President's attorneys can raise.

- 1/ A new Climate Study shows atmospheric CO_2 has reached a high level never before seen by humans and raises doubts about the validity of the Paris climate goals: "*Currently, our CO_2 levels are rising at about 2.5 ppm per year, meaning that by*

2025 we will have exceeded anything seen in the last 3.3 million years."

- 2/ The World Meteorological Organization secretary-general, Petteri Taalas stated: *"This study shows – with a high level of scientific skill – the enormous challenge ahead in meeting the Paris agreement on climate change target of keeping a global temperature rise this century well below 2C above pre-industrial levels and to pursue efforts to limit the temperature increase even further to 1.5C."*

- 3/ The Russian region of Siberia recorded exceptionally high temperatures and the first six months of 2020 the warmest in the history of instrumental weather observations. In a region of eastern Siberia, six miles north of the Arctic Circle the high temperature – reached on 20 June – was 100.4 F and exceed the average high by 32 degrees. Overall, Arctic Siberia saw average June temperatures exceeded by over 5 C.

- 4/ As a result of the high temperatures, vast areas of Siberia have begun to burn – previously, the region was too frozen to burn. The 100 degree June temperatures, effectively fueled an enormous outbreak of wildfires which further melted the permafrost, and scientists sign now believe that the Arctic is undergoing rapid changes that could initiate a cascade effect with global consequences.

- CNN reports and cheers a "NEVER TRUMP" movement that is headed by the Republican Swamp Denizens who gave the nation George W. Bush and the 19-year-old alleged "War on Terror" which has served to strengthen a Jihadist movement and embolden Iran.

- SCOTUS rules on Trump tax returns and denies Congress access while granting the NYC prosecutor the right to subpoena the financial data – the media reports it as a Trump loss, but they ignore the contents of the ruling outlining the Constitutional arguments Trump can assert and the bar the prosecutor must exceed.

- Trump's Attorney Jay Sekulow tweeted: *"We are pleased that in the decisions issued today, the Supreme Court has temporarily blocked both Congress and New York prosecutors from obtaining the President's financial records. We will now proceed to raise additional Constitutional and legal issues in the lower courts."*

- There is an interesting aspect to a subpoena that asks Trump to provide the Tax documents. The NYC DA stated his goal was a criminal prosecution. Trump providing the documents amounts to testifying against himself – the Fifth Amendment states: *"nor shall be compelled in any criminal case to be a witness against himself,..."*

- Self-incrimination by word or document would appear to be unconstitutional. Since the Tax documents exist with the IRS, they should be the primary source; the contained data indicating a crime presented to a grand jury; then the grand jury issues an explicit crime based subpoena.

- It must be noted: the criminal act associated with reporting of income or deductions emanates from that which is actually filed with the IRS, where such filing is then proved to be criminal. Thus, prior to seeking Trump's private notes or inaccurate copies, the NYC DA must obtain the legal filing as submitted to the IRS. For legislative purposes, Congress is also required to use documents filed with IRS.

- In a separate ruling, SCOTUS ruled that, in accordance with treaties not repudiated by Congress, Native American tribes hold jurisdiction over a large portion of Oklahoma. This ruling affects both State and Federal legal jurisdiction. There is the possibility that the House Democrats will, as has been done in the past, demonstrate historic discrimination against Native Americans and nullify or violate a lawful treaty. That would send a message to the international community that has come to rely on about both the word or good faith backing credit and debts of the United States.

-

NOT DATE SPECIFIC

Governments often trust the idea that people will responsibly self-police. But, as we have seen with the various police exclusion zones, this is a misguided trust that results in the descenders turning on and killing, their own.

We are witnessing the return of the counterculture which was the defining element of the Vietnam-Hippy era of 57-years ago. That was also a period overshadowed by the McCarthyism that defined the period 1950-1954 and allowed B-Actor Ronald Reagan to emerge as a devout anti-Russian anti-Communism political force which would eventually bring him to the Oval Office.

Joseph McCarthy was an anti-Semite who could successfully mask his bigotry behind the term "Marxist." As we know, the term has continued as the description of Socialism – something that Marx envisioned as Capitalism utilizing "surplus capital" to benefit those who – for whatever reason – were failing to survive in the capitalist environment.

In many regards, Marx had taken the culture of the 1840s and imposed an Old Testament mandate regarding those who were sick, widows, orphans, or who found themselves, for some other reason, destitute. The Golden Rule mandate – if you were in their place, how would you want to be treated – was the mandate of the Marxist. But it was not the mandate of the Communists. Their mandate dictated the continuation of a Czarist culture under a different name – serf or peasant was now a part of a "commune" that shared possessions and responsibilities. Their leaders simply dropped their hereditary role and title to create another means of obtaining and retaining power.

"Everything is the same, they just change the name, and order of magnitude" This is the rule that governs nature and life. It is seen in combination with a fuzzy cycle of behavior whose mathematics are too complicated – too many decimal places or active functions – to be easily and exactly codified.

The Bible defined it as three or four generations from the starting point – we know it as the sins of the parents unto the third or fourth generation. A generation is about 25 years, which means the birth of the third generation from the individual who committed the initial act would be a child, grandchild, and the great-grandchild at the age of eight-years-old. Why eight? As the ancients said, "Give me the child for the first seven years of their life, and I will return the adult." And when we combine two average generations with eight additional years, we get the 57-year-cycle which appears in my books over the past decade.

In 1990, Robert Fulghum related the idea in his book, *"All I Really Need To Know I Learned In Kindergarten."*

Fulghum related the idea that: *"I believe that imagination is stronger than knowledge. That myth is more potent than history. That dreams are more powerful than facts. That hope always triumphs over experience. That laughter is the only cure for grief. And I believe that love is stronger than death."*

Inherent in that idea is that a positive outlook is critical. Now we are seeing a period when negativity dominates.

That third or fourth generation is a time when the children finish what their grandparents began – biblically, it's the sins of the parents unto the third or fourth generation; factually, it is the cyclical nature of the driving forces that define evolution and a period of change.

Right now, the leaders are, for the most part, those we call the "Silent Generation." As the rear cover illustration shows, they were born between 1925 and 1945, so we can say when they were eight – 1933 to 1953 – they had been shaped by the adults 57-years-earlier. They reflect the values and beliefs that existed, or prevailed, in 1876 through 1896. That is, the period of massive American expansion and a wave of immigrants escaping imperial Europe.

That was a period when people really had to work. There were none of the social programs we know today, and communication was slow. We still carry a mentality from that period which was at odds with the Bible and the ideas that Marx put forward – this opposition to "freeloading" or "getting something for nothing" even though we all love free things.

Fulghum tells us to *"Remember, most of us got something for nothing the first time just by showing up here at birth. Now we have to qualify."* How do we earn the rewards we are given at birth? Is it done by being jealous of the rewards others have received, or by moving forward and then being able to grant to our children greater rewards?

We are in a period of negative population growth; that means we have no children upon whom to bestow the fruits of our labors and accomplishments. That being the case, we bemoan what we do not have and so lose all we could have had.

Again, Fulghum shows kindergarten knowledge: *"I get tired of hearing it's a crummy world and that people are no damned good. What kind of talk is that? I know a place in Payette, Idaho, where a cook and a waitress and a manager put everything they've got into laying a chicken-fried steak on you."*

In the 1960s, the Hippy Generation was a manifestation of the transitional wartime-post-war Silent-Boomer generation whose work ethic was rewarded with a minimum wage sustained self-sufficient living or the pursuit of higher education.

The advent of the television presented what can now be seen as conflicting cultural views of the "wild west", "stay-at-home" mom, and individuals who bent or skirted the law. Then there was "The Many Loves of Dobie Gillis" and with Bob Denver as the beatnik cum hippy Maynard G. Krebs. The series ran from 1959 to 1963 and thus was the role model for the wartime babies born after 1943.

The counterculture was part of the after school indoctrination afforded by television comedy. If we look back, it's possible we could find a combination of characters or series that would be the model for the 2020 'cancel culture.'

With all the 'bad guys' and 'criminals' we see talked about, could it be that the youth of today are looking for "The Sopranos" in "The West Wing"? Or, maybe the 'cancel culture' has confused itself with some version or variation of the characters on "Lost."

Unfortunately, erasing history while ignoring the present is not a way to build a future. You don't destroy the foundation and then try to build the house.

It would be silly. But consider...

It's funny how, just when the 'cancel culture' generation was being born, Fulghum was already declaring he was *"tired of hearing it's a crummy world and that people are no damned good."*

But, all Fulghum was saying is that he was tired of the mantra of the Right-wing Conservatives who saw Reagan as their lord and master. Reagan was 1980, so the generation time that he trained were the parents of those being born to that generation of children whose kindergarten knowledge took shape around 2005.

George Santayana wrote: *"Those who cannot remember the past are condemned to repeat it."* What he wrote has been repeated in various forms – *"Those who forget the past are condemned to repeat it."* But, how about those who destroy their common past?

The 'cancel culture' is working to erase the past. They think the South was racist and the north wasn't. But both north and south were dominated by the same exact bigotry we see today. Granted, the slaves are no longer formally enslaved – unless they are in prison and put to work as California wildfire fighters. Today's slaves are those working full-time and still in need of public assistance, or those who cannot work and are told they need to engage in "workfare" and provide their energy to some non-profit in order to get assistance.

But, Covid-19 seems to have crippled that Reagan-era policy.

The stimulus packages have shown that an economy can be kept alive only if the poorest are given the resources to purchase the things they need. Granted, the big corporations found a way to tap the federal piggy bank, but, at the same time, many old names are going out of business and the culture is changing.

Change is inevitable in societies that seek to improve, and it is often strange to see the things that serve as the catalyst for change.

Consider those who are angry about the slave trade – asked them if their ancestors were slaves or masters. Most will look at the color of their skin to find an answer when the true answer lies within or in the genealogy.

But, for the sake of discussion, we'll many will answer slaves. But now they are Americans. If not for the slave trade, their parents and their parent's-parent's would never have met. In fact, the vast majority of their ancestors would never have left Africa. It could be argued that European culture would have entered Africa in the same way it did Asia – the way it did India, China, and South Africa. The slaves came from the central region around Nigeria, so they would have been untouched by any culture other than Arab slave traders.

Is the 'cancel culture' generation honestly angry about having been forced to be Americans, French, or British? Do they think the culture their ancestors were pulled away from is superior to modern European-American society?

If they do, they can always immigrate to Africa.

The Jews have been subject to anti-Semitic bigotry since the time of ancient Rome. Would members of the 'cancel culture' rather be Shakespeare's "Merchant of Venice" or "Othello" – both were set in the culture of Venice, where Othello was a General in the Venetian military, and Shylock was a despised merchant who, acting as a moneylender, we could see as a banker (the still hated elite 1%).

Isn't funny how little society has changed?

Othello was an African-Muslim whose racial ancestry could have been mixed and therefore not too unlike Barack Obama. We can look at Trump and there is the German-English that is common in Pennsylvania and Ohio. But Trump is wealthy and his daughter is an Orthodox Jew – so there is a touch of the Shylock.

Isn't it fun to note the same Right-wing Swamp Denizens who proudly supported Reagan, and promoted the wars of father and son Bush, now have cast their wealth and efforts behind the nomination and election of Joseph R Biden?

When Barack Obama was in office, those same people were propagating the Birthers ideas that Trump willing to accepted as the price of getting the votes of their supplicants. Ah, but isn't that what Shylock would have done, and did?

When it comes to finances, Trump obeys the law. Curiously, that is what Shylock was doing after having been cheated by Antonio so often, when he was asked for money, Shylock offers a contract that demanded the right to take a pound of flesh as security in the event the loan was forfeit. Of course, the loan was not repaid and the law – an anti-Semitic law passed to prevent Jewish doctors from taking on Christian patients – was invoked to both nullify the contract and punish Shylock.

There might be an analogy to the impeachment to be had, but there is also a warped reality related to the actions of 'cancel culture' as it attacks the statues of Confederates who fought to uphold the slave ownership rights they were granted in the Constitution. It seems funny to attack people who fought FOR the Constitution as it was written, and against those who lacked the public support for change in the form of a lawful amendment. Of course, after blood had been spilled and the southern states destroyed, in 1870 America did what Britain had done before 1835.

But, as usual, I'm drifting away from the existential reality of the Trump era and the Covid-19 pandemic. As I write this, more events are unfolding to shape the third-quarter and the realities that the pandemic has brought into general view.

This is an age of change. Biden could finally become POTUS, but the stress will interact with extensive damage resulting from his brain aneurysm and he'll be out of office by November 2023. If he is not elected, people will see the damage affect his private life.

For now, we have a global contraction in GDP, with China able to make a swift recovery while America argues to allow Biden to destroy its GDP.

Biden is known for his law school plagiarism and in July came out with his $700 Billion version of Reagan's Buy America. It is easy to understand Trump, a Republican and PT Barnum type, using the Reagan era ideas in the same way he took the MAGA slogan. But to play the 'Buy America' card you need to do what Reagan didn't.

You need control of borders and migration – which is going to grow as the climate worsens. Even now, above the Arctic, Siberia is showing temperatures that are melting the permafrost and that is going to accelerate climate change. And when that happens, the northward migration of unskilled illiterates and tropical diseases is only going to get worse.

This brings us to our closing numbers and the reality that the current pandemic is proving excessively deadly to those of African and Latino heritage. But that reflects the oriental origin of Covid-19, over the next decade, in the western hemisphere, the disease origins will be from the "Latino" nations that are currently being hardest hit by the Asian pandemic. And a segment of Americans are yelling they want to open the borders to those emerging diseases – they became Reagan Democrats, promoting Reagan policies, and expecting there will be a different outcome than that which defines Reaganomics and policies.

Remember history. At the end of World War One, a Spanish Flu epidemic killed 50 million people and reduced the global GDP by 6%, while causing 11.4% unemployment over the three years between 1918 to 1921.

Nature also plays games – climate yielded the dust storms of the Depression Era. Named the "Dust Bowl," it destroyed agriculture across the regions whose modern agricultural production provides the basis for America's balance of trade surplus. Unless America has industrial and technological resources – now outsourced – restored, Global Warming will restore Dust Bowl conditions. That could mean poverty in excess of 45%, and unemployment above 25%.

If America keeps its reliance of fissile fuels and continues to brag about its oil production, the result will be a permanent collapse of the nation by 2030 – and no later than 2035. The nation needs to devote its vast intelligence and skills to the production of renewable energy sources to power every home and building.

For now, we have the misrepresentations about the severity of the pandemic. The media loves to talk about the increases in cases in the third most populous nation on the planet. And they compare to nations a sixth of America's size.

On Social Media, there are even those who foolishly assert the comparisons should be done against a standardized measure such as population – so cases or fatalities per million. Accordingly, we will conclude this book with the numbers that existed on 10 July 2020, when the book went to the final edit.

On 5 July, Trump was blasted for saying: *"...we have tested over 40 million people. But by so doing, we show cases, 99 percent of which are totally harmless. Results that no other country will show, because no other country has testing that we have — not in terms of the numbers or in terms of the quality."*

Ok, based on the data from 213 jurisdictions, let's look at the top 15. For consistency, the top fifteen are used for all the final data presented. The United States ranks twelfth in the number of cases relative to its population. Globally, 0.16% of people are affected.

FATALITY% COUNTRY

#	FATALITY%	COUNTRY
1.	3.66%	Qatar
2.	2.06%	San Marino
3.	1.91%	French Guiana
4.	1.85%	Bahrain
5.	1.62%	Chile
6.	1.50%	Vatican City
7.	1.25%	Kuwait
8.	1.11%	Andorra
9.	1.05%	Oman
10.	1.04%	Armenia
11.	0.99%	Mayotte
12.	**0.83%**	**USA**
13.	0.98%	Panama
14.	0.96%	Peru
15.	0.83%	Brazil

It appears that only ten countries have more than one percent of their populations infected and both the United States and Brazil have less than that.

How about the fatalities per case. Is the United States really bad? At 4.17% it ranks 56th in the world– and yes, once again we find the U.S. in the "magic number" range and almost 57.

#	FATALITY%	COUNTRY
1	26.38%	Yemen
2	22.22%	Namibia
3	19.23%	Sint Maarten
4	17.57%	France
5	15.69%	Belgium
6	15.50%	UK
7	14.40%	Italy
8	14.04%	Hungary
9	12.50%	British Virgin Islands
10	12.07%	Netherlands
11	11.88%	Mexico
12	10.28%	Bahamas
13	10.00%	Western Sahara
14	09.44%	Spain
15	09.09%	Montserrat

However, the significant measure of handling of the virus is not the fact that the third most populous nation in the world has the most cases. As the sixth most populous nation, it follows that the cases in Brazil would grow quickly – especially when the evidence indicates Latino's are highly susceptible to Covid-19 and that means Brazil second in the number of cases. And, as of this writing, India – the origin point of Indo-Europeans – is third.

In 2021 or 2022, we will have the final numbers and will be able to compare them to prior years. That will tell us how many of the deaths would have happened anyway, and how many can be attributed exclusively to the virus. The results might well show the dishonesty of the media and the accuracy of Trump's one-percent.

On 10 July, a late news report showed that in New York City 68% of those tested evidenced the Covid-19 anti-bodies. That means that areas of the City where the virus was most intense could be on the verge of Herd Immunity.

New York State registered 425,783 cases and 32,371 deaths, which means over 24% of the deaths in America were in New York. In terms of cases, NYC accounted for roughly 13.4% of all the cases in America. That means New York was the problem and not the way Trump handled the nation. In terms of fatalities, New York City is a mess – globally, the 10.42% fatality rate places it in the top twelve.

Borough Deaths/Total cases = Fatality Rate

Borough	Deaths/Total cases = Fatality Rate
BRONX	4,789/49,139=9.75%
KINGS	7,163/6,2175=10.52%
MANHATTAN	3,114/29,751=11.52%
QUEENS	7,099/67,465=9.75%
RICHMOND	1,066/14.464=10.47%
City Total	23,231/222,994=10.42%
STATE TOTAL	32,371/425,783=7.60%
Exclude NYC	9,140/202,789=4.51%

If we look at the emerging epicenters – Florida and Southern California – we see ties to New York City. California has 312,087 cases with 6,952 deaths (2.23%); Los Angeles accounts for 127,358 case and 3,738 deaths (2.94%). Florida has 244,151 cases and 4,102 deaths (1.68%) and Miami-Dade has the highest caseload, 58,341, with 1,118 deaths (1.9%).

It's interesting that Trump made Florida his home and it is the proposed site for the Republican Convention, while California is the state he protected when he put that "xenophobic" travel ban on China. But in NYC, De Blasio was placing sick patients in elderly care centers where the virus quickly spread, while also telling city residents it was OK to travel the subways.

Nancy Pelosi's San Francisco 12th Congressional district – which is 44% White and 33% Asian – has 4,316 cases with 50 deaths (1.16%).

It will be interesting to see how the numbers change in book ten. Will it still be an "*Existential* cancel culture" existence?